HOW TO STUDY LITERATURE
General Editors: John Peck and Martin Coyle

HOW TO STUDY A SHAKESPEARE PLAY

Second Edition

How to Study

Series editors: John Peck and Martin Coyle

IN THE SAME SERIES

HOW TO STUDY A SHAKESPEARE PLAY

Second Edition

John Peck
and
Martin Coyle

MACMILLAN

First edition 1985
Reprinted five times
Second edition 1995

Published by
MACMILLAN PRESS LTD
Houndmills, Basingstoke, Hampshire RG21 2XS
and London
Companies and representatives
throughout the world

ISBN 0-333-64126-4

A catalogue record for this book is available
from the British Library.

10   9   8   7   6   5   4   3
04   03   02   01   00   99   98   97

Printed in Malaysia

For Matthew
and
Penny and Steven

Contents

General editors' preface

EVERYBODY who studies literature, either for an examination or simply for pleasure, experiences the same problem: how to understand and respond to the text. As every student of literature knows, it is perfectly possible to read a book over and over again and yet still feel baffled and at a loss as to what to say about it. One answer to this problem, of course, is to accept someone else's view of the text, but how much more rewarding it would be if you could work out your own critical response to any book you choose or are required to study.

The aim of this series is to help you develop your critical skills by offering practical advice about how to read, understand and analyse literature. Each volume provides you with a clear method of study so that you can see how to set about tackling texts on your own. While the authors of each volume approach the problem in a different way, every book in the series attempts to provide you with some broad ideas about the kind of texts you are likely to be studying and some broad ideas about how to think about literature; each volume then shows you how to apply these ideas in a way which should help you construct your own analysis and interpretation. Unlike most critical books, therefore, the books in this series do not simply convey someone else's thinking about a text, but encourage you and show you how to think about a text for yourself.

Each book is written with an awareness that you are likely to be preparing for an examination, and therefore practical advice is given not only on how to understand and analyse literature, but also on how to organise a written response. Our hope is that although these books are intended to serve a practical purpose, they may also enrich your enjoyment of literature by making you a more confident reader, alert to the interest and pleasure to be derived from literary texts.

John Peck
Martin Coyle

Preface

THE purpose of this book is to provide you with some broad guidelines about how to build a critical approach to a Shakespeare play. The book itself is divided into two parts. Part One is concerned with looking at the basic moves you can make to come to grips with a Shakespeare play: the first chapter explains how best to approach a play and how to begin shaping a critical response. The next three chapters then demonstrate how to construct a critical reading of the text by using a sequence of steps to build your argument. We look at how to tackle a history play, a tragedy and a comedy, in each case offering a number of examples that should allow you to see how the method applies to the particular play or plays you may be studying. After these chapters come two chapters which deal with how to discuss an extract from a Shakespeare play and how to write an essay.

Part One of the book is intended for students who are just getting started in criticism and are unsure about what is involved in studying a Shakespeare play. In Part Two, which is entirely new and appears for the first time in this 'Second Edition', we discuss some of the new approaches to Shakespeare. In recent years there has been a flood of new thinking in literary criticism, and a whole range of new critical approaches have appeared; students at university, in particular, soon become aware of terms such as deconstruction, feminist criticism and New Historicism. Part Two illustrates these new approaches in action, and suggests ways in which you can absorb this new thinking into your own work.

Part Two is at a more difficult level than the first part, and is intended to show you how you can take your studies on a stage further. By the end of the book, therefore, you might find that you are dealing with some unfamiliar ideas, but do try to see that the method is exactly the same as in the first part, that of building an analysis from the evidence in the text. This is because even the most innovatory approaches are built upon close examination of the words on the page. And this, in essence, is the message of the book as a whole, that criticism starts from the close reading of the text.

University of Wales   JOHN PECK
Cardiff   MARTIN COYLE

Part One

1

How to approach a Shakespeare play

What problems am I likely to encounter when I study Shakespeare for the first time?

SHAKESPEARE is often the first dramatist people study. You might have read, seen, and even acted in plays, but Shakespeare could well be the first writer whose plays you are expected to analyse and discuss. Consequently, when you start to study Shakespeare you might have little idea about what you are supposed to look for or say. You might sense that criticism must amount to something more than just retelling the story, but nobody expects you to have an instinctive awareness of how to discuss a play. The principal aim of this book is to provide the kind of guidance you are likely to need, showing you how to make an appropriate and valid response.

There is, however, a problem that precedes this question of how to discuss a play. This is the basic problem of reading the text. You will not be alone if you find it very difficult just trying to follow the story of a Shakespeare play. Part of the problem is the language: you will have to read a great many speeches, mainly in verse, where the characters seem to be saying far more, and in a far more peculiar way, than if they were involved in similar situations in real life. The language is not only old-fashioned but also complex and dense. The meaning of much of what is said is likely to escape you. Coming to terms with Shakespeare must obviously include coming to terms with his language, but at the outset the best tactic is to slide over the speeches you do not understand, ignoring the difficulties. Concentrate on trying to follow the action on the simple basis of who is involved and what happens next. Indeed, reading a Shakespeare play for the first time, it is a considerable achievement if you can grasp the broad outline of the story, even if there are many parts of the play that you cannot understand and even if you have no idea of the significance of what you have read.

Following and understanding the story of a play does, however, become a lot easier if you have some ideas about what you might or should be looking for. In other words, knowing something about how to make a critical response can actually help you in your initial reading of a play.

How do I start to shape a critical response?

We must stress that the way of studying Shakespeare described in this book is only one of many possible approaches. One approach, for example, is to produce and act the play as a group, so that the play begins to make sense from the experience of performing it. This is a way of approaching the play from the inside, but such an approach is not always possible or practical. What we are more concerned with is how, as an individual, you can develop your own ideas about a play, and the best starting-point for this is probably from the outside, with some ideas about drama in general. What we mean by this is seeing how much all plays have in common, in terms of both structure and theme. Shakespeare is obviously an uniquely gifted writer, but if we know what he has in common with other dramatists this will give us something solid to hold on to which can help shape our response. Our starting-point, therefore, is the shared conventions of drama.

What does Shakespeare have in common with other dramatists?

All plays by all dramatists have a great deal in common. This becomes apparent if we consider the structure of a play, or even the structure of an episode from a television series. Every play can be said to fall into three stages, generally referred to as exposition, complication and reso-lution. The play begins with the exposition stage, where we are intro-duced to the characters and the situation they find themselves in. At the outset the characters might not seem to have any particular pro-blems, but there would not be much to interest us if we were simply confronted with characters who were living happily, continued to live happily, and lived happily ever after. Very soon, often in the first scene, a problem develops: something happens which looks as if it is going to disrupt the characters' lives. One way of putting this is to say that a kind of order prevails at the beginning of the play but that very soon this ordered life is thrown into disarray.

The central and longest stage of a play is the complication stage. Shakespeare's *Romeo and Juliet* can provide an illustration of what happens here. In *Romeo and Juliet* there are two families, the Montagues and Capulets, who are sworn enemies. There are brawls between the members of the two families, but for the most part there is an uneasy calm so long as they keep their distance. But then Romeo, a Montague, falls in love with Juliet, a Capulet, and so a complication has arisen. The consequence is that the established state of affairs that exists at the opening of the play breaks down, and we get a long sequence of scenes in which social disorder takes over, with family set against family, and child against parent. What Shakespeare is looking at are those human passions, feelings and instincts that make life complicated. In doing this he does what all dramatists do: he takes a situation where things are relatively peaceful at the outset, but then shows how the actions of people disrupt that established social order. If we think about a conventional detective series on television we find a similar pattern: characters are going about their normal business when a crime takes place. Often the crime is violent: what we see are the anti-social tendencies of certain characters shaking the established order of society. A detective series presents this disruption of order in extreme and simple terms, in that the villains are obviously acting in an unacceptable manner, but the dramatist does not have to present overly anti-social behaviour. As in *Romeo and Juliet*, he or she can present natural instincts in people that challenge, or react against, the pressures and expectations of the society in which they live. Nor does the dramatist have to treat subjects seriously: comedy, for example, can present an irrational quality in people that undermines any possibility of a rational order in society. In all plays, however, what happens is that the behaviour of the characters creates confusion and social disarray.

This leads us on to the third stage in a play, the resolution stage. In a detective series, the crime is solved, the villains are brought to justice, and a sense of social order is reassuringly re-established at the end of the episode. Stage plays can end as neatly as this, particularly comedies, but often the ending of the play is far less tidy. Sometimes, for example, as in tragedy, the social order is so thoroughly destroyed that civilised behaviour yields to violence, and the play ends with the death of the principal characters. The situation is thus in a way resolved, but what we are principally left with is an impression of the precariousness of the whole idea of social order.

What we hope has become clear here is that not only do all plays follow the same structure of exposition, complication and resolution, but also that, at least in the broadest terms, all plays have a lot in common thematically. Plays deal with threats to or disruption of the established order of society. That might sound very abstract, but what makes plays interesting is that they present these problems in human terms: they present and explore the experiences of characters caught in problematic situations brought about by their own or other people's behaviour.

How can I make use of what I now know about plays in general?

We have argued that in all plays we see some threat to or disruption of the established order of society. Passions, instincts, forces, and feelings are unleashed that undermine any established order. Such ideas are, however, only valuable if you can start making use of them to help you in your reading of specific plays. One immediate use of these ideas is that they can help you follow the story of a Shakespeare play when you are reading it for the first time. You know that at the outset you will be introduced to various characters and that soon a problem will begin to define itself. Some act, or series of acts, will take place that alters the way of life that has existed. During the course of the play things will become more and more chaotic, so that by the central point of the play life will have become completely topsy-turvy. At the end, however, things will sort themselves out in some way: order might be re-established, or there might be a feeling of temporary peace and taking stock of what has happened, but it could be that the chain of events leads to the death of one or more of the characters. If you know that this is the standard pattern of a Shakespeare play you then have a framework which can help you see the shape of the story in the particular play you are studying. Whole sections of the play might continue to baffle you, but the thing to do in a first reading is to ignore the complications and look for the broad pattern in the text.

These general ideas about drama do not, however, just help you follow the story of a play. They can also provide a framework for your entire critical analysis of a play. A common mistake students make is that they put a tremendous effort into studying every aspect of a play, so that they are able to comment in detail on every character, every scene, and every theme, but all too often they fail to see the play as a whole. They fail to see how everything holds together. The point we are making is that, if you can see the broad pattern of the text, you have a framework which can help you make sense of and interpret every local complication and detail. In the simplest terms, it can be argued that every play is built upon a tension between an idea of order and the reality of disorder in society. If you can grasp this, you have a framework for making sense of every detail in the play – the actions that take place, the characters, their speeches, the language used, and the range of themes explored – for every detail must reflect the tension between the idea of order and the reality of social disorder.

Isn't this approach too simple?

The advice given here might seem limiting, for we seem to be saying that plays always deal with the same issues. And to some extent they do, for they deal with those problems that affect us all as human beings who have to live with other human beings. We must all be aware that we live in a world that is far from peaceful and ordered. There are always tensions, disagreements and conflicts that create discord, yet the aspiration towards a better state of affairs is one that most people share. What the dramatist does is to explore and re-explore this perennial problem that confronts humanity. While the broad pattern in all plays might be the same, however, it is developed and presented in a different way in every play. The general ideas outlined so far should help you get a purchase on a play, but for the most part criticism is concerned with the particular way in which the issues are developed in a specific play. What we are saying is that the broad significance of a play is easy to see – how plays are concerned with the reality of living in a disordered world where people's unruly instincts repeatedly create discord – but the real skill in criticism lies in seeing how this theme is brought to life and made distinctive in the play you are studying. It is to this question of how to start building a full critical response that we turn now.

What should I be trying to do in a critical response?

This is a summary of the critical method illustrated in the following chapters. The first step, as already discussed, is **look for the broad**

pattern of the play. Look for the action or actions that trigger off the complications of the play: almost invariably one of the characters acts in a headstrong, or foolish, or ill-conceived, or possibly evil way. The act that takes place creates discord; the alteration in the established state of affairs throws life into disarray. Order yields to disorder. The greater part of the play will then be devoted to presenting scenes in which people are at odds with each other, and in which conflicts and disagreements or confusion and misunderstandings dominate. As the following chapters on histories, tragedies and comedies show, these initial moves which enable you to get a hold on a play are likely to prove even more productive if you **have some ideas about the particular characteristics of the kind of play you are studying**. If you know what to look for in a tragedy, for example, you can make additional advances in getting hold of the pattern of the play you are concerned with.

So far, however, your critical analysis is relying on the assumptions you can bring to a play. This means that you are likely to be stressing what the play has in common with plays in general and other plays of its kind. **The real task of criticism**, however, **is to capture the distinctive qualities of the play you are studying**. You want to explore and convey something of the unique nature of this play. A sense of what is special about a play will, in fact, begin to become clear the moment you **start looking in more detail at the plot**. The danger here is that you might lapse into just retelling the story. What you have to remember is that you are not only interested in what happens but also in the significance of what happens. There are, fortunately, two fairly straightforward ways of organising and disciplining your discussion of the plot. One is to remember that the general framework we have used, which helps you see the overall pattern of the story, can also be used as a key to help you interpret any part of the story. This means that you always have at hand a way of commenting on the significance of what is happening. The other point to bear in mind is that if you attempt to discuss too many scenes you are likely to lapse into merely summarising the action without commenting on its significance. It is far better to **concentrate on a few scenes**, working on the assumption that those scenes on their own are bound to tell you a lot about the play as a whole. To illustrate these points: you might have chosen a scene from around the middle of one of Shakespeare's plays. As you start to describe what is happening you are putting together a set of perhaps rather confused impressions. What can help you organise these impressions is if you call upon the idea that the scene is presenting a picture of social disorder, as it inevitably will be. But your abstract idea will come to life as a result of describing concrete and specific details in the scene. Remember, though, that a play is likely to maintain a constant tension between order and disorder. Look for evidence that the characters feel there is something wrong with the disorderly state of affairs: implicit in every scene will be the idea that life should be more orderly and rational, even though it is in the nature of people to disrupt harmony. As you use these large controlling ideas to illuminate small areas of the text you will begin to move towards a sense of what is distinctive about a particular play.

Our critical method has so far gone through two steps: it starts with ideas about plays in general, and then, on the basis of analysis of a few scenes, moves towards a sense of what a particular play is about. But there is more to a play than the overall significance and meaning of the plot, and as you look at individual scenes you are likely to be noticing a number of things of interest. It helps if you are aware of the kind of **things you can focus on**. The six areas of interest in a play were first listed by the Greek philosopher Aristotle: these are **plot, character, thought, diction, music and spectacle**. What we have been talking about so far is the significance that can be found in the plot, but in studying a play your attention is also likely to be caught by the other elements Aristotle mentions (with the exception of music: music is important in some of Shakespeare's plays, but it is not of primary importance in his work as a whole). You are bound to respond to the characters, and if you analyse a scene, as suggested above, you will almost inevitably find yourself talking about them. The problem with talking about characters, however, is that you might just have a vague, ill-defined feeling that they are interesting or complex. What you need is a way of focusing and disciplining your impressions, and again the large ideas we have been working with provide a way of organising your response. It can be shown how **the main characters are caught between opposite impulses**, how they are attracted by an idea of orderly and reasonable behaviour yet often find themselves acting illogically and irrationally. The broad pattern of the plot reproduces itself in the experiences and personalities of the major characters, so that there is a constant tension both in the play as a whole and in the central characters between orderly and disorderly behaviour. It can also be shown that the minor characters play an important dramatic function in this pattern, as they often serve to comment on or draw attention to the gap between how things ought to be in an orderly world and the disorderly state of affairs that prevails in the play.

The same tension is reflected in the language of a play (the element Aristotle refers to as diction), where **images of order are constantly set against images of disorder**, and in the thought of a play, which we more commonly refer to as a play's themes. All manner of themes can be identified in a Shakespeare play, but they can all be said to come under the more general heading of a tension between order and disorder. In addition, what we see on the stage, the spectacle, will reflect the same tension, for the action will either be violent or chaotic, or more disciplined and organised. In the chapters that follow we discuss these elements of drama as and when they seem appropriate for discussion, mixing them in with our broader comments on the plot, but we also make the point that a critical response can concentrate on one element if you want to construct a more rigorous scrutiny of one aspect of a play.

This discussion of how to construct a critical response is obviously very abstract, but the method should become easy to understand in the following chapters as we discuss specific plays. We do hope, though, that our main point has come across, which is that a few simple controlling ideas – primarily the idea that plays are built around a tension between social order and social disorder – can provide a key to interpreting the whole of a play, and that if you combine these large ideas with close attention to specific details of the text you should be able to capture and express what is special and distinctive about any individual play.

What, if anything, is Shakespeare trying to say in his plays?

As Shakespeare returns again and again to passions that disrupt social order it might be felt that he writes with the intention of warning people against acting in an anti-social or unruly way. We want to stress as strongly as possible that this is an inadequate view: good literature never carries this kind of simple message about how people should behave. What, then, is the purpose of the plays? Well, it is something more indirect than a purpose. Shakespeare is exploring the reality of human experience, the way in which people do act. He is making us aware of how society is complex because people are complex; of how individual instincts and passions disturb any ideal of a harmonious society. He does not write to condemn unruly instincts, but rather to explore both the good and bad qualities in human nature. He is concerned to ask questions about how we can or should behave in such a complex world, rather than to offer any answers. At the end of a play we do not come away with a message but with an increased awareness of the problems and choices and difficulties that humanity has to face up to.

What distinguishes Shakespeare from other dramatists?

We have stressed how much all plays have in common. They focus on the realities and problems of living in a disordered world. But, if this is the pattern of all drama, what distinguishes Shakespeare from other dramatists? The answer must be that the plays present a fuller and more complex sense of the nature of experience than all other writers. But how do they do this? It is tempting to start talking about Shakespeare's genius and the quality of his mind, but these are vague and unhelpful terms. Every element in the plays is, of course, important, but the really special thing about Shakespeare is his language. It seems a silly thing to say, but Shakespeare is the greatest writer because he writes so much better than anyone else. One aspect of this is that every speech carries a tremendous weight of meaning. This is one reason why the speeches can prove hard to take in when we are first reading a play, as the characters are not simply saying things that advance the action but constantly raising all the larger questions implicit in the play about the whole relationship between a harmonious vision of life and the messy reality of experience. The effect of this is that every Shakespeare play seems to raise fundamental questions about the whole nature and meaning of life. It is this that makes Shakespeare's plays difficult and demanding, for they always raise more issues than any single reader can ever fully comprehend. Yet, even if we cannot hope to grasp a Shakespeare play in its entirety, this very richness of the speeches can help us when studying the plays, for whatever speech we turn to can be guaranteed to be raising many of the questions raised in the play as a whole.

Why does Shakespeare write in verse?

The answer students most frequently give to this question is that it was the convention, that most dramatists wrote in verse at this time (around

1600). There has, however, got to be a better answer than this, an answer which manages to connect Shakespeare's choice of method with the content of his plays. What we have stressed so far is that behind the plots and characters of Shakespeare's plays is a level of larger significance in which questions are being raised about the whole nature of life in society. Writing in verse is, in fact, in itself an effective way of forcing these larger questions on to our attention. We are confronted with an action sufficiently stylised to be not just a mirror image of life, but something at a tangent to real life, so that we do not simply become absorbed in the action but realise that there is a larger pattern of significance inherent in the play. But it goes further than this. Poetry is highly ordered language: when Shakespeare writes in verse his lines are usually in blank verse – that is, unrhymed lines, each line containing ten syllables. This ordered quality of poetry relates to the issues we have been discussing, for not only is there always a tension between the idea of order and the reality of disorder in the content of the plays; this tension is also in evidence in the form of the speeches. Time and time again it is the case that in an ordered verse form a character will be talking about the disorder of experience. There is thus, in Shakespeare's preference for verse, a constant tension between the desire for neatness, symmetry and order and the awareness that life itself always burgeons out of control. Consequently we can argue that the preference for writing in verse is at one with the thematic substance of the plays, for verse raises the same questions about order and lack of order in life. Shakespeare does not, however, always write in verse: there are often scenes and speeches in the plays where he obviously feels prose is more appropriate. Our general ideas should again help us explain this: presumably at such moments we are closer to the mundane reality of life where order and disorder jostle together. We are closer to the daily shambles of experience, and, for the moment, any more inspiring vision of order in life has been eclipsed.

What we have explained so far is Shakespeare's overall preference for verse, but we also want to stress one of the particular ways in which his verse works, the way in which it allows him to concentrate a great deal of meaning into a few lines. We can make the point most clearly if we refer to Hamlet's most famous soliloquy:

> To be, or not to be – that is the question;
> Whether 'tis nobler in the mind to suffer
> The slings and arrows of outrageous fortune,

Or to take arms against a sea of troubles,
And by opposing end them? . . .
                                    (*Hamlet*, iii.i.56–60)

Hamlet is debating with himself whether to commit suicide. His life is
full of problems and troubles, and Shakespeare uses warfare and sea
images to help clarify and make vivid Hamlet's dilemma. But the use of
imagery (words from one area of experience or life to describe another
area of experience) also adds to and complicates the meaning of the
lines. Hamlet's 'troubles' are only his personal feelings of unhappiness,
but, by associating his feelings with such large and chaotic subjects as
warfare and the sea, the individual experience is linked with vast
aspects of life. Within the space of a few lines Shakespeare thus
manages to incorporate questions and concerns that go beyond the
stated subject matter, with the result that the speech is not just about
Hamlet's feelings but becomes a huge statement about the whole
nature of life in a giddy, disordered world. We get the impression that
Shakespeare is not just dealing with the immediate situation but with
the whole complex nature of life.

    This soliloquy, and the way in which it works, sums up much of
what we have been talking about so far. We can see how it focuses on
the disorder that erupts in Hamlet's life, and on his baffled response,
his uncertainty how to act. We can see how Shakespeare is doing more
than just telling the story of one person, how he is raising questions
about life in general, and that the most effective way of doing this is
through the use of verse, often because, as here, the imagery manages
to extend and broaden the issues involved. But the method of analysis
we have employed is also important: we moved from our general ideas
to discussion of a particular passage from the play. This is always the
most productive approach: using a few, simple controlling ideas, but
then focusing on details which can give a more precise and more vivid
idea of what the play is about and how it works.

Isn't this becoming too complicated? Wasn't Shakespeare essentially a working
playwright who wrote enjoyable plays to entertain people?

Some people argue that the academic way of looking at Shakespeare
gets it wrong, that it places too much emphasis on the ideas and language of the plays, and loses sight of how well his plays work as thea-

trical entertainments, and of the marvellous parts he creates for actors. And certainly it is very important to try to appreciate how the plays work on the stage. But it is also the case that any appreciation of the theatrical qualities of any play has to be based upon and must follow on from some understanding of what the play is about. Otherwise, we can end up knowing a great deal about how a play might be performed without understanding the logic behind the performance. In the pages that follow we have therefore tried to relate any discussion of staging to a discussion of meaning in the plays. Nevertheless it is true that this book is intended principally for those of you who are studying Shakespeare for examinations, and the sort of things we say reflect the kind of emphasis there is in examination questions on Shakespeare. The system as it exists is far more likely to ask you to talk closely about a speech than to discuss a production of a play you have seen, and the direction this book takes simply reflects and responds to that state of affairs.

Do I need to know anything about Shakespeare's life and times?

Our whole emphasis has been on the productiveness of working with a few general ideas and then turning to specific scenes and speeches. But can it all be done this way? Isn't it necessary to know something about Shakespeare's life and the period in which he wrote? One of these questions we can provide a very short answer to: you do not need to know anything about Shakespeare the man behind the plays. Stories about Shakespeare's life might be interesting, but they will not help you understand the plays.

Knowing about the times in which Shakespeare wrote, however, is useful, although the amount of information you need is very small indeed. Shakespeare was writing around 1600 in an era that is sometimes referred to as the Renaissance period. This period sees a major cultural shift as the medieval world yields to the modern world, resulting in an extraordinary flood of great literature. There is a shift from an essentially religious world view to an essentially secular world view as a new sort of dynamic society based on trade and commerce comes into existence. A central aspect of this change is that people came to feel that they were living in a less familiar, somewhat more disturbing world. The medieval period offered people a secure image of a divine order in the universe: there were problems, of course, but the world seemed both well ordered and comprehensible. This gives way, very slowly, to a less stable, less confident world view. Shakespeare's acute sense of the disorderly nature of experience could be said to be due to his instinctive feel for what was happening. Throughout Shakespeare's plays there is a sense of a traditional order that is being torn apart. The people upsetting things are often characters of a certain kind: they are self-interested and ambitious. The plays thus reveal a sense of a new spirit of individualism which is in conflict with the traditional religious order. Individuals are increasingly presuming to take the initiative in a world where it used to be the case that everyone knew their place and trusted in God.

Where do I go from here?

This chapter has concentrated on the assumptions and ideas you can bring to your reading of Shakespeare. We have said a little about how you can construct a full critical response to a play, but the usefulness of such comments is obviously limited in the absence of examples. It is in the next three chapters that we turn to discussing specific plays. It might well be that we fail to discuss the Shakespeare play or plays that you are studying, but try to see how these chapters are concerned with showing you how to construct a reading, rather than with providing you with full analyses of plays. We suggest a sequence of steps for looking at a play, and the same sequence is repeated with every play we consider. The method of analysis itself is most fully discussed in the analysis of *Richard II* which appears in the next chapter, and you might find it useful to read this, even if you are not studying a history play, as it spells out the technique for studying a play. The principal thing the three central chapters of this book attempt to do is to illustrate this systematic approach, but we do provide some additional pointers about what you might want to look for in certain plays.

The way to use these chapters is to take as much or as little from them as you want to. The most important thing is to read and reread a play so that you really know it well: this repeated reading of a play will teach you more about it than any teacher or critical book such as this can do. The next three chapters might, however, help you organise and discipline a response. What we say is obviously far from everything that can be said about Shakespeare: if you have ideas of your own it is important that you express them. Criticism would be a very drab affair if everybody read books in the same way and found the same things in them: what will make your criticism personal and worthwhile is if you have the courage to develop your own insights.

So, it is a case of reading the play, and then working on the play – taking what you want from this and other books and from your teachers, but also developing your own ideas. In the study of literature, however, more than in the study of any other subject, the way in which you express your views is as important as the views themselves, and in chapters 5 and 6 of this book we focus on how to write essays and answer examination questions on Shakespeare. The advantage of having a good essay-writing technique is that it not only enables you to develop your own work on the text, it also helps you begin to take on more advanced critical ideas. This is something we turn to in the second part of the book, where we look at new approaches to Shakespeare and apply them to some of the plays discussed in the next three chapters. The intention is to show how the same method of analysis will serve you well at all levels in your work on Shakespeare.

2

Studying a history play

THE ENGLISH HISTORY PLAYS

SHAKESPEARE'S principal English history plays are *Richard III*, *Richard II*, *Henry IV Parts One and Two*, and *Henry V*. The two we discuss here are *Richard II* and *Henry IV Part One*. It might be that you are studying one of the others, but try to see how the approach we demonstrate can be used to analyse any of the history plays. Remember that the pattern of all plays is that some action takes place at the outset that triggers off a problem, and that the greater part of the play is then devoted to presenting the ensuing conflict. We can, however, be more precise about the particular pattern found in a history play, and it is this which provides us with a starting-point for our analysis of *Richard II*.

Richard II: constructing an act-by-act analysis

1   *Read the play, then think about what kind of play it is and what sort of broad pattern you can see in the plot*

Richard II is a history play, and history plays have common characteristics. They present famous historical figures at moments of crisis in their lives. In Shakespeare's English history plays the emphasis falls upon the problems a king has to face: these take the form of rebellious elements within the kingdom and/or the foreign wars he has to fight. If we consider the plot of *Richard II* we can see that it conforms to this pattern. Richard banishes Bolingbroke and then confiscates his lands to help finance a war in Ireland. Bolingbroke consequently invades England and deposes Richard; he then ascends the throne as Henry IV. Almost immediately Richard is murdered, and the play ends with Bolingbroke's troubled awareness that Richard had to be murdered to make his own position as King secure. What we thus see is a king

17

overthrown by rebels. We should, just by reading the play, be able to see that this is the central action, but, if we cannot, an awareness of the standard format of history plays should help us see the pattern in the plot. There is more that can be said about this pattern of kings and rebels, but it might prove most helpful in this first illustration if we relate this to a discussion of the opening scenes of *Richard II*.

2   *Look at the first two or three scenes, trying to achieve a sense of what is happening in this particular play*

The best strategy with the opening scenes of a play is to look at what is happening and then move forward to a sense of the significance of what is happening. The scenes need not be discussed in any great detail as the intention at this stage is simply to establish a sense of the particular issues in this play. *Richard II* begins with Bolingbroke, Richard's cousin, accusing Mowbray of treason. Richard orders that their quarrel be settled by armed combat. After a short second scene, scene iii takes place on the day of battle, but Richard intervenes and banishes both men – Mowbray for life, and Bolingbroke for ten years, which he immediately reduces to six.

It might seem difficult to start commenting on the significance of these events, but the way to approach the problem is to have some ideas about history plays in general, and then to interpret the action of the play in the light of those ideas. Implicit in history plays is an idea of a well-ordered society in which everyone is content and everyone fulfils his or her social role. In the hierarchical society of Shakespeare's history plays, this would be a society where the King, as God's representative on earth, carried out his duties carefully and responsibly, with his subjects respecting and serving their king. Such a settled state of affairs is, however, only an ideal: real life is never like this. Real life is always characterised by conflict and disagreement. It is the gap between how things might or should be and the reality of how things are that the history plays explore.

The events at the beginning of a history play can always be interpreted in the light of these ideas. In *Richard II*, the play immediately plunges into a conflict with Bolingbroke accusing Mowbray of treason: we are immediately confronted by the kind of disagreement between people that creates problems in society. Can you see how our method of constructing a critical response to the play is to concentrate on specific details which we interpret in the light of the simple controlling ideas we have established? If we look at the actions of Richard, we see him mishandling the dispute between Mowbray and Bolingbroke, first deciding on one course of action and then changing his mind. The significance we read into this is that Richard is not providing very good leadership. In the course of the opening scenes, therefore, an implicit idea of a well-ordered, peaceful society is set against the messy reality of how things actually are, with noblemen in dispute and the King failing to control them. If you can perceive such a pattern in a history play, how the untidy reality of life is set against an idea of how things might be, then you have really got hold of the play as a whole.

In addition, however, you also have a framework for interpreting individual scenes, actions and speeches. Let us consider, for example, Richard's action in suddenly changing Bolingbroke's ten years of exile to six. One thing worth asking yourself about any detail is whether it reflects an ordered state of affairs in society or whether it seems to have more to do with the disordered side of things. In this instance, a clear-cut ten year sentence of exile might reflect a king who is acting decisively to preserve order in the country, but Richard's quick change of mind seems to indicate that he is weak and indecisive, that things are unstable under his rule.

If you went through the events in the first three scenes of a history play, every action could be discussed in this kind of way. A picture would develop of what the particular issues are in the particular play you are studying. It does help, however, if you know that the king is going, on the whole, to appear as either an effective monarch or as a weak (or, in the case of *Richard III*, a perverse) figure, and that the rebels are not necessarily out to create disorder in the state but indeed are often honourable figures who find themselves caught up in conflicts that get out of hand.

3   *Choose a scene from Act II, and try to clarify your impression of what this play is about and how it is developing*

The procedure with the opening scenes is to look at what is happening and then beyond this at the significance of what is happening, how the play is presenting a dramatic picture of the tensions and problems that exist in political life and the governing of a country. A large part of the secret of producing good criticism, however, is learning not just to talk about the text in these general terms, but discovering how you can make use of specific actions and details to illustrate vividly what the issues are and how they are brought to life in a particular play. It would be possible to work through a play discussing every scene in this kind of way, but such a thorough approach can sometimes accumulate facts at the expense of understanding. We suggest, therefore, that you look at one or two scenes from each act, so that you focus on how the issues in the play are developing. As good a scene as any to choose is the first scene in each act, but, if this scene seems difficult or puzzling or not particularly revealing, you can move on to a more promising scene. Or there might be a scene that you found especially interesting and which you particularly want to discuss. We, however, have decided to look at the first scene of the second act of *Richard II*. We need to build on the ideas and impressions we have established so far, but our approach, as in the first act, is to describe what is happening and then to comment on the significance of what is happening.

John of Gaunt, Bolingbroke's father, is dying, and wishes to see Richard. The King visits him and listens to a rebuke from the old man, but dismisses it. Gaunt is carried off and dies, whereupon Richard immediately confiscates his estates, despite York's warning against this. The scene ends with Willoughby, Ross and Northumberland conspiring against the King. This is what happens. We now have to move forward to discussing the significance of these actions, and after that we should be in a position where we have a reasonably confident sense of what this play is about. That, of course, makes it sound easy, but, despite the fact that we have talked about a method of analysis, the chances are at this stage that you will still find it very hard to talk about the significance of the action rather than just describe it. This is where the simple formula of labelling actions and details as orderly or disorderly, that we used in discussing the sentence Richard passes on Bolingbroke, can help so much. In this scene, the old man who is dying gives the King his advice, but Richard rejects it. It would seem reasonable to say that Gaunt is the good counsellor whose duty is to advise the King and that his speech offers us an image of how England should be. The reality, however, is Richard's foolish lack of respect for Gaunt's advice and for the traditional order of things in England. This idea of the traditional order being flouted is immediately underlined by the forfeiture of Bolingbroke lands, which is a vivid way of illustrating how Richard's actions are throwing the country into disarray as he overturns the established laws of inheritance. What we are doing is working from our controlling idea of the gap between an idea of the well-ordered state and the reality of how things are, interpreting the details in the light of this, asking ourselves whether actions seem to contribute to a sense of a desirable state of affairs or whether they reflect a disorderly state of affairs. Our main impression of this scene is that Richard's actions undermine the established order of things he is supposed to represent, so that even such men as York are becoming disaffected. His failings as a monarch are leading to civil unrest, and the scene effectively sums this up at the end when we see three men launching a conspiracy against him.

In looking at the first two acts of *Richard II*, we have kept to the idea that a history play explores the gap between how things might be and how they really are, seeing how this idea is brought to life in the action of the play, and the result is that we can now be rather more specific about the particular issue this work presents. It seems to us that Shakespeare is examining the problems that ensue when a king fails to live up to what is expected and required of him. We must stress, however, that this is only our interpretation of what is revealed in the first two acts: you do not have to accept our reading of the play. What we are principally concerned to do is to illustrate a method of analysing a play – a method which involves working with a few simple, controlling ideas and interpreting scenes in the light of these ideas – and one of the virtues of this method, we hope, is that it should not only help you organise and discipline your response but also leave you plenty of freedom to establish your own view of the play on the basis of what you discover in the scenes you select for discussion. This technique of establishing a coherent view of a play is far more important than the particular reading we offer.

4   *Choose a scene from Act III to see how it develops the issues you have identified so far, and now begin to pay more attention to the principal characters in the play*

So far we have established a view of what this play is about. There comes a point, however, when it becomes necessary to start investigating the issues more closely. We suggest that the place to start doing this is with Act III, having used the first two acts to establish the solid foundations of an analysis. One advantage of focusing more closely at this point is that the third act is often very revealing, for by this stage we are in the middle of the play's complications. This is evident at the beginning of Act III of *Richard II*: Bolingbroke, offended by the taking of his lands, has now returned to England. The confrontation with Richard has yet to take place, but Bolingbroke has captured Bushy and Green, two of the King's flatterers, and in the opening scene of the act he orders that they be taken away to be executed. As with earlier scenes, the easiest way of getting to grips with this is to ask yourself whether the details tend to reflect a state of order in society or social disorder. Here, the country is at the opposite extreme from social order, as England is actually in a state of civil war. When Bolingbroke presumes to order the execution of Bushy and Green he assumes for himself the right to exercise justice, a right which, it must be clear, can only be the King's prerogative: it is a graphic illustration of how the established order has been overturned.

We have spent long enough, though, establishing the general picture: we now need to look more closely at the characters caught up in these events. We also need to start looking more closely at the words of the play and what we are seeing on the stage. All of this will enable us to gain a fuller sense of the experience of the play. The most productive move to make at this stage is to select one of the principal characters for closer investigation and then to look closely at what he says in part of one of his lengthier speeches. Bolingbroke, as one of the two central characters in the play, is obviously the person to look at here. In this extract he is explaining to Bushy and Green why they are to be executed:

> You have misled a prince, a royal king,
> A happy gentleman in blood and lineaments,
> By you unhappied and disfigured clean;
> You have in manner with your sinful hours
> Made a divorce betwixt his queen and him;
> Broke the possession of a royal bed,
> And stain'd the beauty of a fair queen's cheeks
> With tears drawn from her eyes by your foul wrongs:
> Myself – a prince by fortune of my birth,
> Near to the King in blood, and near in love
> Till you did make him misinterpret me –
> Have stoop'd my neck under your injuries
> And sigh'd my English breath in foreign clouds,
> Eating the bitter bread of banishment,
> Whilst you have fed upon my signories,
> Dispark'd my parks, and fell'd my forest woods . . . .
>   (III.i.8–23)

The speech amounts to a catalogue of their crimes: they have misled the King, created a division between Richard and his wife, and robbed Bolingbroke of his birthright. You might feel that you could work out the literal meaning of the speech, as we have done here, but would then feel unsure what else to say about it. This is where we can introduce one of the most important ideas you have to grasp in studying Shakespeare: this is that the themes of the play as a whole are reflected in every aspect of the play. Every character, every speech, every detail, reveals and reflects the larger concerns of the play. Here, for example, an idea of the natural order of things – a happy king, a stable marriage, Bolingbroke on his own estates in England with the confidence of the King – is set against Bushy and Green's destruction of that order. Try to see how Shakespeare uses imagery to convey this tension. Bolingbroke says, for example, that Bushy and Green have 'disfigured' the King and 'fell'd' his forest woods. Disfiguring suggests a deforming of the body, while felling of woods suggests destruction of the order of nature. The effect is that the issue is broadened, so it is not just a matter of misleading the King but of a violent destruction of the entire natural order of things, from order in the body politic through to order in the natural world.

The key to interpreting the words of a speech such as this, then, is to see that, although the language is complex, the idea that informs and shapes it is the idea we have worked with all along of the order that should be as opposed to how things really are. Once you have realised this, criticism becomes somewhat simpler, for you do not have to rack your brain puzzling away about what to say, but can move back and forth from simple ideas to analysis of how vividly these ideas are brought to life in the text. And good criticism amounts to nothing more than clear ideas about the text which you can illustrate and support from the evidence of the text.

Analysis of the words of a speech is essentially a matter of seeing how images of order are set against images of disorder. The personality of Bolingbroke, or of any of the main characters, can be discussed in very similar terms. From this speech alone we can see that Bolingbroke is motivated by a concern for the well-being of England. He is reluctant to blame the King for the problems that have developed. What he says is that Bushy and Green have corrupted the natural order of things. Yet this puts Bolingbroke in an awkward position, for he too is challenging the King and thus challenging the natural order. Nor are his motives entirely clear: he seems to be acting in the public interest, but he resents the stealing of the lands, so is also partly motivated by self-interest.

The impression of Bolingbroke that comes across, therefore, is of a complex character, but what we have to see is that the basic tension is very simple. People might aspire to be good and to create a better world, but their very ideals can create problems, and they are also likely to reveal quite ordinary human failings. The secret of producing good criticism, however, is to move from these general ideas to specific extracts from the text which bring these ideas to life. On the basis of the speech we have examined, for example, we can say that Boling-broke is essentially a good and honourable man who has a great concern for the well-being of England, yet his sense of how things should be is inevitably bringing him into conflict with the King. In addition, there is a streak of individual self-interest in his actions. If we wanted to fill out this picture of Bolingbroke we would have to look at other sections of the play where he appears, but what we would always find is a tension between Bolingbroke as the servant of the state and Bolingbroke the man. We should find a very similar division in Richard's personality.

5   *Choose a scene from Act IV and attempt to build upon everything you have established so far*

Our method of analysis involves working with a few, simple controlling ideas and interpreting extracts from the play in the light of these ideas. Our basic idea is that there is a huge gap between how things should be in England and the more complex reality of how they actually are. Day-to-day life is complex because society is made up of individuals who are not content to be mere robots obediently serving the state. Each of the main characters is likely to have individual characteristics which clash with his or her social or political role, or to have ideals which bring him or her into conflict with other characters about how the state should be run. The simple fact is that life will never be stable and peaceful as people cannot suppress their individuality.

The way to appreciate how these issues are brought to life is to focus on short extracts from the text. What might surprise you is the very small amount of text we discuss at each stage. The reason for this is that an analysis will probably become unwieldy if one tries to discuss too much. It is much better to tackle a manageable amount of material.

In turning to discuss Richard, therefore, we are going to work from a
very small section of Act IV rather than attempt to consider everything
that happens to him in the play.

The section we have chosen is where we see Richard and Bolingbroke together, as Richard hands over his authority. If you are unsure
what part of a scene to select for discussion, a good rule is to choose a
moment when some seemingly significant stage direction appears. Here,
for example, we look at a passage where Richard, having just surrendered the crown to Bolingbroke, calls for a mirror. Looking into the
mirror he says,

> No deeper wrinkles yet? Hath sorrow struck
> So many blows upon this face of mine
> And made no deeper wounds? O flatt'ring glass . . . .
>
> (IV.i.277–9)

As with looking at Bolingbroke's speech, it is not immediately obvious
what we can say about this, but what we have to remind ourselves of is
the fact that the idea of the difference between how things should be
and the reality of how things are, which permeates the play, must be in
evidence here. Richard is surprised that his face does not reveal the
sorrow and blows he has experienced. He is, after all, a king who has
had to hand over his power to an usurper. To his surprise the mirror
reflects back an image of his kingly self.

What we have is a difference between the image of Richard as
king and the reality of Richard as a man. He might have the appearance of a king but he lacks the necessary authority and personality. He
has been expected to play a public role, a role which was in fact
beyond him, but what is revealed to us here is the suffering and pain of
the individual who finds himself in this situation. A full character analysis of Richard might expand on his bravery in defeat and the pathos
of his life and death, but any fuller analysis of Richard has to be based
on an understanding of the gap between the role he is expected to play
in the state and his nature as a man.

As always, there is a sense of the nature of individuals making life
more complicated than any ideal image of how life should be. This
impression is confirmed at the end of this scene: Bolingbroke looks as if
he will prove to be a far more capable leader of the country, but the
scene ends with the possibility of further civil unrest as a new rebellion
is planned by Aumerle against the new king. What we see is that the

idea of the well-ordered state remains a remote ideal: the reality is that people will always be led by their own instincts rather than just prove docile servants of the state.

6   *Choose a scene from near the end of the play which shows how the issues are resolved, and which will enable you to draw together the threads of your critical analysis*

To conclude an overall analysis of a play the most logical scene to look at will usually be the very last scene. At the end of *Richard II* Bolingbroke, as Henry IV, has replaced Richard as king, but the country is not at peace. News of fresh outbreaks of civil commotion is repeatedly delivered at court. This is what we might expect to find at the end of a history play: the issues in the play have been resolved and a new king begins his reign, but the real problems have not disappeared. Dissent and division are still prominent as individuals will always have different views of how the country should be run and will also want to defend their own interests. Bolingbroke is also troubled by his awareness that Richard had to be murdered in order to make his own position as King secure. He is aware that murder is an offence against any notion of how things should be organised in society, yet murder served his interest as a man who aspired to be the king. Richard's coffin on stage is a grim reminder of what happens when order collapses in society, of how things can lapse into anarchy and uncontrolled violence even as people aspire towards a better state of affairs.

What you should try to see, though, is that Shakespeare is not writing with the intention of providing answers to political and social problems. People sometimes suggest that Shakespeare's history plays are about the qualities needed by a good king, as if Shakespeare is saying that if the king exhibited certain qualities then the whole of society would be in better health. But Shakespeare is far less concerned with how things might be in a perfect world than with how they are in the real world. He is not offering us messages about how people should behave, but examining the reality of how they do behave. At the same time, however, we need to recognise how strong the sense of order is in the plays, how the picture of individuals creating discord in society is only so powerful because all the actions and all the speeches include a sense of that well-ordered society which is not being achieved.

Our analysis of *Richard II* has focused on how it presents the tensions of political and social life, tensions which are created by the personalities of the characters involved. You might find, however, that you are more interested in the personal element in the play, in particular the presentation of the suffering of Richard, and this is a perfectly legitimate focus of interest. Indeed, what is important and interesting in any play is what you find important and interesting. It is the case, however, that a reading of *Richard II* will lean either towards discussing it as a history play – which involves paying attention to the political issues it raises and will mean paying as much attention to Bolingbroke as to Richard – or towards discussing it as a tragedy – which will involve a greater degree of concentration on the experiences and suffering of Richard. The full title of the play is, in fact, *The Tragedy of King Richard the Second*, and if we looked at it as a tragedy, rather than as a history play, we would see it somewhat differently. A tragedy focuses on a suffering individual caught up in a chaotic situation. This clearly provides us with a way of talking about Richard and his experiences. If we pursued this line there would be a rather different idea at the centre of our reading of the play. Whereas we have emphasised the gap between the ideal of the well-ordered state and the reality of the disordered state, an interpretation of the play which examined its tragic qualities might well focus on the disorder of life, but is likely to balance this with a sense of the courage of the central character who displays so much of humanity's potential for greatness even amidst the tragic waste of life. This is too big an idea to explain fully here, but is the controlling idea in the following chapter, which deals with the tragedies. Several of Shakespeare's English and Roman history plays can, in fact, be regarded as being both histories and tragedies, and so this is a point that we shall return to in the course of this chapter.

7   Pursuing aspects of the play

If you make use of the method of analysis illustrated here, by this stage you should have a coherent view of *Richard II*. The only qualification we should make to this statement is that, whereas we have looked at just two extracts from the third and fourth acts, you might find it necessary to look at two or three further passages from Acts III and IV before a clear picture emerges. By this stage, too, you should have sufficient ideas and enough material to write a very reasonable essay. You could, of course, add to this overall analysis by looking at further extracts from the play. It might be the case, however, particularly in preparing for an examination, that it could prove more rewarding to look at a variety of aspects of the play, these being character, themes, language, and staging. This does not necessitate launching into new ideas, as everything you might want to say on these topics should be an extension of what you have already discovered. In other words, looking at an aspect of a play does not involve searching for new ideas but rather it involves developing your analysis in a particular direction by focusing on that aspect. What you do need to remember, however, is that, whatever aspect of a play you are considering, the way to write effective criticism is to make use of the text. If you choose to talk about a character, for example, your ideas can be simple, but what will bring your ideas to life is the degree to which you focus on what the character does and says in the play, using specific illustrations to make your points.

(a) *Character.* The characters are obviously absolutely central in a play. What sometimes goes wrong when students look at characters, however, is that, while they can see they are interesting individuals with interesting personalities, they fail to see that the main characters are part of the larger pattern of the play. This is easy enough with minor characters, who usually act as commentators on the action, such as the gardeners in Act III, scene iv. But what you must see is that the main characters also serve a function, that they embody the issues which are at the heart of the play. To take Bolingbroke for example: it would be possible to construct a very full character analysis of him in which you talk about his good and bad qualities, but such an analysis will lack a sense of direction and purpose unless you see that he is initially reluctant to challenge the traditional God-given authority of the King but feels that he has to do so in the public interest. As the play goes on, however, a degree of self-interest becomes more apparent as he grows ambitious for power. The division in him is a split between public-spirited idealism and more selfish motives. When you focus on extracts from the play in which he appears it should become apparent that he is never totally good or totally bad, that there is always an ambiguous mixture of motives. Bolingbroke is thus one embodiment of the larger issue of the play, how the complex reality of humanity's fallible nature is at odds with any simple idea of order. The same is true of Richard. Again, you could construct a full but purposeless character analysis, whereas what you have to see, and illustrate from the evidence of the text, is that the complex nature of his personality as a man comes in conflict with the role he is expected to play as king.

What is true of these two characters is to some degree true of every important character in the history plays. The plays examine the gap between the ideal of a well-ordered state and the reality of disorder in the state, and each of the main characters in the plays experiences the same division, being torn between loyalty to the role he or she is expected to play and the instincts in his or her personality that rebel against such disciplined obedience. It is the nature of people – not evil people, but people who have ordinary human weaknesses and ambitions – that prevents a peaceful and stable society from coming into being. One way of putting this is to say that the central characters are torn between what their heads tell them to do and what their hearts tell them to do. You can only show this, however, if you select and discuss passages in which the character or characters you are interested in appear. It is a case of selecting details, as we did in our act-by-act analysis, and showing how the details make concrete and bring to life your broader ideas.

At the same time, it is also important to remind yourself that the central characters in a play are not two-dimensional figures with fixed personalities but are likely to develop as they confront different situations or to change under pressure from events. As they change, or as new, perhaps contradictory aspects of their personalities are revealed, so too your response to them may shift. Richard's actions in the opening acts of *Richard II*, for example, might make him appear weak and foolish, but his speeches in Act IV, as he surrenders his crown, may well evoke not only your sympathy but also a sense of his greatness, that he is able to see and voice a sense of humanity's plight in a chaotic world. Stripped of power he is forced to re-examine his understanding both of the world and of himself. It is this facing up to the world and to his own position which most clearly identifies the change in Richard.

(b) *Themes.* By theme we mean an issue which is being dealt with in a play. For example, typical themes in Shakespeare's English history plays are honour, rebellion, war, truth, time. In analysing a play as a whole you will have developed your own ideas about its themes. Often, however, you will come across the suggestion that other themes are central. For example, in discussing *Richard II* we identified its main theme as the gap between how things should be in a well-ordered world and the more complicated reality of how things actually are. Some critics, however, suggest that the central theme of the English history plays is 'kingship', and the theme of *Richard II* is sometimes identified as 'the problem of deposing a king'. What you have to see is that these are only other ways of talking about the same idea. Take 'kingship': Shakespeare might be interested in the qualities that make a good king, but he is aware that people are fallible, that the King might find it difficult to live up to what is expected of him and that the King's subjects will often prove reluctant to serve him in a docile manner. We return, therefore, to the idea that there will always be a gap between the simple ideal of order and the reality of life's disorder, but under a different heading: the same issue is being discussed, but here the particular focus is on the gap between the ideal and reality of kingship. 'The problem of deposing a king' is similarly a matter of the conflict between accepting the traditional order in which the King is seen as God's deputy or an ideal figure, and the difficulty of accepting that traditional order. The point we are making is that every additional theme which might be mentioned is not a completely fresh subject that you have to consider in the play, but simply another way of describing and focusing a discussion of the issues which you have already noted as central in the text. If you decide to look at 'kingship', for example, search for those speeches in the play which make explicit reference to the problems of being a king, but try to see how the ideas you have already formulated give you an organising framework for talking about this subject.

(c) *Language*. Nothing frightens people as much as being asked to discuss the language of a play, yet in some ways it is the easiest thing to talk about, primarily because the speeches in a Shakespeare play are so rich and so full of meaning. In looking at a speech you should be trying to see how it expresses the larger themes of the play, and almost invariably Shakespeare does this by setting images of order against images of disorders. All the histories make use of war imagery, setting an ideal of peace against the bloodshed of battle, and also religious imagery, cosmic imagery, legal imagery and imagery from nature. In this way an idea of something perfect or natural or just is set against its disorderly opposite. Such images always help create a vivid impression of the tension in the plays between the ideal of order and the reality of disorder.

It is, then, possible to approach a history play knowing in advance something about its language. In addition, however, each play has its own characteristic images. *Richard II* is very rich in garden imagery and sun imagery. Again, these serve to make clear the contrast in the play between ideals and reality: there is both the contrast between how England should be – an idyllic, well-ordered garden – and how it is, and between the God-like ideal of kinship and the human reality of kingship. But what you also have to grasp about such images is how, as in Bolingbroke's speech in Act III, scene i, they broaden the meaning of the play so that what is involved is the whole idea of order in life through from order in the heavens to order in society and in nature. Our analysis of Bolingbroke's speech (*see* p. 22) provides one example of how to discuss Shakespeare's language, but we offer a far fuller discussion of this in chapter 5, where we tackle the problem of how to discuss an extract from a play. What you have to remember, however, is that there is little point in talking loosely and generally about the language of a play, saying, for example, that *Richard II* is full of religious imagery; the only way to get to grips with the issue is to see how the language operates in specific passages.

(d) *Staging.* Talking about staging primarily involves reporting on the visual impression the play offers, on what we see happening on the stage. This might seem difficult if you are just reading the play, but what you have to do is to visualise what the words tell you is going on. And it is again the case that the issues of the play, which permeate the text, will be apparent in what we see on the stage. For example, in *Richard II* there is a great deal of ritual and pomp in the opening scene: this offers an impression of Richard's surface grandeur as a monarch. Very soon, however, we see Bolingbroke and Mowbray arguing: the real tensions of life disrupt the surface appearance of things. The visual effects of a play are, in fact, bold, simple and fairly easy to talk about. As the society is consumed by civil war and chaos the movements on the stage become increasingly frenetic. This is an example of just how direct the effects on the stage are.

In talking about staging, however, it is always worth looking at any scene where you feel the visual impression is particularly striking. One such scene is where Richard descends from the walls of Flint Castle (III.iii). This is visually arresting, but it also carries within it the larger tensions of the play. We know that he is the King and are therefore all the more struck by the indignity of this event. It is a world away from the ritual that surrounded him in Act I and altogether closer to the messy, painful reality of life. The King who is to be deposed is here literally brought down. The point with staging, then, as with talking about characters, themes or language, is that in order to appreciate it you have to have a solid idea of what the play is about, but, in actually looking closely at how the play brings this idea to life on the stage, you capture and convey something of its unique dramatic nature as a play that is both seen and heard.

Henry IV Part One

To illustrate how the method of analysis described above can be applied to any of the history plays, we now want to look at *Henry IV Part One* (Shakespeare wrote two separate *Henry IV* plays: *Part Two* continues the story of *Part One*, but they are distinct plays with a quite different tone). Our discussion of this play will be briefer than our discussion of *Richard II*, however, as we now want to concentrate on showing you how you can construct your own reading of a history play rather than to provide you with a full analysis. The purpose of this book, after all, is to show you how to study a Shakespeare play, not to study the plays for you. As always, the place to start is with a consideration of the kind of play you are reading and the general pattern of the plot. The first two acts can then be looked at to establish a sense of the particular issues in the play, and then, as you turn to Act III, you should be attempting to report in rather closer detail on the experience of the text.

1   *Read the play, then think about what kind of play it is and what sort of broad pattern you can see in the plot*

Henry IV Part One is a history play. The subject matter is the troubled reign of Henry IV. Attempting to impose his authority on the country he has alienated various noblemen who helped him achieve power. The most prominent of these are Hotspur, Northumberland and Worcester, who organise a rebellion, hoping to unite the Scots, Welsh and northern rebels against the King. Another worry for Henry is more domestic: his son Hal (the future Henry V) is consorting with rogues, most notably Falstaff, in the London taverns, and seems unconcerned about playing his role as heir to the throne. The play deals with the

rebellion, which the King puts down, but even at the end of the play
he is still uneasy as there is the possibility of further rebellion and more
battles. One development, however, is that during the course of the
play the apparently dissolute Prince Hal mends his ways, and is valiant
in support of his father.

Such a summary, and even a reading of the play, might well leave
you baffled, but try to see the standard pattern of a history play in this
plot. Try to see how the play deals with the problems the King has to
face. This is the conventional pattern of a history play, but you also
have to be aware of the significance of this pattern, the way in which
the play makes use of the idea of a well-governed, peaceful society, but
sets against this the reality of how things actually are in the country.
You can assume that the play is dealing with the gap between the idea
of a well-ordered society and the disordered reality of life.

2   *Look at the first two or three scenes, trying to achieve a sense of what is
happening in this particular play*

You have some general ideas and expectations; you now have to start
interpreting the action of the opening scenes in the light of these ideas.
In the first scene the King is in his palace in London. A period of civil
war is over and Henry plans to go off to fight in the crusades, but news
comes of fresh disturbances and he announces that he must abandon
his idea of a crusade. Further news then comes that Hotspur, one of
the King's followers, has defeated the Scots. Hotspur's conduct makes
the King think of the unsatisfactory behaviour of his own son Hal. We
then learn that Hotspur refuses to hand over his prisoners to the King.

The way to start interpreting the events of the scene is to ask
yourself whether the details reflect an ordered or disordered state of
affairs. The King's ideal plan is for a crusade, but the plan has to be
abandoned because of fresh troubles at home. What you have here is a
simple example of how the idea of an ordered existence, in which the
King tries to make plans for the future, is undercut by the reality of
day-to-day life. You can interpret other details of the scene in the same
way, seeing, for example, that Hotspur, in refusing to hand over his
prisoners, proves to be something other than a totally loyal servant of
the King. Henry is also worried by the disorderly behaviour of his own
son. As you select details for comment, and find your own way of

expressing the significance of these details, you will begin to produce your own distinctive account of the play. Your controlling framework, however, is the idea that a notion of order in the state and even in the family is being set against the untidy complications of life.

Given the nature of this opening scene, the second scene of the play might appear rather surprising. You might expect a serious dramatisation of Henry's problems in running the country, but scene ii features the King's son, Hal, and his drinking-companion, Falstaff. They exchange insults and banter, and Falstaff is generally disrespectful of the whole idea of the serious business of running a country, being concerned only with a life of drinking and indulgence. Hal and Falstaff plan a robbery, but then Hal arranges with another character, Poins, that they will subsequently rob Falstaff. All the scenes with Falstaff are good fun, and vastly entertaining on the stage, but it can prove hard to see their function in the play. The material about Falstaff is, in fact, a subplot, a fully developed story that runs alongside the main sequence of events in the text. What you need to know is that a subplot, and Shakespeare uses them frequently, usually illuminates the main plot: the issues being presented are the same issues as in the main plot, but they are presented in simpler terms in the subplot. The subplot is thus a useful thing to look at because it helps you understand what the play is about. To think about a subplot, use the formula of asking yourself whether details of the play suggest an ordered or disordered state of affairs. You can see that Falstaff is a fat rogue who spends all his time drinking and thieving. Does such a character strike you as belonging to the order or disorder side of things? The answer, obviously, is that this is disorder on a grand, even if rather ludicrous, scale: here is someone who has no respect for law, authority or moderation.

What you need to do now is to pursue the question of Falstaff's function in the larger pattern of the play. At first he might just seem to be an example of irresponsible behaviour and so simply to be disapproved of, but there is clearly something very attractive and enjoyable about Falstaff and, indeed, about his complete lack of respect for authority and discipline. It soon becomes apparent in *Henry IV* that Henry is a far stronger king than Richard II and unwilling to countenance rebellion in any form. Falstaff, however, refuses to be tied down by laws and rules, and his presentation in the play seems almost a celebration of individual instincts which act against uniformity and order in society.

We mentioned earlier in this chapter that *Richard II* can be regarded as both a history play and a tragedy. *Henry IV Part One* is a history play, but a history play with a comic subplot, and one of the main ideas in comedy (as chapter 4 explains) is that it shows us how foolish and irrational people are, how they are so motivated by foolish desires that social life is always close to collapsing into chaos. If you examined some of the details of the presentation of Falstaff in this second scene or other scenes where he appears you could show how his actions and words serve to deflate through comedy the whole idea of any kind of dignified and stable order in the state. This is not the main emphasis of the play, but related ideas feature in the main plot where the refusal of a character such as Hotspur to be a docile servant of the King seems both heroic and natural. The difference is that, whereas the subplot laughs at and enjoys disorderly impulses, the main plot gives serious consideration to the problems caused by people's instinctive unruliness. We might add as an aside that, because it does seem so ready to celebrate individual instincts, *Henry IV Part One* is a fairly happy play even though it deals with serious political issues, but that *Henry IV Part Two* is a far grimmer play. In *Part Two* Hal rejects Falstaff, and the King stamps out rebellion. Order is achieved in the state, but it is not an attractive or desirable order as it is brought about through a rigidity which suppresses individuality.

If you managed to come to terms with the first two scenes of *Henry IV Part One*, you would now be in a position to sum up your impressions so far. You know that all history plays deal with the gap between how things might be in an ideal world and how they are in the real world, but you need to pinpoint the specific issues in this play. What you might decide is that, whereas *Richard II* focuses on the problem of a weak king, *Henry IV Part One* is more concerned with an instinctive rebellious and self-interested streak in people that makes them challenge the authority of the King.

3   *Choose a scene from Act II, and try to clarify your impression of what this play is about and how it is developing*

Act II starts with a curious scene between two carriers or porters. The scene is so curious that you might find it hard at this point to fit it into your overall scheme of things. When this happens, when a scene baffles you, move forward to the next scene. So, scene ii features the robbery carried out by Falstaff, and then Hal robbing Falstaff. We are going to talk about this scene in as simple terms as possible. Let us suppose that you had not been able to make anything of the first act, but hope to work something out here. All you need is the idea that history plays concentrate on the gap between the idea of the well-ordered state and the messy reality of life. Crime is part of the untidy reality of everyday life, so, if nothing else, Falstaff's robbery provides an illustration of one of the problems that exists in society. When Hal robs Falstaff, the play shows what a tangled web of confusion there is in the country. All act for themselves, even double-crossing their friends, and thus the play dramatises how it is in the nature of people to create discord. Yet Hal, as the heir to the throne, ought to be on the side of order, not adding to the confusion. As ever, even amidst the disorder, there is a sense of how people should act, and it is this that creates the dramatic tension in this scene.

All we have done here is look at the action on stage and inter-pret it in the light of our controlling ideas. It will often be the case that if you start your analysis of a scene by thinking about what happens on stage in this simple fashion you will achieve a concrete sense of the play while also clarifying your ideas about its staging. Here, for example, it is not difficult to imagine the comic effect as Falstaff first terrifies the travellers and then is put to flight by Hal and Poins. Both actions convey a vivid sense of disorder. Part of the comedy lies in the use of dramatic irony. Dramatic irony is in evi-dence in plays when the audience knows something that the character or characters in the play do not know. Here we know Hal is going to rob Falstaff and so can enjoy the fat rogue's threats and bravado in the anticipation that his mettle will be tested more severely. Dramatic irony always works in this straightforward way in a play, putting us in a position where we know more than the characters on stage, but it is also reflected in the very arrangements of the staging. As we watch Hal watching Falstaff steal we are aware of a distance between them, of a tension between Falstaff's bulky disorder and Hal's seeming disorder. This visual tension adds to our impression of a confused state of things in the country, of how appearances might be deceptive. The larger point we are making here, though, is that it is always helpful to think about the visual impact of a play, and how it serves to realise the themes and issues.

4   *Choose a scene from Act III to see how it develops the issues you have identified so far, and now begin to pay more attention to the principal characters in the play*

You now have some idea of the issues in this play, in particular how it focuses on the unruly nature of people. The next step is to start looking more closely at how the issues are brought to life in the play. Act III begins with Hotspur and others who are now actively conspiring against the King. They make their plans and then Hotspur takes leave of his wife as he prepares to go off to fight. Hotspur's name gives you a clue to his character: he has a hot, fiery temperament that resists being told what to do. But the rebels also feel that they have a justified grievance: they feel that they have not been sufficiently rewarded for their part in deposing Richard II.

At this stage it is a good idea to start focusing on particular speeches. We have chosen a section that features Hotspur and his wife, primarily because it is the kind of passage that you might find hard to interpret since it appears so peripheral to the main action of the play. What you need to remember, however, is that every scene, speech and detail reflects the larger concerns of the play. Hotspur's wife, Kate, urges him to sit still and listen to some music, but he is impatient to be off to fight. In that detail alone there is an idea of harmony, here associated with music, being set against more wayward impulses. But Hotspur does sit and listen, and then urges Kate to sing. She says she will not, adding the phrase 'in good sooth'. The politeness of this phrase amuses and angers Hotspur, who says:

> Swear me, Kate, like a lady as thou art,
> A good mouth-filling oath; and leave 'in sooth'
> And such protest of pepper-gingerbread
> To velvet-guards and Sunday-citizens.
>
> (III.i.254–7)

The way to make sense of his comments is to look for an opposition between images of things orderly and images of disorder, and, indeed, Hotspur sets the whole world of manners, polite turns of phrase, and conventional behaviour against an idea of vigorous and earthy swearing. It is very much of a piece with Falstaff's disdain for correct behaviour: a tension is thus constantly in evidence in the play between an idea of a polite and civilised society and human impulses that resist this. The problem is, however, that if people do not try to create order in society the country will slide into violence and chaos, and this is what is about to happen, for when Hotspur leaves a civil war will be under way. Yet Hotspur is not simply a trouble-maker: he does not enjoy mindless violence for its own sake. The very fact that we see him with his wife suggests that he enjoys the order of domestic life, while his decision to challenge the King is prompted both by his sense of the need to restore his own honour and by his concern for the well-being and honour of England. What you have to take account of, therefore, in assessing Hotspur is that, like all the central characters in the history plays, he is pulled in two directions at once. There is a mixture of motives which includes idealism but also self-interestedness and sheer instinctive rebelliousness.

5   *Choose a scene from Act IV and attempt to build upon everything you have established so far*

As you can see, the strategy in looking at Act III is to select a small section, or perhaps several small sections, of the text for analysis, so that you can talk with some precision about the issues of the play and how they are brought to life in the words, actions, and presentation of characters. The next character you will want to look at is Prince Hal, who is a far more central figure in the play than his father. The crucial point to grasp about Hal is that as a prince he should be working to create harmony in the state, not spending his time in the company of Falstaff. By Act IV civil war has broken out. Hal only makes a brief appearance in this act, but he begins to appear in a different light. He is still in the company of Falstaff, yet preparing to fight in support of his father. It is again the case that if you want to say something really precise about Hal then the best tactic is to focus on a small section of the text, but the problem here is that Hal's appearance in Act IV is so brief that there is not a substantial speech to work on. The answer is to keep turning the pages until he makes a more promising appearance; and in Act V, scene i, he can be found talking about his conduct, and also taking about Hotspur.

> I do not think a braver gentleman,
> More active-valiant or more valiant-young,
> More daring or more bold, is now alive

To grace this latter age with noble deeds.
For my part, I may speak it to my shame,
I have a truant been to chivalry . . .

(v.i.89–94)

So far we have represented Hal as a waster, but this speech makes clear that he is alert to how princes should behave and is conscious of the shortcomings of his own conduct. It is, in fact, the case that if you looked at any of Hal's earlier speeches in the play you would see how he does distance himself from Falstaff and is always conscious of how he should behave as a prince. But the really surprising thing about this speech is that what you might have previously considered as rebellious belligerence in Hotspur is represented by Hal as noble. Hotspur is seen as possessing all the social virtues of being a brave gentleman, valiant, daring, bold and chivalrous. There is something inspiring about Hal's words: whereas the play as a whole has set correct social conduct against unruliness, it is as if Hal can see these individual energies of people as contributing to, rather than harming, the well-being of the country. It can be argued that his life in the London taverns has been educative in that he has seen the reality of how people are, and has a vision of how there could be a stable society which none the less accepted and coped with the individuality of people's natures. In Hal, then, there is a promise of a more harmonious society in the future, for he seems ready to recognise and accept those instincts in people that react against docile obedience to the state.

6   *Choose a scene from near the end of the play which shows how the issues are resolved, and which will enable you to draw together the threads of your critical analysis*

You are likely to find yourself responding positively to Hal in this promise of something better, but it is only a promise. Shakespeare is far too wise to provide us with glib solutions to life's problems. At the end of the play an idea of how life should be is still being set against the disorderly reality of life. Hotspur is killed and lies dead at Hal's feet. In the final scene, the King has defeated the rebels but fresh civil disorder is imminent. In summing up the play, therefore, you might well want to draw attention to how human beings inevitably and invariably create discord. Yet, as much as the play presents a picture of a society beset with quarrels and disagreements, an ideal of order is always present in the text. This tension is not just there in isolated examples, such as the presentation of Hal in the play, but is built into every speech and the presentation of every character. You might feel that your act-by-act analysis has only just begun to achieve a sense of how such an issue is presented in the play, but if you have come this far you have a coherent view of the work, and are therefore in a position to turn confidently to other scenes and speeches to fill out and develop your impression. Equally, you have a solid base on which to build further comments about the play's characters, themes, language and staging.

If, for example, you wanted to talk about staging, the most practical way of doing this is to select particularly striking moments in the play where you feel it makes a strong visual impact. For example, you might be interested in seeing how ideas of order and disorder are dramatised in the battle scenes. War itself suggests an idea of chaos, but in any detail we look at we can expect to find an opposition or tension. Take the fight between Hal and Hotspur in Act v, scene iv. Hal defeats Hotspur and then stands over his body. On stage too is the corpse of the seemingly dead Falstaff. For a moment it seems as if Hal has overcome both the unruly honour of the headstrong Hotspur and the corpulent disorder of Falstaff, as if order has been established and Hal's reputation redeemed. But Falstaff is not dead, and, after Hal has gone, rises. We see that life, in the comic form of Falstaff, refuses to fit into a neat pattern to suit the needs of the state.

We have moved through *Henry IV Part One* quickly. You might, therefore, find our comments more frightening than helpful, but try to see how simple the critical moves are that we have made. We started with an idea of the standard pattern of history plays. We then looked at the first two acts, trying to gain a more precise sense of the issues in this play. After that, we started to focus more closely, looking in particular at the characters, and putting sections of speeches, and obviously you might find it necessary to look at more extracts than we have done here, under a kind of critical microscope. By focusing as closely as this, we could say fairly precise things about the play, so that as we reached the final act we were in a position to draw together the threads of our critical analysis. The same ideas and the same approach can be used to study any of Shakespeare's history plays, including the Roman history plays, to which we turn next.

THE ROMAN HISTORY PLAYS

As well as the English history plays, Shakespeare wrote three Roman history plays, *Julius Caesar, Antony and Cleopatra* and *Coriolanus*. What we can predict, even before looking at them, is that these plays, like all history plays, will present famous historical figures at moments of crisis in their lives. *Julius Caesar* presents the assassination of Caesar when he is at the height of his power both as a soldier and as ruler of Rome. *Antony and Cleopatra* presents the famous Roman general lured away from his responsibilities by his love for Cleopatra. *Coriolanus* presents a general who wins a great victory for the Romans against the Volscians, but who is then turned on and rejected by the citizens of Rome; he goes over to the Volscian side, where he is again victorious as a general, but they also turn against him and he is cut to pieces by the mob. As with the English history plays, order and stability in the state seem elusive: there are rebels who create problems, and the heroes themselves are no less fallible. It is the easiest of the three plays, *Julius Caesar*, that we discuss here, and as with *Henry IV Part One* we try to provide guidance about how you can construct your own response. We also, however, provide a note about the other two plays at the end of this chapter, and take up the point that all three of these plays can be described either as history plays or as tragedies.

Julius Caesar

1 *Read the play, then think about what kind of play it is and what sort of broad pattern you can see in the plot*

Julius Caesar is a history play. It begins with Caesar returning to Rome after his military triumphs. Various people in Rome are, however, beginning to turn against him, and a conspiracy develops in which even Brutus, an old friend of Caesar's, becomes involved. The conspirators murder Caesar. Mark Antony, who has not been involved, swears vengeance for Caesar's death. Antony is victorious in the subsequent battle at Philippi, and Brutus kills himself. There is more to the plot than this, but the complications can be ignored for the moment.

Your starting-point is trying to detect the standard pattern of a history play in the plot. Order seems to exist at the beginning of the play: Caesar has been triumphant, and one would expect a feeling of

national unity and achievement to be dominant. Yet the conspirators
are disaffected and keen to dislodge Caesar. Any idea of a well-ordered
state becomes more and more remote as the country slides into a civil
war. The wounds do, however, seem to be healed by the end, when
Mark Antony is victorious, but the ending is possibly not as straightforward as this. As with all history plays, the play seems to focus on the
gap between the ideal of an ordered society and the complicated reality
of life. As yet, however, you do not know what the particular problems
are in this community; this should become clearer as you look at the
first two acts.

2   *Look at the first two or three scenes, trying to achieve a sense of what is
happening in this particular play*

Your method here is to describe what happens, and then to move on
to an impression of the significance of what happens. In the first scene,
two tribunes, Flavius and Marullus, encounter a group of workers who
are preparing to welcome home the victorious Caesar. The two tribunes criticise them, urging them to return to their work. If you read
their speeches carefully you might gather why they feel this way, but
for the moment it is enough to say that here is just a slight note of
discord in a day of victory. The first seed of the subsequent tension of
the play has already been sown.

Caesar, his wife Calphurnia and Mark Antony make their first
appearance in scene ii. An old man tells Caesar to 'Beware the ides of
March' (a detail we shall return to), and then the scene moves on to a
conversation between Cassius and Brutus. Cassius attempts to persuade
Brutus to join a growing movement against Caesar. The way to interpret these actions is to ask yourself whether the details suggest an
orderly or disorderly state of affairs. The conspiracy against Caesar is
clearly a threat to the order of society, and if you looked closely at this
part of the scene you might be able to point to evidence that men envy
Caesar his success and power. Yet you might also gain the impression
that Cassius is not entirely motivated by self-interest: he is worried
about the power Caesar is assuming for himself. There is, then, a
mixture of self-interest and genuine concern for the national interest in
what Cassius says. As in all history plays, *Julius Caesar* is already presenting those instincts and convictions in people that bring them into
conflict with their leaders. Caesar must take some of the blame for this,

for if you examine the scene you will find evidence that he is becoming too powerful, that he is beginning to abuse his position as leader.

What makes *Julius Caesar* a relatively easy play to study is that it focuses such issues quickly and clearly and keeps them central. As with all history plays, it focuses on the gap between the ideal of a well-ordered society and the untidy facts of life. The problems are caused by the members of the society. In this play, both the leader and his subjects have good qualities and shortcomings. Caesar is a great leader, but his vanity and love of power create disaffection among his subjects. Those, such as Cassius and Brutus, who rebel against him are not evil men: indeed, they are acting from the most honourable of motives, believing that they are working for the general good of Rome, but there is also a degree of self-interest in everything they do. The clash of competing interests and of people with competing ideas inevitably leads to discord. All the central characters are interested in the well-being of Rome, but their different visions of how the national interest can best be served, and their understandable flaws as human beings, inevitably create conflict in the state.

3   *Choose a scene from Act II, and try to clarify your impression of what this play is about and how it is developing*

We have devoted a fair amount of space to talking about the framework of ideas that informs *Julius Caesar*, as it always helps if you can see the logic behind a play, but criticism is primarily concerned with how the play dramatises and brings to life its themes. You would, therefore, need to work on Act I, showing where and how it presents such issues, and again, as you turn to Act II, you must look closely at the text. In the first scene of this act, Brutus is visited by the conspirators and persuaded to join them in the killing of Caesar. It is not a decision he arrives at lightly, but he decides it must be done for the good of Rome. Choose a manageable section of the scene to look at: use the formula of looking for details which suggest order and details which suggest disorder. What you are likely to find is a number of contradictions: that Brutus desires to be loyal to Caesar yet also desires to be loyal to Rome, that his respect for the civilised life of Rome might involve killing a man, that the point where the public interest stops and private interest begins is far from clear. Such ideas could easily become unmanageable unless you focused on a small section of text to discipline your argument. The underlying idea, however, is simple: that harmony in society becomes elusive the moment we take account of the complex nature of the people who make up that society.

4   *Choose a scene from Act III to see how it develops the issues you have identified so far, and now begin to pay more attention to the principal characters in the play*

In the first scene of Act III the conspirators kill Caesar. After this, Mark Antony and Brutus emerge as the central characters, and it is these two that you will want to look at in most detail in your analysis of the play. Mark Antony has not been involved in the conspiracy. Apart from this, however, you are not likely as yet to have achieved any very clear notion of his personality. All you know, from the play as a whole, is that he and Brutus become involved in a power struggle and it is Mark Antony who is the victor. This seems a good moment to establish a clearer view of his nature and of his function in the play. In the second scene of this act, Brutus explains to the Roman crowd why Caesar had to be killed. The conspirators have, however, agreed that Mark Antony can address the people of Rome after Brutus. He enters bearing the body of Caesar and delivers a long speech over it, constantly drawing the crowd's attention to it, a point we shall return to later. For the moment we want to concentrate on what Mark Antony says. These lines come from towards the end of his speech:

> Good friends, sweet friends, let me not stir you up
> To such a sudden flood of mutiny.
> They that have done this deed are honourable.
> What private griefs they have, alas, I know not,
> That made them do it . . . .
>
> (III.ii.210–14)

Initially these might strike you as the words of an honest man who cannot understand the motives that lead people to create disorder in society. Indeed, Antony pleads for sanity, asking the crowd to curb their mutinous instincts (which would be directed against Brutus and his fellow conspirators). He seems to be saying that the all-important thing is the maintenance of peace and order in the country. But look at how he addresses the crowd: 'Good friends, sweet friends . . . .' Isn't this slightly suspicious because it is excessive? Can you see how Mark

Antony might be a skilful politician, cajoling and manipulating his audience? The more you look at what he says, the more likely you are to feel that this is a cunning, rather than an honest, speech. What you have to do now is relate this impression to your larger ideas about the play. A simple, but wrong, reading of the play might be that bad men kill the good man, Caesar, but then another good man, Mark Antony, comes along to punish them. But what this speech seems to suggest is that Mark Antony is an opportunist, interested in seizing power for himself. Again, a simple, but wrong, reading would be to say that this makes him a bad character, but ambition is an important part of human nature. Mark Antony, however, is not simply ambitious: he is also loyal to Caesar and grieves over his death, so that our impression of him is a complex one, divided as he is between unswerving loyalty to Caesar and more selfish motives.

This division is brought out most clearly in the staging of the scene. We mentioned earlier the fact that Mark Antony makes his entrance carrying in the murdered body of Caesar. This powerful spectacle creates an immediate effect of Mark Antony's loyalty and grief. But the second point to grasp about the staging here involves seeing how Mark Antony uses Caesar's body as a theatrical prop to manoeuvre the crowd's sympathy, timing his references to it and building up to the horror of the murder by showing them where Brutus stabbed Caesar through his cloak. As he does so we recognise those ambitious instincts in Mark Antony and his skill as a political leader able to turn events to his advantage, with the result that our response to him shifts and changes from a fairly simple one to a much more ambiguous and ambivalent one.

What we see, therefore, is how the issues and tensions of the play are evident everywhere in the text, in its language, staging, even how they are at the heart of the presentation of the central characters. A well-ordered, peaceful society is the ideal we all aspire to, but the presence of individuals in a society, all of whom have different interests and different ideas of how a better society can be brought into being, creates discord. In the same way, no character can be simply an obedient robot content to serve the state. Every important character is motivated by a mixture of idealistic and self-interested motives. But it isn't good enough just to talk about this in general terms: you need to look at extracts from the play, such as this speech of Mark Antony's which illustrates how Shakespeare makes the themes of the play vivid and concrete.

5   *Choose a scene from Act IV and attempt to build upon everything you have established so far*

Brutus is the other character who demands attention; he is a more like-able character than Mark Antony, but a tension between idealism and self-interest should again be observable in the scenes in which he features. Mark Antony's speech has turned the crowd against the con-spirators, and by Act IV civil war has broken out. Mark Antony is the leader of one party, Brutus the leader of the other. You could look at any of Brutus's speeches in this act, but we have chosen an extract where he and Cassius are quarrelling: Brutus accuses Cassius of taking bribes and then refers to the death of Caesar:

> Did not great Julius bleed for justice sake?
> What villain touch'd his body, that did stab,
> And not for justice? What, shall one of us,
> That struck the foremost man of all this world
> But for supporting robbers, shall we now
> Contaminate our fingers with base bribes,
> And sell the mighty space of our large honours
> For so much trash as may be grasped thus?
>   (IV.iii.19–26)

The grammatical structure of this is somewhat strange, so it may be hard to follow, but what Brutus is saying is that surely they stabbed Caesar to promote justice, not because of a desire for personal gain, and surely things have not now arrived at the point where they are going to stain their characters by taking bribes.

If you wanted to talk about the language of this speech, the approach, as always, is to see how images suggesting order are set against images suggesting disorder. Here a whole series of words and phrases suggesting admirable qualities and high principles (for example, 'great Julius', 'justice', 'mighty space of our large honours') are set against images of baseness and corruption (for example, 'villain', 'robbers', 'contaminate our fingers', 'so much trash'). As always, the broader issues of the play are reflected in every detail of the play, the emphasis here being on the opposition between the very best and very worst qualities in people.

But what of Brutus? Surely Brutus himself is untainted, for he is so vigorous in his denunciation of self-interest. He clearly does not reveal himself to be an opportunist in the way Mark Antony does. And certainly the impression of Brutus that comes across in the play is of a man with very high ideals. Even though he has acted from the best of motives, however, he has helped contribute to the creation of disorder in his society. The play, therefore, illustrates again that the moment we take account of the nature of human beings, even good men such as Brutus, the creation of a well-ordered society seems an impossible dream. In addition, although Brutus is not corrupt and not hungry for power, there is a kind of self-interest in his pride in his own high principles, in how seriously he takes himself. The simple ideal of a well-ordered society can never become a reality because people are complex, and, as the difference between Mark Antony and Brutus shows, complex in all kinds of ways.

6   *Choose a scene from near the end of the play which shows how the issues are resolved, and which will enable you to draw together the threads of your critical analysis*

The battle between the two sides takes place at Philippi. It is a chaotic battle, and this seems appropriate: it seems to be another way of suggesting how issues in life are tangled rather than ever being clear-cut. Cassius commits suicide, and Brutus, who has seen Caesar's ghost and seems to have a kind of fatal awareness that he is doomed, also kills himself. The idea of fate ties up with the soothsayer who appears in the early stages of the play. His warning to Caesar to 'Beware the ides of March' suggests that there is a larger pattern of fate that determines everything. The idea is not pursued in any great detail in the play, but what the references to fate in both the above instances suggest is that there might be some larger supernatural scheme of things that is beyond the clear perception of people. This idea is not central in the text, but the play does acknowledge that if order cannot be found on earth there might be order somewhere. This, though, is hardly comforting for the characters, for it merely emphasises how they stumble around in the dark, creating problems and conflicts, and how everything in life is beyond their control.

The problems of the play do, however, resolve themselves to the extent that Mark Antony emerges clearly as the victor at the end. The country is at peace again, but the play ends with the victors talking about Brutus. Mark Antony himself refers to him as 'the noblest Roman of them all'. Rather than looking to the future, therefore, the play ends by looking back at the tragic waste of life that this society has experienced. As in the English history plays, Shakespeare has no remedies to offer: he simply offers us an impression of the complex reality of political and social life, showing how people always create discord in society, yet at the same time we are never allowed to forget that aspirations towards a better society are necessary, or else life will deteriorate into anarchy and violence.

We have shown how you can discuss *Julius Caesar* as a history play, but the play is also a tragedy, the tragedy of Brutus, a good man caught up in a chaotic situation which his own actions have helped bring about. If you discuss the play as a tragedy the emphasis of your analysis will differ. In discussing a history play it is important to appreciate how the play presents an impression of the disorder of experience, but what has to be set against this is a sense of the general aspiration towards a better-ordered society that permeates the play. In discussing *Julius Caesar* as a tragedy it is also important to recognise how it presents an impression of the disorder of life, but what has to be set against this is the personality of the central character, who, in his courage, offers us a sense of humanity's potential for greatness even in a chaotic world. Brutus clearly has enough substance as a character to make a worthy and true tragic hero. Indeed, even if you discuss *Julius Caesar* primarily as a history play, you might feel that to capture a full idea of the impression the play makes you need to acknowledge Brutus's stature as a tragic hero.

A note on *Antony and Cleopatra* and *Coriolanus*

Antony and Cleopatra and *Coriolanus* can, like *Julius Caesar*, be regarded as both history plays and tragedies. To take *Antony and Cleopatra* first: Antony, the same Antony as in *Julius Caesar*, is now one of the three rulers of Rome, but he has been diverted from his political duties by his love for Cleopatra. This leads to a situation where Rome, led by Octavius Caesar, and Egypt, led by Antony and Cleopatra, are at war. Believing Cleopatra to be dead, Antony kills himself and, consequently, Cleopatra also kills herself. We have talked consistently of how people create discord in society: with Antony it is the passion of love that leads him to neglect his social obligations. As a history play, *Antony and Cleopatra*, like any of the histories, presents a full impression of the consequences of that element in people that make them something more than just servants of society. But what makes this play so complex is that the disruptive factor here is the finest of all passions, the passion of love. Antony's head might tell him to do one thing, but his heart tells him to do another, and the love between Antony and Cleopatra is presented in lavish and extravagant terms. It is, indeed, so extravagant that we seem to be seeing something larger than the examination of political and social realities that generally characterises the histories. In order to make sense of the impression this play offers we do need to regard it as a tragedy. What we have to see first is how Antony's actions create discord in society, so that the play offers a vivid impression of life becoming chaotic and disorderly. But what we have to set against this is a sense of the greatness both of Antony, who reveals many of the best qualities of human beings even in such a chaotic situation, and of Cleopatra. The beauty of the verse in *Antony and Cleopatra* is important in this: on the one hand we have an impression of the disorder, chaos and waste of life, but, on the other, the eloquence of Antony and Cleopatra is in itself a demonstration that there is something lyrical and great about humanity.

In looking at the play, then, you will need to get hold of how it creates a picture of terrible disorder in life, but you will also need to look at the way it conveys a sense of the greatness of Cleopatra in her love, despite her failings. In looking at Antony, you will need to identify the division within him, how he is torn between love and duty, how this creates a turmoil within him, but also how his courage in facing this gives us a sense of something positive to set against the picture of tragic waste. As *Antony and Cleopatra* goes beyond the ideas about history plays offered in this chapter, it might well be that the following chapter on tragedies will provide you with more precise ideas about how to study it.

Antony and Cleopatra is, therefore, a history play which demands to be considered as a tragedy. *Coriolanus*, however, has more in common with the other history plays we have looked at. It is, though, a much grimmer and far more bitter play than these. Coriolanus has been victorious as a soldier, but first the Romans and then the Volscians turn against him. The way into the play is to think about the standard pattern in history plays of the division between how things might be in a well-ordered society and the far more complicated reality of experience. What creates problems, as always, are the attitudes and actions of people which work against the establishment of harmony in society.

The problem with Coriolanus himself is that, although he is a marvellous soldier, he is arrogant and conceited. He cannot tolerate his fellow citizens. The other characters in the play, including the mob, are equally lacking in attractive qualities. Indeed, they seem to be motivated only by self-interest and show few, if any, of those finer qualities that distinguish the characters in *Julius Caesar*. The clash of interests in the play, as in all the history plays, leads to disorder in society, but what makes the play seem so gloomy is that its emphasis is so negative. In the other histories there is always the awareness that people create discord, but there is also a sense of an aspiration towards a more rational, better-ordered society. In *Coriolanus*, however, there is not the same sense of an ideal worth pursuing, rather a more jaundiced sense that life will just collapse into violence. This is not to say that we cannot find images of order, of ideals. Indeed, the play is built on them: there is Rome itself, the family, friends, honour, valour, but they are all shown to breed violence rather than harmony.

Similar problems emerge if we consider *Coriolanus* as a tragedy. Coriolanus's failings help create a chaotic situation, and the play presents a terrifying picture of the violence and destructiveness that can consume society. But Coriolanus himself does not possess those awe-inspiring qualities that we usually associate with the tragic hero. He is more of a victim of society than anything else. If the play seems somewhat unsatisfactory, at least when we set it against Shakespeare's major tragedies, it is probably because its emphasis is so negative. It conveys a powerful impression of the disorder of experience, but does not offer anything more positive, either in the way of a vision, or ideals, or a sense of greatness in humanity to weigh against this. It is a late play of Shakespeare's, and probably the most pessimistic view he offers of the world in which we have to live. It is significant that after *Coriolanus* Shakespeare in a sense abandons real life for romance – writing *Pericles*, *Cymbeline*, *The Winter's Tale* and *The Tempest*. The final word we will offer on *Coriolanus*, and the histories generally, is that, if you can see what we mean when we describe *Coriolanus* as a negative play, you have grasped an important point about the kind of tension that is generally in evidence in Shakespeare's histories and tragedies.

3

Studying a tragedy

THE TRAGEDIES

SHAKESPEARE'S four major tragedies are *Hamlet, Othello, King Lear* and *Macbeth.* They are generally recognised as Shakespeare's finest plays. To understand why, it helps if we start by thinking about tragedy as a specific form of drama. The pattern of all plays is that some action takes place or a character does something that throws life into turmoil. To express this in the simplest terms, social order prevails at the beginning of the play, but very quickly we see society in a state of disorder. The effect of this is that a play makes us think about the complex nature of people and the world we live in; we see the gap between our ideal notions of a peaceful, stable society and the reality of a world where people are unruly.

It is important to grasp that those instincts that lead to disorder can either be laughed at or be viewed seriously. The two traditional forms of drama are comedy and tragedy. Comedy laughs at people's unruly instincts and passions. In tragedy, by contrast, the dramatist gives full and serious consideration to the disruptive effects of people's behaviour. Indeed, the consequences are so serious that the disorder presented leads to the death of the main character at the end of the play. Any play that ends with the death of the main character is a tragedy; the pattern is always the same: the society presented in the play has shifted so far from any orderly standard of behaviour that it collapses into violence, and the main character is the principal victim of this violence.

It might occur to you that we can find this pattern in several of Shakespeare's English and Roman history plays as well as in a play such as *Romeo and Juliet.* They all present societies where conventional notions of social order have collapsed, and as order collapses into chaos it becomes clear that the main character is going to die. They are, therefore, quite properly described as tragedies. Usually, however, when people talk about Shakespeare's greatest tragedies they have in mind the four plays mentioned at the beginning of this chapter. There is an awareness that they are in some way different from the history plays that can be regarded as tragedies. Where we can pinpoint this difference is that the great tragedies raise much more disturbing questions about life. In the history plays, when things begin to go wrong, it is because people are weak, or fallible, or ambitious, or resent authority. In the major tragedies, however, the passions that disrupt life are far more extreme: there is a focusing on the evil in human beings, an evil that results not just in the death of the tragic hero but also in the deaths of the innocent and good who seem to be singled out for destruction for no other reason than that they are innocent. The great tragedies, then, force us to ask how such qualities as goodness, love, justice and loyalty can survive in the world given people's capacity for evil and destruction.

If we assume that at the beginning of a tragedy life is much as it always has been (things are far from perfect, but society is at least holding together in some kind of way), some action then takes place that disturbs the *status quo*. The moment the façade of order is shattered, we begin to see the cruel, vicious and murderous side of people, to see the self-seeking, hatred and violence. It is as if a false sense of a civilised life has existed, but the moment the usual social restraints are relaxed an overwhelming force of evil is released, and this creates the terrible disorder of the central stages of a tragedy. In *Hamlet, King Lear* and *Othello* the hero comes up against the evil of those around him; in *Macbeth*, however, it is the tragic hero himself who is revealed as being evil the moment he gives way to his desires. This is one reason why the great tragedies are likely to strike us as particularly ambitious plays: whereas the histories look at people in society and consider the political problems of human behaviour, the great tragedies consider the possibility that human beings are no more than vicious animals. Most people, of course, are not evil, but because these are extreme plays they can consider that potential for evil that history (for example, recent history in the wartime concentration camps) has shown is there in human nature.

The difference between those plays of Shakespeare's that can be seen, quite correctly, as tragedies and the major tragedies is therefore a matter of degree and emphasis. In the histories, the characters, however much they might create discord, are essentially honourable and well-intentioned or weak. In the major tragedies the focus is on evil as a problem in life. This is why *Antony and Cleopatra* is not grouped here with the major tragedies: it is an extreme play, and to describe it as just a history play seems inappropriate, but the extreme disruptive force examined is love rather than evil.

This awareness of evil as a disruptive force helps us search for the basic pattern in a tragedy. Early on we meet the tragic hero, a figure such as a king or a great soldier who has a prominent social role. He has to be a great figure who has achieved or can be expected to achieve much, for one of the things that is going to be examined is the possibility of human achievement in the face of evil. Then, through his own actions or through what he discovers, his life and the life of those around him is thrown into disarray. As in any play, we are confronted with disorder in the central stages, but in tragedy what we see is an extreme form of disorder where the whole of life seems close to chaos and meaninglessness. This terrible disorder then leads directly to the death of the tragic hero.

By focusing on extreme passions in people, specifically their potential for evil, the plays raise fundamental questions about the whole nature of existence, asking whether human beings are anything more than violent animals disguised in the clothes of civilised human behaviour, even asking whether there is any order or meaning in life. The other thing to be aware of in the basic pattern of a tragedy, however, is the tragic hero himself, who, amidst this vision of the worst face of people, offers us a sense of the best face of people. The major tragedies might seem to present a bleak and disturbing vision of life, but through the tragic hero we are given a sense of the human potential for greatness even in such a chaotic world. One of the problems with Shakespeare's major tragedies, however, is that, although they share this common pattern, each play is very different. Shakespeare's histories have a lot of common characteristics, as do his comedies, but the four major tragedies are ambitious not only in what they say but also in the extent to which each is unique.

Hamlet

1   *Read the play, then think about what kind of play it is and what sort of broad pattern you can see in the plot*

Hamlet is a tragedy. What you might be more aware of, however, when you first read it is that it is a very long play which might prove hard to summarise. In summarising one of the histories it is reasonably clear how one events leads to another, but *Hamlet* appears to lack this causal narrative drive, seeming to lurch from one scene to another. Our ideas about the basic pattern of tragedy should, however, enable us to find some kind of shape in the story. The basic pattern of tragedy is that something happens that disrupts the established order of society. Evil is then unleashed and we witness terrible disorder. Set against this is the tragic hero who tries to confront the chaos he sees, but is overtaken by it and dies. As we look at the plot of *Hamlet* we should be able to see that it conforms to this pattern.

The play begins with some guards talking about a ghost who looks like Hamlet's father, the former King of Denmark. The ghost tells Hamlet that he was poisoned by Claudius, Hamlet's uncle, who is now King and married to Hamlet's mother Gertrude. The ghost instructs Hamlet to revenge his murder. Hamlet, however, delays doing so, and spends most of the play debating his inability to take revenge. By mistake he kills Polonius, one of the King's courtiers, and is sent to England, supposedly mad. On his return he fights a duel with Polonius's son Laertes and is killed by a poisoned sword. Before he dies, however, Hamlet kills Claudius. Gertrude, drinking from a poisoned cup, also dies.

In any play we look for the action which triggers off the complications of the plot, and in this play it is the revelation of Claudius's murder of Old Hamlet. The settled pattern of life has been disrupted. Not only is Claudius a murderer, he has also married Hamlet's mother, a marriage Hamlet regards as incestuous: the play thus focuses on the presence of evil and lustful instincts in life. Implicitly, and perhaps explicitly as it goes on, the play will be asking how we can make sense of a world in which a man can commit such an unnatural act as killing his brother. This side of a tragedy, the presence of extreme disorderly impulses in life, is quite easy to get hold of, but what the play does other than dramatise villainy seems more difficult to discover. We would have something positive to hold on to if Hamlet acted decisively against evil, but most of the play just drifts, with Hamlet himself doing very little, until it ends in a bloody final scene. What, if anything, a tragedy offers us other than a vision of people's potential for evil might, however, begin to reveal itself as we work through the play.

2   *Look at the first two or three scenes, trying to achieve a sense of what is happening in this particular play*

We can delay looking closely at the hero until we consider the third act. In considering the first two acts our main task is to try to achieve a more precise sense of the nature of the disruptive force in this society. This involves describing what happens in scenes, then trying to comment on the significance of what happens, interpreting what we discover in the light of our general ideas about tragedy.

In the first scene of *Hamlet* we see two guards. Horatio is also present. He has come to test their reports of a ghost. He sees the ghost, but it will not speak. Confused and frightened, Horatio confirms that it looks like Old Hamlet but cannot explain its presence other than feeling that it must somehow be an ill omen, perhaps of the war that Denmark is preparing for with Norway. It is a difficult scene to interpret, but that does not mean you have to approach it in a complicated way. The best way of coming to terms with any scene is to consider it naïvely but methodically, using the framework of order and disorder that we have used throughout this book, asking yourself whether something seems orderly or disorderly, even whether it seems good or bad, reassuring or disturbing. The main dramatic event in this scene is the appearance of the ghost. A ghost is obviously baffling and frightening. It worries and disturbs people, unsettling the normal pattern of their lives. Other details in the scene fit in with this: the talk of war, for example, suggests another way in which life in this society is about to be disrupted. The opening scene, therefore, creates a feeling of unease, that upheaval can be expected.

Scene ii starts with Claudius as King dealing with the business of state. He sends ambassadors to Norway, grants Laertes permission to go to Paris, and then seeks to console Hamlet for his late father's death. So too does Gertrude. Hamlet, however, seems withdrawn and hostile. When they leave he gives vent to his feelings about his mother's remarriage so soon after Old Hamlet's funeral, and then Horatio enters and tells him about the ghost. To interpret the scene we can again apply our order/disorder formula. The significance of the first part of the scene, where we see Claudius conducting the affairs of state, must be that Shakespeare wants to create an impression of the normal, stable face of society. The scene as a whole, however, is far from reassuring.

There is Hamlet baffled by his mother's marriage, unable to explain her choice, her gross sensuality which has poisoned the world for him. When he hears about the ghost it confirms his feeling that something is wrong, even though things appear all right on the surface. Quite what is wrong, however, is not yet being very sharply defined. There is a sense of unease, of a mystery, but the play is holding back from defining its themes explicitly.

In scene iii we see Polonius, a courtier, bidding farewell to his son Laertes, who is off to Paris. Polonius gives the young man advice on how to conduct himself. Polonius then talks to his daughter, Ophelia, telling her not to believe Hamlet's words of love. This is the start of the subplot: these characters are to some extent peripheral to the main action. The thing about a subplot is that it helps to define the concerns of the main plot, because it deals with the same issues but presents them in simpler terms. If we think about this scene we can see that Polonius gives Laertes advice on how to conduct himself in an orderly and civilised manner. With Ophelia, he warns her not to trust Hamlet's words of love, that his feelings might be more complex than they appear. We feel that this scene allows us to sum up an impression of the issues so far: there is the apparent order of life, exemplified in the surface appearance of Claudius's court and the manner in which Laertes is advised to conduct himself in society, but the play has constantly pointed to a sense of something more disturbing that lurks beneath the surface: there is the ghost, the sensuality that might characterise Gertrude, and the idea that Hamlet might be concealing lustful designs in his words of love to Ophelia.

With most plays, having looked at three scenes, we would now move on to Act II, but, as it is the ghost that has triggered off the mystery of what lies beneath the surface, it seems appropriate to look at the last scene of this act, where Hamlet encounters the ghost of his father. The ghost tells Hamlet that he was poisoned by Claudius, and that if he loved his father he must revenge his murder but not harm Gertrude. Hamlet swears revenge. His companions then come in and he asks them not to mention the ghost and not to say anything even if his behaviour seems odd. At last the issues are defined rather more clearly. Claudius has acted in an evil way, murdering his brother. We have seen the apparent stability of the state he runs, but here is an extreme act which makes the whole semblance of things as secure appear false. However much Claudius might try to present an impression of life proceeding as usual, beneath the surface things are very,

very wrong. As readers of the play we have been presented with a strong and concrete example of evil: the desire for power and sexual lust that made Claudius a murderer.

Why, though, has Shakespeare delayed this revelation by the ghost till the end of the act? Why has such a sense of mystery been created? The point is that Claudius's behaviour focuses an idea of concealed impulses, but the play is not just dealing with the baseness of one villain. The opening scenes have created a far more general sense of base and disturbing impulses that lie beneath the surface. The play holds back from defining a specific problem as it is concerned to convey a comprehensive impression of something disturbing but concealed and inexplicable in human nature that makes life complex. A sense is created of the mysteriousness of life: that beneath the surface of things are irrational forces.

In analysing these opening scenes you will spot different details from those we have noticed, and in articulating your impression of their significance you will be establishing your own distinctive grasp of the play. But, whatever line you take, and however you place the emphasis – for example, you might decide to make more of the ghost and the supernatural than we have done, tilting your discussion towards the idea that there is an incomprehensible world that lurks behind the comprehensible – your basic idea is likely to be of something irrational that disrupts the surface calm of society. It is a simple idea, but one that should help you make sense of any detail or aspect of the plot. For example, you might be fascinated by the character of Ophelia, Hamlet's girlfriend, who goes mad and drowns herself. Hamlet's killing of Polonius, it could be argued, leads her to confront her own concealed feelings. She cannot maintain a role as dutiful daughter and devoted lover, and, as a result, the irrational forces within her personality well up and consume her. Throughout the play we feel the confusing and complex nature of people behind their social identities, behind the social roles they usually play.

3   *Choose a scene from Act II, and try to clarify your impression of what this play is about and how it is developing*

What happens in the first scene of Act II is that Polonius tells a servant to spy on his son in Paris. Ophelia then tells him of Hamlet's distraught behaviour to her and he determines to tell the King that Hamlet has gone mad for Ophelia's love. Let us start with the first half of the scene. Laertes has departed for Paris with good advice from his father. There is nothing wrong with that, but the reality is that his father is distrustful; there is something underhand about having his son spied on. As with all the details, it reinforces our awareness of the more suspect reality concealed behind the social appearances of things. What, though, are we to make of the fact that Hamlet appears to have gone mad? As it is a difficult detail to interpret, the best strategy as always is to approach it naïvely but methodically, asking ourselves whether it suggests order or disorder. It must be clear that if Hamlet is mad then his mind has disintegrated into a state of total disorder. Perhaps he has yielded to the irrational forces within himself. There is, however, some uncertainty about whether he is really mad or feigning madness. Let us consider what he has recently discovered: he has come to believe that his uncle is a murderer and that his mother has contracted an incestuous marriage. It is a shattering confirmation that the world is not a sane, reasonable place, but that people are motivated by evil instincts that have no reason. It causes him to lose all faith in sane and reasonable behaviour and either go mad or act the part of a madman. Again, then, we see the play plunging into the dark side of life, acknowledging the mysterious world that lies beneath the veneer of a civilised existence. But, if humanity is motivated by irrational and base instincts, Hamlet as yet seems simply to be yielding to these instincts himself. We cannot yet see why he should be regarded as a tragic hero. In turning to Act III, however, we can make a real effort to come to terms with the character of Hamlet.

4   *Choose a scene from Act III to see how it develops the issues you have identified so far, and now begin to pay more attention to the principal characters in the play*

Those at court cannot see what Hamlet is so disturbed about; they cannot fathom his irrational behaviour. As a result, they spy on him. Polonius and Claudius send Ophelia to speak to him, and watch as he cruelly and perversely abuses her. This baffles them, but we should be able to see that Hamlet's horror at his mother's behaviour makes him distrust any simple emotional relationship. He is conscious of a level of lust and sexual corruption that might lie behind the simple face of love. This same idea of the false surface appearance of things is again present in a play about a king who is murdered which Hamlet arranges for some players to put on before the court. He wishes to see if Claudius will react in a guilty way. Play-acting gives us the idea of feigning a role, but in addition there is the idea of trying to get at the truth behind appearances. Repeatedly in *Hamlet* the emphasis is on the difference between playing a part and the murkier truth that lies below the surface.

But our problem with this play, the problem we have yet to solve, is what to make of Hamlet's role in all this. You might well feel that, having sworn revenge, he should simply get on with it and kill the King. So why does he delay? Revenge would seem to solve everything, striking out the cause of the original problem and so restoring order in the state. Rather than speculating on Hamlet's reasons for delaying you should try to find an explanation in the actual evidence of the text. The most productive approach is to focus on a speech, and in Act III we have probably the most famous speech in the whole of literature, the 'To be, or not to be . . .' soliloquy. Clearly an analysis of the play is going to be incomplete if we fail to look at this speech. Here are the opening lines:

> To be, or not to be – that is the question:
> Whether 'tis nobler in the mind to suffer
> The slings and arrows of outrageous fortune,
> Or to take arms against a sea of troubles,
> And by opposing end them? To die, to sleep –
> No more; and by a sleep to say we end
> The heart-ache and the thousand natural shocks
> That flesh is heir to. 'Tis a consummation
> Devoutly to be wish'd. To die, to sleep;
> To sleep, perchance to dream. Ay, there's the rub;
> For in that sleep of death what dreams may come,
> When we have shuffled off this mortal coil,
> Must give us pause. . . .
>
> (III.i.56–68)

Hamlet is considering whether to kill himself. But why? The speech tells us, although it will always be the case that every reader of the text will interpret the evidence in his or her own way. Our interpretation of the evidence is that Hamlet is oppressed by what he has discovered about life: he speaks of 'The slings and arrows of outrageous fortune' and 'the thousand natural shocks / That flesh is heir to'. What he has discovered is the baseness of his uncle and mother: it is as if he has lifted up a large stone and discovered all kinds of vile things beneath.

Why, therefore, does he not kill himself? The problem is that death might seem to promise eternal rest, but if life is so baffling then he might still be disturbed by all sorts of dreams even in death. In short, there is no easy answer to his problem. The moment he considers an answer he finds that all kinds of doubts intrude that unsettle the neatness of the solution; every time he considers a way of putting his life in order (even if death is one of the answers he considers) a sense that everything is disordered intrudes.

We can move from this speech to a consideration of the bigger problem of why Hamlet delays killing Claudius. Our emphasis has been on the fact that he can find no answers to his problems. It could be argued that killing Claudius would solve very little; one evil man would be eliminated, but it would not solve the broader problem of how irrational and base instincts seem pervasive in human behaviour. You might find other ways of explaining why he delays, but do not fall into the trap of just talking about his indecisive character. Such an explanation reduces the issue, making Hamlet just a man with a personality flaw, and loses sight of the broader issue of how Hamlet tries to come to terms with the problem of evil in human nature and the whole complexity of existence.

What you should be able to see from what we have said so far about Hamlet is that the tragic hero is not a superman figure who can stride in and eliminate the villains and clear up all traces of mess and corruption. The dilemma of the tragic hero is that he is caught in the middle, between a desire for a well-ordered world and an awareness of just how corrupt life can be. Although the tragic hero is not a superman he proves himself great in the way he wrestles with the worst face of existence. One particular form this can take is, as with Hamlet, where the hero tries to understand what life amounts to in such a world. In the very act of thinking about the worst face of life, Hamlet exemplifies some of the best qualities of human beings. The pattern of a tragedy, therefore, is that it presents a pessimistic view of how evil can permeate life, but the positive thing it sets against this is the tragic hero who demonstrates the noble qualities of humanity. The 'To be, or not to be . . .' soliloquy, or any of Hamlet's speeches, can be used to illustrate this and to show how Hamlet uses his intellect to try to understand the nature of life and death. The eloquence of his speeches is important in this: such an ability to use words to talk about every aspect of life is, in itself, a forceful demonstration that there is more to people than animal-like brutality.

5   *Choose a scene from Act IV and attempt to build upon everything you have established so far*

Often in the play Hamlet distances himself from the action and comments on life in general; look at these soliloquies and speeches as they will provide you with the evidence of how Hamlet as tragic hero grapples with the problem of trying to make sense of a world which he has seen as nasty and vicious. There are, though, moments when Hamlet does act, such as when he kills Polonius mistakenly believing that he is Claudius. This might seem to contradict what we have said previously about his reasons for not killing the King, and also what we have said about Hamlet using his intellect to try to understand the nature of life. In such an incident Hamlet might appear as corrupt as his opponents. But the fact that Hamlet acts badly at times adds to the play, for Shakespeare presents a general infection of baseness that affects even the hero. Hamlet is seen wrestling with a general corruption of humanity in which even he is implicated. His struggle is both with the world and with himself, as he discovers the evil instincts in his own nature.

After the killing of Polonius, Hamlet is shipped to England, where Claudius has arranged for him to be murdered. Laertes returns from France: his father is dead and by the end of Act IV his sister, Ophelia, will have drowned. Hamlet, having escaped assassination in England, returns to Denmark where Claudius arranges a duel: Laertes and Hamlet will fight, Laertes using a poisoned sword. We could look at any of these details, interpreting them in the light of what we have established so far, but the central focus of interest is so much Hamlet himself that we have decided to look at a further extract from one of his soliloquies:

> What is a man,
> If his chief good and market of his time
> Be but to sleep and feed? A beast, no more!
> Sure he that made us with such large discourse,
> Looking before and after, gave us not
> That capability and godlike reason
> To fust in us unus'd. Now, whether it be
> Bestial oblivion, or some craven scruple
> Of thinking too precisely on th'event –
> A thought which, quarter'd, hath but one part wisdom
> And ever three parts coward – I do not know

Why yet I live to say 'This thing's to do',
Sith I have cause, and will, and strength, and means,
To do't. Examples gross as earth exhort me . . . .

(IV.iv.33–46)

He is wondering why he cannot simply take revenge. He does not know why himself, yet his speech does to some extent reveal why. What we want to do, however, is look at this speech in the light of our ideas so far. It starts with the idea that people are no more than animals, but then moves on to talk about those nobler qualities of 'capability' and 'reason' that distinguish people from animals. Yet the moment Hamlet turns his reasoning on his own behaviour he finds contradictions, that it is partly wisdom but perhaps more the baser instinct of cowardice that prevents him from taking action. He ends by saying that it should not be difficult to act, as the world is full of gross examples. The opposition, then, is between an idea of rational beha-viour and gross behaviour, but the problem is that there is no such thing as clear-cut rational behaviour: all actions are tainted and ambig-uous. We mentioned earlier that *Hamlet* lacks the strong narrative drive of most of Shakespeare's plays, and it does seem repeatedly to grind to a halt because it sets up impossible problems. Life repeatedly seems so complex that there seems no way of making sense of it. This is one reason why *Hamlet* is the most complex play you will ever read, because it consistently points to the disorder that prevails in everything. In many plays each scene advances the action decisively, but in *Hamlet* we burrow down into the impossibility of making sense of such a proble-matic world.

6   *Choose a scene from near the end of the play which shows how the issues are resolved, and which will enable you to draw together the threads of your critical analysis*

At the end of *Hamlet* Laertes and Hamlet fight a duel. Laertes wounds Hamlet but they exchange swords and Laertes himself is killed. Ger-trude drinks unknowingly from a poisoned cup Claudius has prepared. Hamlet kills Claudius, and as he dies learns that Fortinbras and the Norwegian army have arrived. Fortinbras takes over the state. We can again make use of our order-and-disorder formula here. Initially the scene might seem to present a vision of complete disorder and to be wholly negative: just about everyone is dead, killed by poison. Poison here can be seen as a metaphor for the evil that infects all actions at all times in the play. In addition, Denmark is now under foreign rule, as if the whole country has been consumed and defeated. The play as a whole has seemed to ask how to make sense of or act in a corrupt world, but at the end there seems to be no answer. What we have to set against this is the fact that Claudius is dead and that in Fortinbras's last speech there is clear recognition of Hamlet's greatness, of his heroic qualities. But we should also see that Hamlet's attempts to understand life, even if he only discovers that it is an incomprehensible mystery in which everything that might seem good is tainted with evil, is heroic and powerful in itself. There is, too, the sense that Hamlet, having confronted the worst facts about human nature, achieves clarity of vision as a result of his suffering, so that the final effect of the play is to re-establish a sense of positive values even amidst the chaos we see.

7   Pursuing aspects of the play

What we have said about *Hamlet* might seem complicated, but in essence it is not. All we have tried to show, from specific scenes and details, is that the play reveals how people are sometimes evil and that the moment we scratch the surface we begin to find murky and suspect instincts in everybody. This, really, is the overall picture tragedy offers us of the disorder of life. What we have also argued is that set against this is something more positive in the figure of Hamlet, for he at least tries to understand the base nature of people, even if he has base elements in his own personality. A vision of people as no better than animals is balanced by an impression of a man using his reason to try to understand the world and himself. It is not, then, merely a bleak picture: the evidence of Hamlet's powers of speech, reasoning and intellect creates a powerful counterweight to the impression of people as no more than beasts. At the same time, we cannot avoid the fact that it is an extremely difficult play, because it does so consistently batter us with an idea of the complexity of everything. Some readers are puzzled that Hamlet never seems to do anything, never seems to take the initiative, but this is of a piece with the way in which the action fails to advance steadily and purposefully. What we have instead are scenes and speeches in which Hamlet turns inwards, assessing the complexity of all actions, all thoughts and all behaviour, questioning and doubting everything.

Your ideas about the play will be different from ours, but our main point is that quite a simple argument, showing from specific examples in the text how the play sets a vision of extreme disorder against an idea of something positive in human beings, can serve as the basis of a very good essay on *Hamlet*. Indeed, you are likely to find it almost impossible to convey a clear sense of the complexity of the play if your basic argument is not clear and simple, as you need a coherent frame in which subtleties of understanding and interpretation can be accommodated. The main effort of criticism must obviously go into responding to the play as a whole, but, in preparing for examinations, you might also want to focus on specific aspects of the play. The things to look at are the characters, the play's themes, its language, and how the play works on the stage, and we deal with these briefly here. Much of the general advice we gave in the previous chapter on pursuing aspects of a history play (*see* p. 27) applies equally to the tragedies.

(a) *Character.* The basic point to grasp about the main characters in a play is that they all embody the wider division in the play of a gap between a simple idea of how things should be and the instincts that disrupt order. A tragedy, in a more extreme form than any other kind of play, exposes base instincts, but an idea of a well-ordered society is constantly articulated as well. These ideas of order are simple: order in the family, order in the state, and a secure place in God's universe. So, for example, Polonius is presented as a distrustful character who arranges to have his son spied on, but when we see him with his children he voices the common-sense wisdom of rational and reasonable behaviour. This division is also apparent in Claudius. As the King he should represent order and justice in the state, but he is a murderer. In Act III, scene iii, we see him at prayer, confessing his guilt to himself and God. He is a man who has surrendered to his own evil instincts, but in this scene we see him in turmoil, wrestling with his conscience, mindful of his crime and God's laws. There is, then, even in Claudius a tension between his evil, disorderly instincts and his awareness of how one should behave. All the central characters are similarly pulled in two ways: they are aware of the claims of reasonable, decent behaviour, but they are also aware of or tainted by instincts that act against the general good of society. In a sense they all experience the same dilemma as the tragic hero himself: they are caught between a sense of how people should behave in society and the baser reality of how people do behave. The other characters may not see Hamlet as mirroring their dilemma or see themselves in him, but we have to. What sets the tragic hero apart is that he is at the very centre of the play, feeling most acutely the presence of the evil that can infect life and also trying to confront and understand why there is such a gap between how human beings should act and the reality of how they do act.

(b) *Themes.* A theme is an important subject or issue in a play. There are a lot of themes in *Hamlet,* such as revenge, conscience, evil, justice, love, death, damnation, the supernatural, and acting. You might wonder why there are so many. If we were asked to define in a word our sense of the theme of *Hamlet* (or any play), we would say the theme was 'life'. Against an orderly vision of how life should be, the play presents an impression of how complex and diverse life is when we start to consider the nature of humankind. A tragedy reveals both what is base in human nature and the qualities of greatness in people. By working in such extreme terms, showing the worst and best faces of people, it creates a space in which just about every aspect of life can be discussed. This is why there are so many themes in *Hamlet.* What you have to understand, however, is that these themes are only ways of focusing and making concrete the broader issues of the play, the complex nature of people and the complex nature of life. For example, revenge: very often when students write about revenge in *Hamlet* they concentrate only on the fact that Hamlet delays taking vengeance, sometimes arguing he is right to delay, sometimes arguing he is wrong. The point to grasp, however, is that revenge is a particular example of the wider issue of social order and instincts that can wreck social order. Revenge might seem a simple means of restoring order to Denmark, but what *Hamlet* shows us are all the complications that attend revenge. So, if you were to look at Hamlet's speeches, you would see how revenge is presented sometimes as a duty, as something honourable that a son ought to do to prove his love for his father, but at other times as a brutal, irrational act. Again, with Laertes we see how revenge is associated with murder and poison. At the same time, however, the play makes us aware that because Claudius, who should be the fountainhead of justice, is corrupt, there seems little alternative to the violence of revenge. What we can see in the theme of revenge, therefore, is how it is one aspect of the whole problem of how there can be no simple scheme of things in life, how life is always tangled and complex. We discover something similar if we look at the theme of death: in a simple, ordered world we would lead a good life, die, and go to heaven. But in the real world death is more complex: as the play shows, some people fear death (Claudius), others puzzle over it (Hamlet), others joke about it (the gravediggers), others do not rest peacefully even after death (Old Hamlet). The point is that the play makes us feel the complex reality of death as a factor in human existence. The play sets the simple *idea* of death against the complex *reality* of death.

An idea of the gap between how things should be and the reality of how they are is explicitly present in some of the themes of the play. If we consider madness or evil, for example, these are themes which seem to demand attention to their opposites, sanity and goodness. In the same way, if we consider love as a theme we also have to consider lust. Sanity, goodness and love are all positive: they would all be characteristic qualities found in a well-ordered society. But the play examines the baser or more irrational instincts in human nature that destroy all simple ideas of order. Can you see, therefore, how, whatever theme you talk about, in order to do justice to it you have to see how it reflects the broader issues of the play? If you can see this it gives a direction and a sense of purpose to your analysis of a specific theme: if you are asked to talk about madness in *Hamlet*, for example, the danger is that you might just go round in circles talking about whether Hamlet is really mad or just feigning madness, but setting the idea of sane, orderly conduct against insane, disorderly behaviour gives you a framework for a worthwhile discussion of how the theme fits into the play as a whole.

(c) *Language*. In looking at the language of a Shakespeare play we can expect that in any speech an idea of something ordered or good will be set against an idea of something disordered or corrupt. We can also predict that in many speeches the meaning will seem to expand beyond the immediate issue so that there is a much more wide-ranging sense of the whole nature of existence being discussed. This is achieved primarily through the imagery. For example, light-and-dark imagery is prominent: when it is used we seem to move beyond the apparent subject matter of the speech to a broader idea of the positive force of light competing with the negative force of dark in the whole of life. All the tragedies make use of light-and-dark imagery, and also animal imagery, clothes imagery, body imagery, cosmic imagery, sea and war imagery, and music imagery. In this way an idea of something being calm, or in good order, or harmonious is set against an idea of storm, or decay, or lack of harmony. Such images make vivid the tensions of the play, but also expand the meaning of a speech so that it becomes a more general commentary on order and lack of order in life.

Each play, in addition, also has its own characteristic images. Some of the most common in *Hamlet* are images of sickness and decay. Again, this is a way of making vivid an idea of the disorder that affects Denmark in the play, but it also broadens the meaning of the play, so that we are not just considering a particular problem in one country but issues that are fundamental to the whole of life, the whole idea of a healthy society. The way to talk about the play's use of language is, as with everything else, to focus on specific scenes and speeches, seeing what words are actually used, but using the framework of your controlling ideas to make sense of, and give significance to, what you discover.

(d) *Staging.* The staging of a play is one of the easiest things to talk about because it represents the issues of the play in very clear and powerful terms. In *Hamlet*, for example, the ghost at the beginning is frightening and offers us a sense of the mysteriousness of experience, especially as it refuses to talk or explain its presence. The final scene, with bodies littered on the stage, vividly illustrates how this society has been consumed by disorder. The mad Ophelia wandering round the stage clearly indicates how insanity is more and more disturbing the settled appearance that Claudius would like to maintain at court. But perhaps most of all the figure of Hamlet prowling about, dressed in black, detached from the others, never making real contact, often speaking to himself, conveys a sense of the kind of tragic hero he is: one who, ever mindful of death, looks at the world and talks about it and tries to understand it.

There are, however, scenes in *Hamlet* where the staging takes on a more complex form than this, especially in Act III, scene ii, where Hamlet has some players act a play within the play. The problem you might encounter here is that, while you can see this creates a complicated dramatic effect, in which we watch characters on stage themselves watching a play, you might find it hard to specify exactly what this effect is. What will help you is if you remind yourself that the inner play must reflect the themes of the main play. This means that you should be able to see how the details of the inner play parallel or mirror the main action. For example, in the play-within-the-play we see a poisoner come on and kiss the crown before killing the sleeping king (III.ii.131). It is not difficult to see how this is intended by Hamlet as a parallel to Claudius's poisoning of Old Hamlet and how it dramatises the idea of evil ambition. There is, however, an important difference: while the poisoner is very clearly a villain, Claudius's evil is disguised behind his appearance as King of Denmark. One of the effects of the play-within-the-play, then, is to emphasise by contrast how much more complicated the problem of disorder is in Denmark. Shakespeare quite often uses the device of a play-within-a-play, and it is usually the case that there is this kind of contrast between the play-within-the-play and the main action. It is a way of reminding us that life is always more complex and ambiguous than it appears on the surface.

We have provided a very full discussion of *Hamlet*, offering more direct guidance as to what it is about than with any of the other plays in this book, because it is the most difficult and demanding of Shakespeare's plays. The accounts that follow of the other tragedies are much shorter, as we feel that we can now concentrate more on the transmission of a method of analysis, than on providing lengthy analyses.

King Lear

1   *Read the play, then think about what kind of play it is and what sort of broad pattern you can see in the plot*

King Lear is a tragedy. It begins with King Lear dividing his kingdom between his daughters. He intends to divide it in three, but one daughter, Cordelia, refuses to say how much she loves him and so is rejected, the other daughters, Goneril and Regan, being given everything. Lear tries to keep some power, but this is stripped from him by Goneril and Regan. He is forced out in a storm and goes mad. Cordelia finds him, but their reunion is short-lived: she is hanged and Lear dies over her body. There is also a subplot involving Gloucester and his two sons Edgar and Edmund. Gloucester is blinded in the play, and Edgar, deceived by Edmund, is banished and forced to disguise himself to save his life, but at the end the good son, Edgar, kills Edmund. Goneril and Regan also die, Goneril committing suicide and Regan being poisoned by her sister.

Look for the standard pattern of a tragedy in this plot. Life is thrown into disarray when Lear divides his kingdom. Goneril and Regan reveal themselves as hungry for total power, turning on their father and on each other. An evil appetite has been unleashed. Notice how simple the essential concepts of order and disorder are: whereas order is a loving relationship between parents and children, disorder is children turning on their father. This is also evident in the subplot, where the evil Edmund is happy to see his father suffer. These base passions that erupt throw the country into chaos, and the central stages of the play, where Lear is forced out of his home, are characterised by a sense of the whole order of civilised life and the whole natural order having fallen apart. At the end of this play, though, there is a much clearer reassertion of positive values than in *Hamlet*, with Lear being reunited with Cordelia and Gloucester with his good son Edgar. The disorder that has been unleashed, however, destroys the lives of most of the characters. Only Edgar survives at the end, promising that things will never be as bad as this again.

What we have in the play, then, is a clear setting of humane values against evil passions that can destroy life. We are made to think about the nature of humankind, that there are animal-like instincts in people which can wreck all our illusions that we live in a civilised world. But the presence of Cordelia and Edgar, and a loyal servant of Lear's called Kent, offers us something more positive to hold on to than in the all-questioning world of *Hamlet*, where the contagion of base passions seems to infect everything and everybody.

2   *Look at the first two or three scenes, trying to achieve a sense of what is happening in this particular play*

In considering the first two acts of a tragedy your main task is to try to achieve a more precise sense of the nature of the disruptive force in the play. You know, however, that you can expect to see base instincts exposed that are usually kept concealed in civilised life. Our analysis of these opening acts is deliberately sketchy as we simply want to provide an illustration of how you can set about interpreting this play.

In the opening scene Kent and Gloucester are discussing Lear's proposed division of his kingdom. Gloucester then introduces his illegitimate son Edmund to Kent. Lear and his daughter enter and Lear says he is going to divide his kingdom between them according to how much they love him. Goneril and Regan declare their love, but Cordelia refuses to do so. Lear curses her and gives her to the King of France without dowry. Kent tries to intervene but is banished. Then Cordelia goes, leaving Goneril and Regan to discuss how they are going to manage Lear. In selecting parts of this scene and beginning to talk about them you will start to put flesh on the bare bones of your ideas about tragedy. You might, for example, choose to talk about Gloucester and his bastard son Edmund. Gloucester jokes about the fact that Edmund is illegitimate. To interpret the detail apply our order/disorder formula. Gloucester appears to be an honourable elder statesman, but there is something suspect in his fathering of an illegitimate child, just as there is something callous and distasteful in his facetious attitude as he tells Kent about it. Immediately you have the idea of the appearance of things in society but other instincts lurking beneath the surface. In talking about the detail you will begin to characterise how the standard pattern of base instincts that disrupt life is presented in this play. We have deliberately selected a minor detail to demonstrate how this idea permeates the entire play. The same approach, therefore, can be used for whatever part of the scene you want to discuss: in the main part of the scene, for example, order would be exemplified by a natural love between parent and child, but Lear's vanity in wanting to hear this love expressed is destructive.

Lear's division of his kingdom unleashes the evil instincts of Goneril and Regan, but you should also try to see that Gloucester and Lear have a less worthy side to their personalities. The second scene develops the Gloucester subplot. Edmund hates Edgar and convinces Gloucester that Edgar intends to kill Gloucester. Again, look for the intrusion of baser instincts here, not only Edmund's but also those of his father, who if he were a better man would know and trust his son Edgar. Remind yourself that the subplot echoes the main plot: Gloucester, like Lear, is deceived into believing that a faithful child does not love him.

The pattern in *Lear* is quite easy to detect: it is a clear case of unworthy instincts surfacing and disrupting life, and in looking at the first two acts you should find it relatively straightforward to characterise how things get more and more out of hand. The secret of producing good criticism, however, is to avoid just saying 'Things get out of hand in the first two acts': the secret of good criticism is to point to, and then discuss as fully as you feel necessary, specific incidents which illustrate this.

3   *Choose a scene from Act II, and try to clarify your impression of what this play is about and how it is developing*

What happens in this act is that Edmund tricks Edgar into fleeing; Goneril and Regan, though distrustful of each other, turn even more against their father, and at the end Lear goes off into the night beginning to fear for his sanity. Any scene you select to discuss here should demonstrate how things are beginning to collapse into chaos; the details you focus on should present a vivid impression of how evil and villainy are beginning to consume this society. There might, however, be scenes, characters and details that you find it hard to relate to your overall impression. You can ignore such details or return to them later, but really, with a little thought, everything should fit together. One puzzling character, for example, is the Fool, who is constantly in Lear's company, forever cracking jokes and posing riddles. What helps here is if you know that the fool or clown always serves the same function in Shakespeare's plays: he is a commentator on people's follies and pretensions. He comments on social imposture, and his games with language undermine the polite phrases people use in society and harp on the true instincts that motivate people. To pinpoint this with the Fool you would need to look at some of his speeches or songs. For example, in Act II, scene iv, he says,

> Fathers that wear rags
>   Do make their children blind;
> But fathers that bear bags
>   Shall see their children kind.
>   (II.iv.47–50)

He is saying that children will appear affectionate while their father has money, but when the father has nothing to offer them they will turn against him. It is another expression of the idea, which permeates the play, of a more complex reality underlying social appearances.

4   *Choose a scene from Act III to see how it develops the issues you have identified so far, and now begin to pay more attention to the principal characters in the play*

In the third act of a tragedy there are two principal things to be aware of. One is that a sense of disorder dominates: this is conveyed to us in this play by the fact that Lear, close to madness, is driven out of doors onto the heath in a terrible storm. The storm seems to suggest a tremendous tumult in the whole universe, as if the whole of life is violent and chaotic, while the madness of Lear seems to represent a loss of faith in the very idea of any sane order. Look at scenes and details which will enable you to convey an impression of this disorder. The other thing that becomes clearer in the central act, however, is the role of the tragic hero. He has seen the worst face of people and is wrestling with the whole problem of evil instincts in humankind that seem to undermine any confidence we might have that we live in a sane world. Focus closely on sections of Lear's longer speeches. We have selected a speech from the second scene where Lear is raging in the storm:

> Blow, winds, and crack your cheeks; rage, blow.
> You cataracts and hurricanoes, spout
> Till you have drench'd our steeples, drown'd the cocks.
> You sulph'rous and thought-executing fires . . . .
>
> (III.ii.1–4)

You might prefer to look at a longer extract than we have provided here, but the same principles always apply. At first we could not think what to say about these four lines, but we decided to employ our usual approach of looking for ideas or images of order and disorder. The disorderly images of the rage and violence of the storm are fairly easy to spot, but images of order seem more difficult to find. The only ones appear to be the references to the 'steeples' on the churches that have been built, and to the 'cocks', the weathercocks people use to predict the weather, both of which will be drowned: the idea is that all signs of God's order and human ordering of the elements will be obliterated and destroyed. The pattern, then, within the speech reflects the pattern of the play as a whole, in which violent forces are unleashed that seek to destroy everything that is part of civilisation.

At this stage of the play these forces include Lear himself, who, in his anger and fury, wishes to see all order undone and vengeance visited on Goneril and Regan. He has yet to recognise his own sin of banishing Cordelia and dividing the kingdom. By the end of this scene (III.ii), however, Lear has begun to change from the vain old man we see at the start of the play: his self-pity is mixed with concern for the Fool and then, in Act III, scene iv, there is a growing concern for the plight of poor people, embodied in the figure of Poor Tom. The appearance of Poor Tom marks the beginning of Lear's madness and the collapse of his reason. The order of reason, though, is replaced by the reasoning of madness as Lear tries to confront and understand the world from his new perspective of pain, suffering and compassion for others.

Lear's character, then, changes and develops in Act III, and this is what we might expect in the central act of a tragedy, where things are at their furthest remove from any sense of stable order. As he changes so he comes to serve more and more as a commentator on the whole chaos of life. Throughout his speeches there are references to the collapse of the cosmic and natural order and to the absence of justice in the human world. Like Hamlet, he is at the centre of things, feeling most acutely the disorder of life. If you look at Lear's speeches you should be able to present a full and vivid impression of how he explores the nature of existence in a world where brute forces seem to reign supreme. This sense of the bestiality of life is conveyed especially by the use of animal imagery, but it is also present in the actions of the play, particularly when Gloucester's eyes are torn out. While you might find it difficult to imagine the staging of the storm scenes with Lear, the blinding of Gloucester in Act III, scene vii, should provide you with a very clear idea of how the play conveys to the audience a picture of the very worst in people as Gloucester is bound and first one eye, then the other, is ripped out. But what we have to set against such vileness are the very concrete images of the servant who tries to prevent the blinding, Gloucester's courage in facing his torturers, and finally his recognition of his own folly. As with Lear, suffering leads to a reassertion of positive values, though both old men are still a long way from any full understanding of their actions.

All of this allows us to specify some of the ways in which *King Lear* differs from *Hamlet*. Hamlet as a tragic hero is primarily impressive because of his intellectual readiness to confront and explore life. In *Lear*, however, it is not the hero's intellect that impresses us but rather his recognition, even as he endures the worst life can offer, of the needs of others, of the need for compassion and feeling in the world. Because of this, and because we see a similar development in Gloucester, *King Lear* offers us a fuller sense of something positive to hold on to, a fuller sense of the best qualities of people – underlined in the love and loyalty of Kent and Cordelia – than in the all-questioning world of *Hamlet*.

5   *Choose a scene from Act IV and attempt to build upon everything you have established so far*

The blind Gloucester and the mad Lear both wander to the cliffs at Dover. They have been stripped of everything. They meet in Act IV, scene vi. What you might find hard to cope with here is that Lear's speeches often seem close to nonsense:

> Look, look, a mouse! Peace, peace; this piece of toasted cheese will do't. There's my gauntlet; I'll prove it on a giant. Bring up the brown bills . . . .　(IV.vi.89–91)

At other points in the play he seems to have an acute perception in his madness of just what life is like, but sometimes there is nonsense like this. As always, however, search for the easy explanation: his speech is disordered, illogical, falling to pieces, but he has understandably lost faith with the ways of reason. If the world is mad, why bother to participate in the sham of logical behaviour? As with Hamlet, see how Lear as the tragic hero is not a superman who can take on and defeat evil, but a man who wrestles with the problem of the irrationality of life, confronting even his own irrationality.

Instead of concentrating on Lear's madness, however, you might prefer to look at a scene where the positive values of the play are more evident. One reason why *Lear* is a rather easier play to study than *Hamlet* is that it does offer us a clearer sense of something positive to set against the picture of the disorder of experience. The place to find this is in the scenes involving Cordelia, in particular the reunion scene where Lear rediscovers his love for his daughter (IV.vii). If you look at this scene, try to see how the staging itself creates a sense of order and calm after the storm: there is the music used to awaken Lear, his fresh clothes, the kneeling of the old King to ask his daughter's forgiveness, all signs of a new harmony in the play. Look, too, at the language, to see how storm and animal imagery are now countered by images of sleep and tears as the dark world of madness gives way to the returning light of sanity in Lear.

6　*Choose a scene from near the end of the play which shows how the issues are resolved, and which will enable you to draw together the threads of your critical analysis*

The most logical place to end your analysis of a tragedy is with the death of the tragic hero. In pulling together the threads of your analysis you need to think about the ideas you have discovered in the play and to shape them into a coherent view. Our view has been that throughout

Lear we are presented with a terrifying picture of the worst in people, but that set against it is a positive sense of some of the best qualities in people. We can see this tension at the end. Lear enters carrying the body of the dead Cordelia: if we think about this spectacle, we should be able to see how its effect is to raise questions about the very meaning of life in a world where the innocent are murdered and where justice seems arbitrary. Similar issues are raised by Lear's speeches:

> And my poor fool is hang'd! No, no, no life!
> Why should a dog, a horse, a rat have life.
> And thou no breath at all? . . .
>
>> (v.iii.305–7)

The animal images here serve to suggest that human life is worth less than that of a beast, and yet the staging itself suggests that this is not the case. Lear's concern is wholly for Cordelia, all thoughts of himself all but forgotten, the fact that his kingdom has been restored to him of no interest. How you see Lear's death, or any of the events in the final scenes, is up to you, but avoid the temptation of thinking that the play ends with an 'answer' or 'message'. What you are most likely to remember, even at the end of the play, is the power of the picture it presents of the self-seeking, vicious cruelty in people, and equally the power of the presentation of Lear's rediscovery through madness of the love of Cordelia. A vision of human bestiality is set against a vision of human ability to endure the worst and to change through suffering. *King Lear* in this respect is a marvellously clear play, as its picture of disorder is balanced by such an awe-inspiring tragic hero whose role is fairly easy to see as he journeys from lack of self-knowledge towards redemption and understanding. In the next two plays we consider, *Othello* and *Macbeth*, the tragic hero is harder to understand because, in the first instance, Othello yields to evil, and, in the second instance, Macbeth himself is the major source of evil in the play.

Othello

1 *Read the play, then think about what kind of play it is and what sort of broad pattern you can see in the plot*

Othello is a tragedy. Othello is a Moorish general in the service of Venice. He has secretly married Desdemona: her father charges him with her theft, but Othello is cleared. He is sent to Cyprus to defend it from the Turks. There, Iago, his officer, dupes Othello into believing that Desdemona is having an affair with his lieutenant, Cassio. Deceived and violently jealous, Othello kills his wife, only to learn she is innocent, and then kills himself. As you begin to think about the story, look for the intrusion of base instincts into the established order of life. Things begin to go wrong when Othello marries. Life, presumably, has been well defined when Othello was just a soldier, but the marriage is a sufficient alteration in the established pattern of things to provide Iago with his opportunity. His evil behaviour throws life into disarray. Othello is initially an heroic general, but his own base passions gain control of his personality. As we said earlier, each of the major tragedies is unique: Hamlet is aware of a rottenness in all human actions, Lear confronts mainly the evil of others, Othello is the victim of Iago's evil villainy, and Macbeth, as we shall see, is evil almost from the start. The essence of the hero, therefore, varies, but in all the tragedies we can see how the less worthy instincts in human beings create havoc in society.

2   *Look at the first two or three scenes, trying to achieve a sense of what is happening in this particular play*

As always, read and interpret these scenes in the light of the general ideas you have about tragedy. *Othello* starts with Roderigo quarrelling with Iago; we gather that Iago has been passed over by the Moor and Cassio made lieutenant instead of him. Iago reveals his hatred for Othello. Watching this scene on stage you would probably find it puzzling: Othello is not even named at the outset, so it is hard to see what the issue is. There are, however, plenty of clues. In the hierarchical structure of general, lieutenant and officer we are given an idea of a defined order. Iago, however, is a soldier who is disloyal. Immediately, therefore, the play presents an idea of suspect instincts in Iago clashing with the social role he is expected to play. Go through the opening scenes of the play, picking up details like this and explaining them in the light of your controlling ideas: you will soon establish a sense of the issues in this play as you uncover evidence of malevolent instincts in people.

One interesting aspect of this is Desdemona's father's objection to her marriage to Othello. He makes the assumption that as Othello is

black he must be a devil, but Othello's eloquence in c
ing of Desdemona convinces the Duke that he is not ɛ
Desdemona's father makes is thinking that evil reveals it.
appearance rather than being a cancer that is hidden
surface. Apart from the intrinsic interest of this detail, our ɔ
for mentioning it is to underline the point we have made all a
the issues of the play are reflected in every speech, every acʈ   and
every detail. It might take time to relate the scenes and details to your
controlling pattern, but the connection can always be made.

3   *Choose a scene from Act II, and try to clarify your impression of what this play
     is about and how it is developing*

In looking at the first two acts of a tragedy your main task is to try to
achieve a more precise sense of the nature of the disruptive force in the
play. In *Hamlet* there is a sense of a general contagion in society, in *King
Lear* there is a sense of brutality. In *Othello* the problem is in some ways
smaller and pettier, though just as destructive, for it is envy, jealousy,
resentment and lack of faith within personal relationships. By this stage
in this book you should be aware that what we have just said is not in
itself good criticism: all we have said is that this is what you might find,
but criticism only has any real substance if the point is made from the
evidence of the text. This stage in your analysis will only stand up as
criticism if you look at what happens in a scene, or, if necessary, more
than one scene, constructing a case from the words on the page, but
also thinking about the play's dramatic effect on the audience. One of
the distinctive qualities of *Othello* is its extensive use of dramatic irony.
Dramatic irony always involves the audience knowing more than the
characters on stage; in *Othello* the source of such irony is Iago's villainy
and plotting. Again, though, what you have to say about this will only
stand up if you focus on a specific example, such as how Iago deceives
Cassio in scene ii. What you might notice about this is how Iago's villainy takes the form of confusing people, using them, contriving little
'plays' to make them appear dishonest. Look at how busy he is, end-
lessly arranging and manipulating events, creating disorder and confusion and violence, as in the fight between Cassio and Roderigo. Such a
simple incident might not seem worth commenting on, but it vividly
demonstrates the power of Iago's evil to overturn the fragile order of
Cyprus, itself threatened from the outside by war.

Choose a scene from Act III to see how it develops the issues you have identified so far, and now begin to pay more attention to the principal characters in the play

By Act III, the evil force that has been unleashed has torn apart any notion of a secure and ordered world. We see this in the scheming of Iago, in his attempts to arouse Othello's sexual jealousy. Ugly passions have surfaced to create an atmosphere of festering unhealthiness. Again, however, you would need to look at specific details to demonstrate your impression of how things are developing. But it is also in Act III that the role of the tragic hero becomes more clearly defined. Iago works on Othello, twisting him, coaxing him, acting the part of loyal friend, but trying to arouse his suspicions. What, however, do we make of Othello? We decided to look at the section where Iago has begun to make Othello doubt Desdemona's faithfulness. It might prove easier to look at a longer extract from a speech than the couple of lines we include here, but the same critical principles would still apply. Othello says,

> Look where she comes.
> [*Re-enter* DESDEMONA *and* EMILIA.]
> If she be false, O, then heaven mocks itself!
> I'll not believe it.
>
> (III.iii.281–3)

The thing is that Othello is going to be consumed by jealousy, but at this point he resists the notion of evil. He desperately clings on to a sense of civilised values. He retains the belief that if Desdemona is false then the whole cosmos must be in a state of disorder, with heaven mocking itself. What we have here is something as simple as a man trying to remain decent and honest in a corrupt world. As with Lear and Hamlet, there is something positive in such an attitude in a corrupt world.

At the same time, as the staging suggests, Iago's evil has begun to shake Othello's whole frame of values. A number of details reveal this: his refusal to let Desdemona bind his head with her handkerchief, his violent seizing of Iago by his throat, but most of all the spectacle that ends the scene. Here we see Othello kneeling and dedicating himself to revenge. As he kneels Iago joins him, so that what we see are two figures as if at prayer or as if at a grotesque parody of a wedding-service. More simply, what the staging reveals at this point is how Iago has reduced Othello to his own level and view of life. There are other ways you might describe the effect of the staging at this point, but the important thing to grasp is how the staging gives concrete expression to the themes and ideas: it is not additional to the language of the play but works with it to create our impressions of the play.

5   *Choose a scene from Act IV and attempt to build upon everything you have established so far*

By this stage of the play Othello has been convinced by Iago that Desdemona is unfaithful. In the first scene, Iago goads Othello. He then talks to Cassio about Bianca (Cassio's mistress), but Othello is deceived into thinking that Cassio is talking about Desdemona. Iago stirs Othello on to strangle Desdemona. Towards the end of the scene Othello strikes Desdemona. Use the simple formula of looking for signs and images of order and disorder. Nearly everything here is distrust and deception, so the scene is also showing that virtue and innocence do exist.

    To develop your case, however, you need to focus on a speech or speeches. We chose Othello's first extended speech in this act. Iago suggests that a woman might be naked in bed with a man and not mean any harm. Othello says,

> Naked abed, Iago, and not mean harm!
> It is hypocrisy against the devil.
> They that mean virtuously and yet do so,
> The devil their virtue tempts, and they tempt heaven.
>
> (iv.i.5–8)

The speech centres on the idea of a devil being set against virtue, and this is really the struggle that is going on in Othello's own character. He has formerly proved himself to be one of the finest of men, yet Iago has unleashed suspicion and unfounded jealousy in his mind, so Othello is being eaten up by the worst instincts in people. A struggle goes on in his mind between sinking into the morass of evil and trying to stand above it. In a tragedy it is always such a struggle against the most adverse forces that is central; the plays assert a sense of something noble and heroic in human beings to set against the alternative vision of people as animal-like. The tragic hero represents the promise and potential of humanity, even if, like Othello, he is consumed by jealousy and finally yields to his own worst nature. A number of factors contribute to the positive impression we retain of Othello. One is his eloquence, first seen in his description of his wooing of Desdemona, and evident in much of the play. Whereas Iago twists the truth and words. Othello's speeches have a grandeur and openness that conveys a sense of what humanity is capable of – until, that is, Iago undermines his faith in Desdemona.

Another important factor is how well *Othello* works on the stage, as we see this impressive and physically dominating character wrestling with ideas and suspicions that devalue him as a man. This is clear in the present scene (IV.i), where ideas swirl in confusion in Othello's mind until he falls into a trance. On stage we see the noble Moor reduced to a state of helplessness, above him the figure of Iago: order has been completely overturned as the soldier rules the general, and evil triumphs over good. It is such ideas that the spectacle suggests, but we are also aware of the savage irony of Iago's comment that his 'medicine' is working (IV.ii.45): the image suggests that both Othello's mind and body are now sick with Iago's evil. It is another example of the dramatic irony that runs through the play and which places us in the position of being able to see the nature of the evil and deception that traps Othello. What this also means, however, is that Othello as a tragic hero differs significantly from Hamlet and Lear. Whereas they see and try to understand the nature of the evil that permeates life, Othello is not clear-sighted. Duped and deceived, he is not an observer or commentator on life but much more the direct victim of evil.

6   *Choose a scene from near the end of the play which shows how the issues are resolved, and which will enable you to draw together the threads of your critical analysis*

In the final scene Othello kills Desdemona. Her innocence is revealed, as is Iago's villainy. Othello, realising the truth, kills himself. He has been misled by the evil in the world and surrendered to his own worst instincts. But, although Othello has yielded to evil, you should try to appreciate the struggle in him between everything that is base and something nobler that sets people above beasts, as seen, for example, in his last speech. There is not the same philosophical dimension to *Othello* as there is to *King Lear* and *Hamlet*, but you should try to see the power on the stage of a heroic, larger-than-life figure struggling against what is sordid and corrupt in existence.

In this brief section on *Othello* we have only been concerned to describe a method of looking at the play, while dropping a few hints about its distinctive character. In moving quickly through *Othello* we have ignored the subsidiary characters and many of the twists and turns of the plot, but all should be explicable in terms of the idea of evil destroying what is potentially good. The same tension should be evident in the language of the play, with words such as 'heaven', 'honest', 'love' and 'fair', set against words such as 'devil', 'whore' and 'black', and in the contrast between animal images and images suggesting purity and innocence. In terms of theme, if you come across the suggestion that the theme is jealousy or perhaps intrigue, try to see how these are ways of talking about underhand motives and passions that disrupt life. With *Othello*, however, we would be inclined to pay special attention to its staging, and to two things in particular. The first is the colossal figure of Othello striding the stage, but then that figure being brought low as he bends an ear to Iago's malicious innuendoes and losing his dignity as he surrenders to his jealousy. We can see this in the stage directions to the play which show Othello gradually brought to his knees and then lying in a trance at Iago's feet. The other important aspect of the staging related to this is the play's powerful use of dramatic irony, the way in which we see Othello being misled by Iago's scheming villainy into the chaos of sexual jealousy and murder.

Macbeth

1   *Read the play, then think about what kind of play it is and what sort of broad pattern you can see in the plot*

Macbeth is a tragedy. It presents the rise to power of Macbeth as King of Scotland. This he achieves by murdering King Duncan. He then seeks to secure his position by further killings, including that of Banquo, for Macbeth has been told by three witches that, although he will be King, Banquo's children will also be kings. Much of the play focuses on Macbeth and his wife, Lady Macbeth, as they murder their way to power, but set against them is the English court of Edward. Malcolm, Duncan's son, flees there and returns with an army to overthrow

Macbeth, who is killed by the noble Macduff. Malcolm succeeds to the throne.

One thing that might strike you is that Macbeth could be discussed as a history play, for it deals with those political rivalries and ambitions, and failings of the monarch, which, as discussed in chapter 2, destabilise the state. *Macbeth* is, however, better described as a tragedy, for in a tragedy it is extreme passions rather than just ordinary human failings that disrupt life, and in this play the extreme passion is the evil of Macbeth. His murder of Duncan throws everything into chaos. You should find it fairly easy to go through the play showing how evil wreaks havoc in society. What you are likely to find more difficult to explain are such curious features of the plot as the presence of the witches and their prophecy to Macbeth, and the role of Macbeth as tragic hero. In the other tragedies the heroes are pitted against villains; here the hero himself is villainous. There might seem to be nothing positive to set against the play's bleak vision of the destructive force of evil.

2   *Look at the first two or three scenes, trying to achieve a sense of what is happening in this particular play*

Look at the opening scenes in the way described in the earlier sections of this chapter. Many of the details should prove relatively straightforward to explain, for you will soon spot destructive impulses which threaten to tear society apart. Some details, however, will prove more puzzling. In particular, the play opens with thunder and lightning; three witches appear and talk of a battle and of Macbeth. As always, the best tactic with a difficult scene is to approach it naïvely but methodically. Ask yourself whether details are orderly or disorderly. Fairly clearly, the storm is disorderly, and the witches belong to a world which is outside the rational order of things. The reason why this scene proves cryptic is that, as yet in the play, there is nothing to set against it. It is a vision of the dark world of evil and you can only make sense of it if you set it against your own ideas of the rational, daylight world of society. By starting the play with witches Shakespeare creates the atmosphere he wants for this play: an impression of mysterious and frightening forces lurking beneath the surface of life. The witches subsequently make prophecies, but these are in the form of riddles which are not fully understood at first. This again creates a sense of something inexplicable which is beyond the comprehension of civilised life. As the play goes on you might well feel that the evil force that motivates Macbeth and Lady Macbeth is equally dangerous, mysterious and incomprehensible.

As always, then, the tactic is to interpret the text in the light of your controlling ideas about tragedy, but as you describe and discuss details you will begin to capture a sense of the distinctive nature of this play. Many of the details should confirm and fill out an impression of a violent world, close to anarchy, where people can be motivated by dangerous and frightening instincts. You cannot hope to discuss all the details. If you tried to do so your account of the play would become unwieldy and superficial, so it is much better to select a few details and really work on them, showing how they create a particular atmosphere and an impression of specific issues in this play.

3   *Choose a scene from Act II, and try to clarify your impression of what this play is about and how it is developing*

In choosing a scene to discuss from Act II you will expect to strengthen your impression of the nature of the disruptive force in this society. Your approach can, even should, be fairly naïve, making the most of simple things, such as so much happening at night, the planning of a murder, and Macbeth seemingly close to madness at times as the horror mounts. You should be trying to convey, from the evidence of the text, a sense of the dark, violent and insane force of evil in this play and its terrifying, bloody consequences for the whole social order. Much of that terror is created by the staging. Look, for example, at the end of scene ii: Duncan has just been murdered, and then we hear violent sounds of knocking at a door. To Macbeth and Lady Macbeth it seems a terrifying noise: in the aftermath of Duncan's murder a sound as commonplace as knocking on a door no longer seems ordinary, but seems instead the portent of something ominous.

4   *Choose a scene from Act III to see how it develops the issues you have identified so far, and now begin to pay more attention to the principal characters in the play*

The growing sense of disorder can be tracked into Act III, but as always in a tragedy this is also a good moment to start paying more attention to the tragic hero. With Macbeth, quite simply, the question is, how can such a villain also be a tragic hero? Where are those noble qualities that promise, or have achieved, so much, but which are squandered or destroyed in such an evil world? Where is that sense of the best of people to set against the sense of the worst of people, for the tragedies are extreme plays in which an extreme sense of human potential for evil is balanced by an extreme sense of human potential for greatness? The problem in this play is that Macbeth is the source of violence and evil in this society.

The only way to answer the question is to look at the evidence of the text, seeing what Macbeth does and what he says. In the first scene of Act III he is seen hiring murderers to kill Banquo. Macbeth talks about him:

> Our fears in Banquo
> Stick deep: and in his royalty of nature
> Reigns that which would be fear'd. 'Tis much he dares,
> And to that dauntless temper of his mind
> He hath a wisdom that doth guide his valour
> To act in safety. There is none but he
> Whose being I do fear; and under him
> My Genius is rebuk'd . . . .
>
> (III.i.48–55)

The speech concentrates on Banquo's wise and heroic qualities. It is a description of some of the better qualities of people, and Macbeth is aware of the value and importance of such qualities. He has a clear idea of how a civilised person should behave, but nevertheless embraces evil and damnation. The violence of Macbeth's behaviour cannot, however, be explained just in terms of an understandable appetite for power. It is not as rational as this: it is more a kind of gratuitous violence and destructiveness as if he is consumed by an insane evil force. Yet the attraction of civilised and rational conduct is something that Macbeth is equally aware of, and so in many of his speeches there is a form of mental agony as the rational element in his personality wrestles with the irrational force that drives him on. He struggles between what is best and what is worst in his own nature, and there is often a tremendous clarity about the way in which he sees and understands this struggle going on in himself. His evil instincts are triumphant, as indeed they must be as they are not forces which can be controlled or tamed by reason alone, but his speeches reveal an awareness of his fear, knowledge, and even terror, of his own evil instincts.

It is this struggle between, and understanding of, people's best and worst instincts that makes Macbeth a tragic hero. But it is not enough just to write about this in general terms: you need to look at his speeches, seeing how they dramatise this tension in his personality. Any speech you select should contain evidence of the quarrel that is going on in his mind. Certain key words are used time and time again: words which suggest admirable behaviour, words such as 'royal', 'valiant', 'noble' and 'worthy', are consistently set against words such as 'murder', 'tyrant', 'damned' and 'bloody', words which suggest the base and irrational elements in people.

5   *Choose a scene from Act IV and attempt to build upon everything you have established so far*

You will need to look at the same issue as you move into Act IV, again focusing closely on small sequences of the action or specific speeches. Your basic idea can remain simple: that in Macbeth we see a struggle between our best and worst impulses. What, however, will bring your critical response to life is the extent to which you provide vivid illustrations of how the issue is presented in the text. If you attempt to discuss too large a section of the text, or if you merely tell the story of what Macbeth does, your comments are bound to be rather thin. But if you take about ten lines of one of Macbeth's speeches then you should, using your controlling idea of a struggle between good and bad impulses, be able to demonstrate the workings of Macbeth's mind, how he is torn between moral and immoral behaviour, how the rational side in his mind recoils in horror at his own evil instincts, yet how he allows his evil instincts to take over. As suggested above, look for simple tensions in the imagery, with words for all the rational and noble qualities of people being set against words which suggest the depraved and vicious side of people, and for the constant tension between images of light and images of darkness and night. In both cases the images being used will suggest a struggle for supremacy going on in Macbeth and in humanity as a whole.

6   *Choose a scene from near the end of the play which shows how the issues are resolved, and which will enable you to draw together the threads of your critical analysis*

At the end, Macbeth dies, but what you might spot is his extraordinary courage. This is not surprising, for what we have been stressing all along is that these are extreme plays where a sense of human evil is balanced by a sense of humanity's capacity for greatness. Macbeth might be evil but, as we see at the end, he can also be brave. What you notice at the end, however, and how you sum up the play, will obviously depend upon the things that you have discovered and decided are important in your own analysis of the text. The only thing that really matters is that your final conclusions must be consistent with what you have decided along the way, so that you establish a coherent view of the text based upon the evidence of the words on the page.

Our discussion of *Macbeth* has concentrated so much on describing a method for analysing the play that we have barely mentioned even such an important character as Lady Macbeth. But what we have said earlier in this chapter remains true: the issue in a play permeates the play. The tension the hero experiences is experienced in a lesser form by Lady Macbeth, who is also caught between her noble and ignoble qualities. If you want to look at Lady Macbeth, start with this idea, but as you look at scenes in which she appears and at some of her speeches you will begin to achieve a more precise understanding of her character and her function in the play. The tension between good and evil impulses also permeates the language of the play, and also underlies any theme we identify. Most commonly, the theme of *Macbeth* is said to be 'evil'; we hope that this chapter has made it clear that you cannot discuss evil on its own, as an irrational, destructive force, without also discussing people's potential for good to set against the idea of evil.

Apart from characters, themes and language, the other aspect of a play you should try to be aware of is how it works on the stage, and as always in Shakespeare the dramatic effects are bold but effective. Concentrate on those scenes or moments where you feel you can see how the staging works rather than try to cover everything. A good scene to look at is that of Lady Macbeth's sleep-walking (v.i), where we are given a vivid impression of the human mind collapsing under the force of evil. Look at how Lady Macbeth's actions are the whole subject of the scene, at how the doctor and servant comment on her appearance, her rubbing of her hands, the light she carries, forcing us in turn to think about her. At this point we possibly see her less as a character than as a symbolic embodiment of the disorder and sickness that Macbeth's evil has created.

Elsewhere there is much that is grisly in the play, simply but powerfully illustrating a violent and destructive force of evil that prevails in the state, in people and in nature. But the play also offers us glimpses of that goodness and innocence that evil destroys. Here you might look at the murder of Lady Macduff and her son in Act IV, scene ii: notice how brutal the murder is, how quickly the action happens. Paradoxically, the most obvious thing to set against this sense of human evil is the dominating presence of Macbeth himself, with many of the play's best lines, who, although evil, provides us with a sense of human greatness. In the great poetry of his speeches, and in the potentiality for thinking and logical behaviour that they reveal, we have perhaps the most positive thing of all to set against the disturbing sense of people as beasts. Here, as in all Shakespeare's tragedies, the richness of the verse is something that does much to counter any view of human beings as mere animals.

4

Studying a comedy

THE ROMANTIC COMEDIES

THE main kind of comic plays Shakespeare wrote are called romantic comedies. The two examples we discuss here are *Twelfth Night* and *Much Ado About Nothing*, but what we say would also apply to *Love's Labour's Lost*, *A Midsummer Night's Dream* and *As You Like It*. They are all light-hearted plays even though they can contain darker elements, but Shakespeare also wrote some rather more disturbing comedies, often referred to as 'dark' or 'problem' comedies, and we consider these briefly later in this chapter. At the end of his career, after he had written the great tragedies, Shakespeare wrote four further comic plays which are conventionally referred to as 'romances', and this chapter concludes with a short discussion of two of these, *The Winter's Tale* and *The Tempest*.

If you get a chance to see one of Shakespeare's comedies your response could well be a divided one. Shakespeare has a tremendous ability to create comic characters and amusing situations. You are likely to find yourself laughing, particularly as the humour of the plays is far more obvious when you see them than when you read them. At the same time, however, you might find yourself wondering what it all amounts to: a Shakespeare comedy can seem little more than an amusing diversion. Whereas with one of Shakespeare's tragedies you are likely to feel that serious issues are being explored, even if you find it hard to pinpoint what these are, you might feel that a Shakespeare comedy has little real substance. Indeed, all you might remember afterwards is that several characters fell in love and that this led to a series of comic mix-ups.

In order to make a critical response you do need to realise, however, that Shakespeare's comedies are, in their way, serious plays. This need not mean that you lose sight of how funny the plays are and how well they work on the stage. Indeed, if you understand the think-

ing that informs the plays you should be better placed to explain why
Shakespeare creates certain kinds of comic characters and comic situations. Our investigation of the plays can start with a general consideration of the characteristics of comic drama. You might be tempted to
think that the structure of a comedy can be fairly loose, that anything
can be included that is likely to make the audience laugh, but a
comedy follows the same structure as any play. It starts with an exposition stage, where things begin to go wrong or get out of hand. This is
followed by the complication stage, when disorder prevails and life is
turned upside down. At the end of a comedy, however, in the resolution stage, the problems are solved: a tragedy ends with the death of
the hero, but comedy conventionally ends with marriage or a dance.
Disorder has been overcome and the ending symbolises a new
harmony.

What we see in the central stage of a comedy is disorder, just as
we see it in any other kind of play. Just as in any other play, the comic
dramatist presents the actions of men and women that create problems,
chaos and confusion in society. The crucial difference, however, is that,
whereas in tragedy the dramatist disturbs us with his picture of the
unruly instincts and passions of people, in comedy the dramatist laughs
at these same instincts. It is a difference of perspective: *Othello*, for
example, could have been written as a comedy rather than as a tragedy
about a suspicious and jealous husband (and in the tragedies generally
Shakespeare is often aware of the comic aspects of a disturbing situation). *Much Ado About Nothing*, which also features a suspicious lover in
the character of Claudio, could have been made into a tragedy. The
point to grasp is that those passions and instincts that disrupt life can
either be viewed seriously or laughed at. In this respect, comedy, as
one of the two main traditional forms of drama, is simply the other side
of the coin of the other traditional form of drama, tragedy. Whereas
tragedy holds up a light that enables us to see into the darker areas of
experience, comedy is much more of a distorting mirror in which we
see an exaggerated version of human folly. The basic pattern to be
aware of in a comedy is, then, the standard pattern of all plays: one or
more actions trigger off a sequence of unruly events. As it is comedy,
however, the emphasis is on the foolishness of people's behaviour. Consequently, we are encouraged to laugh, and can come away from the
play having enjoyed it as merely a piece of entertainment.

Yet, in order to grasp the force of comedy, it is necessary, as we
have suggested, to see that serious issues are being raised, if only indir-

ectly. This serious content of comedy is more obvious in the plays of Shakespeare's contemporary, Ben Jonson. Jonson presents the evil lusts for sex, money and power that motivate people and cause them to create havoc in society. He deals with obvious corrupt instincts in people, but chooses to make such anti-social impulses the subject for laughter, showing how grotesque people appear when they are overwhelmed by greed for money or by sexual desire. Shakespeare sometimes, as in *Much Ado About Nothing* and *The Merchant of Venice*, does deal with mean and cruel instincts in people, but he never just dwells on nasty behaviour as Jonson does, and for the most part the disruptive instinct he presents is the very attractive instinct of love. The simplest pattern in Shakespeare's romantic comedies is that, in a seemingly well-ordered society, characters fall absurdly in love. It makes them act in a foolish way, something that is seen and heard in their actions and words. What we are exposed to is a huge irrational force that can throw life into total confusion. As in tragedy, we are made to see how precarious the rational order of society is, but tragedy focuses on the brutal instincts that are just below the civilised surface. Comedy focuses on the irrational character of men and women that lies behind the masks they present in society. We see the foolish strain in people that is normally disguised by social conduct. The plays do not, however, set out to preach a lesson or make a point: all they do is make us think about the complex nature of people (torn as they are between their social obligations and their more unstable characteristics) and the complex nature of society (as society is made up of people).

We are, however, not profoundly aware of such ideas when we watch a comedy as they are happy plays which take place in a romantic world where problems can be overcome. The way most comedies end sums this up neatly. Marriage provides the answer: marriage is the institution in which the irrational, and yet at the same time inevitable, attractive and important, force of love can be controlled and made to serve the needs of society in the procreation of a future generation. The pattern we have to be aware of, then, as we turn to a Shakespeare comedy, is that passions that are concealed behind the polite surface of society will disrupt life: occasionally these are spiteful passions (as in *Much Ado About Nothing*), but usually it is the attractive passion of love. In the central stages of the play life will be thrown into disarray, but the problem will be solved at the end when the central characters marry. No very serious point is made, but we have learned something about the nature of society and the nature of human beings. We have laughed at an exaggerated version of our own folly, our own failure always to act in a sensible way.

Twelfth Night

1   *Read the play, then think about what kind of play it is and what sort of broad pattern you can see in the plot*

Twelfth Night is a comedy. Orsino, Duke of Illyria, is in love with Olivia, but she has vowed not to marry for seven years because her brother has died recently. Viola is shipwrecked off Illyria and, believing her twin brother Sebastian has drowned, assumes a boy's disguise. Under the name 'Cesario' Viola becomes Orsino's page and acts as his emissary to Olivia. Viola herself is in love with Orsino. The complications arise when Olivia falls in love with Viola in her guise as 'Cesario'. Other characters include Sir Toby Belch, a relative of Olivia's, his foolish friend Sir Andrew Aguecheek, a clown Feste, and Olivia's killjoy steward Malvolio. Sir Toby and his cronies leave a letter for Malvolio, apparently written by Olivia, which encourages him to believe she loves him. Malvolio makes a fool of himself in his advances to her. The main plot, however, concerns the tangled triangle of Viola, Orsino and Olivia. This is further complicated when Viola's supposedly dead brother Sebastian arrives in Illyria. Olivia believes he is 'Cesario' and they become betrothed. Total confusion arises, however, when Olivia confronts Viola, believing her to be Sebastian. The problems are solved when Sebastian reappears. Orsino marries Viola, Olivia marries Sebastian, and even Sir Toby marries Maria, Olivia's gentlewoman. Only Malvolio and Sir Andrew are left outside this circle of happiness.

Even simplifying the plot like this, its twists and turns are confusing, but you should try to see the standard pattern of a romantic comedy in this story. Love, or, as in the case of Malvolio, the belief that one is loved, is the basis of all the complications. The pattern of the play is that sane and rational behaviour is disrupted by people falling in love. The informing idea is presented in its simplest terms, as is so often the case in Shakespeare's plays, in the subplot. At the centre of the subplot is Malvolio, a cold kill-joy who wants everyone to behave decorously, yet the moment he drops his social mask he proves to be the biggest fool of all when he fancies himself to be loved. Yet the subplot, with its emphasis on Malvolio's initial 'correctness', also suggests that it would be a dour and depressing society that could find no place for folly and love, that love is a passion to be celebrated as well as laughed at. The problems are resolved when the play ends with three marriages: our ideas about comedy should help us to see that marriage here serves to reconcile the irrational but important impulse of love with society's demand for rational and disciplined behaviour.

2 *Look at the first two or three scenes, trying to achieve a sense of what is happening in this particular play*

We now have a general sense of what this play is about, but a look at the first two acts should sharpen our impression of what the particular issues are in this play. You might spot different things than we do, and how you interpret scenes is up to you, but it is important that you try to build on the foundations of what you have established at the outset. You might have to think about a scene for a long time, but eventually you should be able to make a valid connection with your initial ideas.

In the first scene of *Twelfth Night* Orsino, besotted with love for Olivia, can talk of nothing except love, but his servant brings him the news that Olivia is in mourning for her brother and has cut herself off from the world for seven years. Already we can see Shakespeare setting up the conventional pattern of romantic comedy: Orsino is drawn away from his responsibilities as a duke by the uncontrollable passion of love. We might well notice how silly and foolish such love makes him. But what can we say about Olivia going into mourning for seven years? The key to interpreting a detail such as this is to use the order/disorder formula which we have used throughout this book. Olivia is trying to order her life for the next seven years, denying herself emotional rela- tionships. It does not take much imagination to see that such a scheme of self-discipline is excessive: she allows no room for her own humanity, no room for the human need for love. The play, therefore, has already set up, in two ways, a tension between socially disciplined behaviour and emotional behaviour.

In the second scene, Viola and a sea captain have been washed up on the shore following a storm. She resolves to disguise herself as a man and seek employment with the Duke Orsino. A good question to ask yourself is why these two characters have been shipwrecked. As with any detail in a Shakespeare play, it is not there just to fill out the plot but must have a meaning and function in the play as a whole. No obvious answer is likely to spring to mind, so again the formula of order and disorder can be employed. A storm is obviously disorderly and destructive, but how does this relate to our sense of what the play is about? What you have to do is seek a connection with the ideas you already have. It could be argued, for example, that the storm is a parallel for the stormy passion of love that creates havoc in society. A more elaborate explanation, however, might be that just beyond society is a wild world of nature that is hostile to humanity (as suggested by Sebastian's supposed death). This helps us understand why people value an ordered social life so highly, as it offers mutual protection from the ravages of the natural world. The order that humanity strives for, however, is always under threat, both from without and from within.

Such abstract thinking might seem at odds with the light-hearted impression *Twelfth Night* makes on its audience, but such thinking is sometimes necessary, particularly if we hope to explain something such as why Viola disguises herself as a man. The easy answer is that Shakespeare always uses people in disguise to complicate his plots, but we have to see that this is more than just a convenient device, that it must relate to the issues at the heart of the play. In seeking an explanation we can again start from our order/disorder divide. Social order depends upon people playing a role in society. By disguising a woman as a man Shakespeare forces us to think about the idea of role-playing. He highlights the difference between the social masks people present to the world and their true natures, and makes us see the artificiality of the social roles people have to play. The argument could be extended from here in all kinds of directions, but the point that is relevant to our discussion so far is that Shakespeare seems not only to be laughing at the irrationality of people but also to be suggesting that conventional social behaviour can be questioned, as it involves people playing such limited and clearly defined roles.

What we are losing sight of so far in this attempt to pinpoint the issues, however, is the fact that *Twelfth Night* is a very funny play which works brilliantly on the stage. As we turn to scene iii, though, which is the first really funny scene, we should be able to move towards a sense of how and why the play is funny. It is at this point that Sir Toby Belch makes his first appearance. He comes across as a drunken but cheerful character who lives for fun and amusement. He is rebuked for his drunken behaviour but carries on unabated, encouraging his friend Sir Andrew to woo Olivia. We can here begin to see the source of the humour in the play: people appear funny the moment they start to diverge from a standard of reasonable conduct. This is at its clearest in the subplot, where Sir Toby is excessive in everything he says and does, where Sir Andrew is a naturally foolish man who cannot understand the rules of social behaviour, and where Malvolio is so correct that he appears pompous and vain. It is important to recognise the kind of tone in which all this is presented. Ben Jonson might have presented these characters as grotesque, but Shakespeare presents them as slightly silly but harmless.

The way to get hold of the tone of this scene, and of the scenes generally in a comedy, is to look at the staging. At the end of the scene we see Sir Toby and Sir Andrew practising their dancing, leaping about ridiculously, enjoying themselves without restraint. The effect, inevitably, is laughter, not a contemptuous laughter but a shared enjoyment of the fun. The laughter in the romantic comedies for the most part is affectionate in that what we see in most of the characters are frailties rather than vices; they are motivated not by avaricious lusts but by something less threatening. In the case of Sir Toby this is just a desire for fun and amusement. In the case of Orsino, Viola and Olivia it is their desire for love. They appear funny when their emotions get in the way of rational behaviour, and the tone is happy and often just gently amusing (as in the presentation of Orsino in scene i) because we are seeing the characters' weaknesses rather than any evil desires motivating their behaviour.

Scene iii, then, tells us something about the nature of Shakespeare's humour, yet it also enables us to pinpoint more clearly the issues in *Twelfth Night*. While there is something foolish about an old man such as Sir Toby behaving in the way he does, his very lack of restraint and disregard for social convention are both funny and attractive. The tension in the play is between social restraint and people's unstable instincts, but in what it says about this the play appears to lean in two directions at once. The presentation of human folly is easy to perceive, but we also see that these unruly passions are attractive. There is something stifling about society with all its rules about acceptable behaviour; it seems to need an infusion of spontaneity and recklessness, as in the dancing at the end of scene iii. Such ideas are apparent in all the scenes we have look at so far. The play starts with Orsino the lover: he might appear foolish, but is no more foolish than Olivia, whose seven-year mourning might be socially correct but is lifedenying. We then meet Viola, who, in disguising herself as a man, challenges social conventions which limit people to fixed roles. And Sir Toby simply prefers debauchery to reasonable behaviour.

3   *Choose a scene from Act II, and try to clarify your impression of what this play is about and how it is developing*

We have moved quickly through the first act as we wanted to introduce a number of points which are relevant to Shakespeare's comedies as a whole, but our analysis could have been a lot simpler. It would have been enough to establish the following points: (i) that, because Orsino talks constantly about love, we are obviously in the world of romantic comedy; (ii) that because Orsino and Sir Toby both act rather foolishly we can see how the play is concerned with the presence of foolish instincts in people; (iii) that the play is amusing when we see characters acting in a way that social convention would regard as exaggerated or extreme.

We now want to discuss the opening scene of Act II in just such simple terms. Initially it might appear a difficult scene to analyse because very little of any apparent significance happens in it. It merely introduces us to Antonio and Sebastian. Sebastian is Viola's brother, and he, too, has arrived in Illyria thinking his twin has drowned. Antonio, the sea captain who rescued him, has become very attached to Sebastian, so much so that despite the fact that he has enemies at Orsino's court he declares that he will accompany Sebastian there.

To tackle a tricky scene such as this, approach it naïvely but methodically, asking yourself whether things are orderly or disorderly, even whether they are good or bad. Here are two men who have just escaped from the chaos of the sea (bad), but they have become close friends (good); Antonio, though, might get in trouble at Orsino's court (bad). We could say that a social virtue – friendship – is being presented, and we see the importance of this in a world that can be threatening. But the complicating factor is that the bond between the two men goes beyond reason, that it is a relationship of affection, and even love. This is the complication that affects the whole play, and indeed all of Shakespeare's comedies, that love is not just a foolish and disruptive passion but an attractive and indeed necessary element in life. It you can see this, how love is both irrational and yet attractive, disruptive but binding, you have got hold of a great deal of the logic behind romantic comedy and why it both laughs at and celebrates people's irrational impulses.

In addition, you have also got hold of much of the logic behind the staging of these plays, why they show people behaving so foolishly. We can see this best perhaps in the gulling of Malvolio in scene v, where he is deceived, or rather deceives himself into believing Olivia loves him. It is a marvellously funny scene, partly because of its dramatic irony – we know Malvolio is being tricked by the other characters, who watch as he finds a letter he takes to be from Olivia – but also because we see Malvolio gradually discard his sober image and take on the role of romantic lover. As he reads the letter his mood changes from discovery to excitement to ecstasy: the would-be paragon of order becomes an example of the irrational force of love, seen in his decision to smile. The facial gesture implied by the text is just one small detail of how the scene creates its effect of laughter, a laughter that appreciates the foolish instinct of love in people.

4   *Choose a scene from Act III to see how it develops the issues you have identified so far, and now begin to pay more attention to the principal characters in the play*

Act III begins with Viola ('Cesario') meeting the clown Feste. They exchange banter, then other characters enter, and there is a lengthy encounter between 'Cesario' and Olivia in which Olivia makes plain her feelings of love. The obvious characters to look at are Olivia and Viola, but there is another aspect to the scene which is so typical of Shakespeare's comedies, and which so many students find hard to understand, that it might be best if we try to explain it directly here.

The scene opens with banter between Viola and Feste. For example:

> FESTE. . . . I live by the church.
> VIOLA. Art thou a churchman?
> FESTE. No such matter, sir: I do live by the church: for I do live at my house, and my house doth stand by the church.   (III.i.3–7)

Shakespeare's comedies are full of such exchanges. Many readers can see that the lines are supposed to be funny but also feel that they are rather pointless and not really funny at all. If we understand the logic behind such lines, however, we might appreciate their humour. What often happens is that, as here, a character pulls apart the normal meaning of words. On other occasions, as with Dogberry in *Much Ado About Nothing*, there are malapropisms, which simply means that characters repeatedly use the wrong words. The logic behind such lines is that they draw attention to the language people share and which makes communication in a society possible. A society, indeed, only functions effectively if everyone speaks the same language. But these speeches play games with language: Feste upsets the accepted conventions and Dogberry cannot even master the conventions. Such games with language are a way of demonstrating how precarious any notion of a sane and sensible social order is, as we see how easily conventional language collapses into near-nonsense. Feste is a clown, and the clowns in Shakespeare's plays are always used in the same way: they are licensed jesters, paid to make fun of people and their social pretensions. They thus serve to remind us that we do not live in a rational world – that even the language we use is artificial and suspect, because, like the social system itself, it is just a system of artificial conventions and rules which can easily break down – and that the world can be seen as rather a mad place. We are back, then, with ideas of social order and social convention and the disruption of that order.

Feste's humour is verbal and witty, and such wordplay is very common in Shakespeare's comedies. It is present in virtually every scene. It is often combined, however, with a more straightforward kind of humour, such as we see in this opening scene of Act III when Olivia makes overtures to Viola in her guise as 'Cesario'. Much of the humour here arises from the fact that we know 'Cesario' is really a girl. We enjoy the confusion this creates. At the same time, though, we can see that the characters appear funny because they are acting in a way that social convention would regard as exaggerated, emotional or extreme. Our laughter, however, as is so often the case in Shakespeare's comedies, is affectionate rather than cruel, for what we see are the characters' frailties rather than any vices.

It is important that you try to describe what you might see happening on the stage in a sequence such as this, as so much of the effect of the play lies in the visual impression of characters acting in a slightly ludicrous manner, but it is also important to look at specific speeches. We have selected Olivia's first substantial speech to 'Cesario'. She starts by referring to a ring that she made Malvolio take to 'Cesario': she is embarrassed about the incident because she sent her own ring pretending it was Cesario's. It was a desperate ploy to make her feelings clear:

> I did send.
> After the last enchantment you did here,
> A ring in chase of you: so did I abuse
> Myself, my servant, and, I fear me, you.
> Under your hard construction must I sit,
> To force that on you in a shameful cunning
> Which you knew none of yours. What might you think?
> Have you not set mine honour at the stake,
> And baited it with all th'unmuzzled thoughts
> That tyrannous heart can think? . . .
>
> (III.i.108–17)

Olivia fears that 'Cesario' will despite her for the openness of her passion. The tension we have been pursuing in the play is between social restraint and the unruly but attractive instinct of love. The easiest way of looking at a speech such as this is to search for this tension here. There are a number of words and phrases that suggest the disorderly power of love: 'enchantment', 'unmuzzled thoughts', and 'tyrannous heart': they are ways of referring to love as a dangerous, uncontrollable force. At the same time, however, there is a great deal about Olivia's social embarrassment: how Viola must despise her, how her honour is threatened. The point is that her social pretensions, all the codes of conduct and self-discipline she lives by as a lady in society, have been threatened by love. It is, in fact, a very simple tension between social convention and the irrational force of love.

What, then, makes Olivia interesting as a character, in this speech and throughout the play, is that she is caught between two competing instincts: the fact that she cannot stay in mourning for seven years demonstrates that social correctness is not enough, that she needs love. And what is true of Olivia is true generally in the play: all the main characters are caught between the demands of society and their own passions that run counter to this, but the complication is that as society is made up of people their emotional needs or weaknesses must be accommodated. At this point, however, as far as Olivia is concerned, social niceties and the pull of love are in total conflict.

As we say, look at speeches to see how the issues in the play are expressed – in this speech it is really quite astonishing how clearly an idea of socially correct behaviour is set against the irrational power of love – but try to combine this with looking at the action on the stage, for it is important to see how the comic confusion can make similar points in a bold but effective way. The moment we see people scurrying around the stage or acting in an undignified manner an impression is conveyed of the gap between socially correct and socially absurd behaviour. Later in this act, for example, Sir Andrew challenges Viola to a duel, and Malvolio makes his romantic overtures to Olivia. She thinks he has gone mad and has him locked up. If we take Sir Andrew first: the scene is comic because we see such a foolish man trying to behave like the kind of knight who fights duels. It is the love that he fancies he feels for Olivia that has made him act in such a way. The same is true of Malvolio: he appeared foolishly correct in his role as Olivia's steward, but is even more foolish as a would-be lover. The humour in the scenes featuring the characters from the subplot is broader than in the scenes involving Viola and Olivia, for not only do Malvolio and Sir Andrew get in a tangle with their emotions, they are equally incompetent in their attempts at acting in a socially correct manner. Characters such as Olivia do know how to act, but cannot always maintain their social poise.

5   *Choose a scene from Act IV and attempt to build upon everything you have established so far*

By the fourth act of a comedy it is likely that confusion will reign. The action on the stage is likely to be fast-paced, chaotic and almost farcical. The comic effects rely heavily on Shakespeare's manipulation of the plot: he has set up all kinds of complications and now contrives situations which bring the characters together.

   We can see this in the first scene of Act IV, where Sebastian reappears and is taken to be 'Cesario' by various characters. The confusion culminates in Sir Andrew starting to fight him, but Olivia intervenes and takes Sebastian home with her. Some of the humour comes close to slapstick comedy, but there is also a great deal of substance to such scenes, as we can see if we focus on a speech. We have selected a passage where Olivia rebukes Sir Toby for encouraging the fight between Sir Andrew and Sebastian:

> Will it be ever thus? Ungracious wretch,
> Fit for the mountains and the barbarous caves,

> Where manners ne'er were preach'd! Out of my sight!
> (IV.i.46–9)

She is angry with Sir Toby because he has breached all the standards of reasonable conduct. She criticises his lack of manners. What we find in the speech, therefore, are references to Sir Toby as a wretch, an animal and a barbarian, and what is set against this is an idea of social restraint. Yet, although what Olivia sees as animal-like behaviour is clearly unacceptable, love is equally a wild passion, and society must somehow absorb and cope with love. As Olivia continues she says to Sebastian,

> I prithee, gentle friend,
> Let thy fair wisdom, not thy passion, sway
> In this uncivil and unjust extent
> Against thy peace . . . .
> (IV.i.50–3)

It is again the case that social virtues (contained in the words 'gentle friend', 'fair wisdom', 'peace') are set against unruly passions; indeed, it does seem that every speech refers to the tension we have identified, but our criticism only has any real substance if we do provide this evidence of how such ideas are evident in the details of the text. Olivia's praise for fair wisdom as against passion is, however, somewhat ironic, as she herself is at the mercy of passion.

6 *Choose a scene from near the end of the play which shows how the issues are resolved, and which will enable you to draw together the threads of your critical analysis*

In a comedy the problems are usually resolved in the last scene. We have anticipated much of what we need to say here, as we have already suggested that marriage is the answer: it reconciles the passionate demands of the individual and the requirements of society. What we remember from the play, however, is not the neatness of the ending but how confusion reigns throughout the greater part of the action. Even the ending, however, is not as neat as it appears, for Malvolio and Sir Andrew are left outside this circle of happiness. In addition, there is a closing song from Feste with imagery of wind and rain, and knaves and thieves. These are ways of acknowledging that there are always problems. Life is always complex because there is always a tension between the desire for order in society and natural forces – both in nature and people – which threaten and undermine order and stability. But the strongest of these forces – the passion of love – is not only foolish and disruptive but also attractive and necessary.

7 Pursuing aspects of the play

As in the previous chapters of this book, we have steered a course through *Twelfth Night*, trying to put together a coherent argument and turning to small sections of the text to illustrate and develop our argument. Of course, it all took much longer than it might seem from what we have said. Initially our overall view of the play was fairly confused. We had to keep on looking at the text and keep on thinking about it as we worked on producing a clear argument. This is worth remembering: do not be put off if your initial attempts at working on the text do not seem to get you very far. If you keep on looking at and thinking about the text you should be happy eventually with your analysis. The most important point to remember is that everything will make sense if you have sound controlling ideas and keep them central. And these controlling ideas can be very simple: with a light-hearted romantic comedy such as *Twelfth Night*, the main thing you need to know is that love creates discord in society. We laugh at characters who find themselves caught up in romantic dilemmas, but we also see that love is an important part of human nature. In looking at the play you are looking at how Shakespeare develops and presents this simple pattern. In preparing for examinations, however, you might want to concentrate on specific aspects of the play, namely character, themes, language and staging, but, as we have stressed in the previous chapters, this does not mean that you have to think up new ideas. Everything you discover can be an extension of the analysis that you have already put together, as we attempt to demonstrate in the next few paragraphs.

(a) *Character*. Our analysis of the play has suggested that the main characters are caught between the demands of their social roles and the passion of love. You can talk about Viola in these terms, about how she is meant to be serving the Duke yet also loves him, and is also having to fend off the advances of Olivia without offending her. As Viola is the central character, you can expect her to embody dilemmas and confusions all the main characters find themselves in, and this proves to be the case if you look at her speeches. The key to the characters, then, is seeing how they are divided between the dictates of their intellects and the dictates of their hearts. Even such a character as Sir Andrew is more than just a comic foil: he tries to act like a gentleman, but is too silly a man to appear anything other than a fool when he attempts to cut a figure in society. The informing idea, then, is simple, but try to see what problems the characters experience as they attempt to reconcile their social roles with their true natures. To explain and explore this with an individual character, look at incidents that they are involved in, seeing how they are pulled two ways, and also look at their speeches to see how the same tension reveals itself there. Here, for example, are just a few words from Orsino to Viola as he instructs her to pay court to Olivia:

> Be clamorous and leap all civil bounds,
> Rather than make unprofited return.
> (I.iv.20–1)

The tension is between an idea of social restraint ('civil bounds') and extreme behaviour ('Be clamorous').

(b) *Language*. The division we have found in this speech will be evident everywhere in the language of the play. Just about every speech will contain words which refer to social restraint and these will be set against images of noise, war, drunkenness, blindness, madness, sea and change. These are also the commonest images in all Shakespeare's comedies, and always serve to emphasise the irrationality and unruliness of love. Your key to analysing a speech is to see how it constantly reveals an opposition between social and extreme behaviour. Our discussion of Olivia's speeches on pp. 98 and 100 provides you with examples of how to do this. To explore the language of the play as a whole you need only look for and describe this pattern in about four substantial speeches by different characters, and you will have established a vivid picture of how the language of the play expresses the themes of the play.

(c) *Themes*. In discussing the play as a whole you will have put together your own ideas about the themes. Often, however, you will come across the suggestion that other themes are central, themes you might not have noticed at all. It is sometimes said, for example, that the twin themes of *Twelfth Night* are deceit and self-deception. By deceit is meant the pretence played by Viola, by self-deception something like Olivia pretending to herself that she can turn her back on the world for seven years. What you have to see is that, if somebody states that these are the main themes, this is only another way of expressing what you have already discovered to be central in the play. We have talked of social conventions and irrational passions. Deceit can simply mean that things are not as they appear on the surface, that there is a more complex truth behind the social masks people present to the world. Self-deception refers to the way Olivia, for example, tries to maintain social pretensions and self-discipline in the face of love. Similarly, some people might refer to the theme of appearance and reality in the play. What you have to see is that this is just another way of expressing the idea that beneath the way things appear in society are more complex emotions which make life difficult. If an essay question asks you to discuss a certain theme in the play, try to see how this is a way of focusing an impression of the play as a whole. Your ideas about the play can remain the same, but you will have to search for the incidents and speeches which illustrate the theme, and then interpret them in the light of your controlling ideas.

(d) *Staging*. Throughout your discussion of a play you should try to be aware of what an audience would see on the stage and how they might respond. If you are asked to pursue this further it is a good idea to look at moments of turbulent activity and at visually arresting incidents in the play. What you are striving to do, though, is to show how the action on stage reflects and realises the themes that you have decided are central. There is no point in talking without any sense of direction about what a fool Malvolio looks when he makes his advances to Olivia: the visual effect of the yellow cross-gartered stockings he wears is only significant if you can say why it is striking. The explanation, however, is simple: previously he has been very 'correct', but now he appears preposterous as he starts acting irrationally. Another thing to talk about in the staging are those places where dramatic irony is in evidence, where we know more than the characters. For example, when Malvolio comes on in his lover's garb we know that he is the victim of a trick designed to expose his vanity and self-love and anticipate the moment with relish. But the other point to grasp here is how the irony serves to underline the theme of the play. It is another way, like Olivia's wooing of 'Cesario', of illustrating the tension between social conventions and the irrational force of love.

Much Ado About Nothing

Our basic idea in looking at *Twelfth Night* has been that love creates discord in society. It is an idea which is central in all of Shakespeare's comedies. Initially, however, you might find it difficult to see how this can, for example, relate to *A Midsummer Night's Dream*, as most of the action of this play takes place in a wood ruled over by fairies. The fairies, however, have as much trouble with love as anybody else. It not only creates chaos and confusion in the lives of the human beings in the play but also disrupts the lives of the fairies. What we see, then, is the same tension between the idea of a well-ordered world and disruption of that world as we find in *Twelfth Night*, and marriage again provides the answer at the end, representing a harmonious balance between social demands and unruly instincts. *A Midsummer Night's Dream*, like *Twelfth Night*, is a very light-hearted play, but in both works there are just hints of something darker. Malvolio, for example, may seem ridiculous, but there is also a streak of vicious intolerance in him which is slightly disturbing. It affects our response to him in the play: we do not simply laugh at his foibles but take a sort of cruel delight in seeing him get his just deserts.

Shakespeare as a comic writer, however, can give far greater prominence to mean, repressive or unpleasant characteristics in people than he does in *Twelfth Night* or *A Midsummer Night's Dream*. Indeed, we can say that generally Shakespeare's comedies seem to lean in one of two directions: either towards a sense of people as absurd but amiable, as in these two plays, or, as in *The Merchant of Venice* and *Much Ado About Nothing*, towards a greater emphasis on mean and cruel instincts in people. These are still romantic comedies (though *The Merchant of Venice* might equally be described as a problem comedy), and love is still the source of the complications, but they present something else alongside and in addition to amiable, irrational instincts in people. Both plays, for example, include characters opposed to the happiness of comedy and to the spirit of love. They are tricky plays to study because it can prove difficult to balance a sense of their comic form with an awareness of their more disturbing qualities, but we hope that our discussion of *Much Ado About Nothing* might provide an idea of how they can be approached.

1   *Read the play, then think about what kind of play it is and what sort of broad
pattern you can see in the plot*

Much Ado About Nothing is a comedy. It begins with the happy return
from war of Don Pedro and his retinue, who are to be entertained at
Leonata's house. Claudio falls in love with Hero, Leonata's daughter,
and gets Don Pedro to woo her for him. Don John, the villain of the
play, hates Claudio and plots to wreck his marriage to Hero: he contrives to make Claudio think she is unfaithful. In the meantime the
other characters contrive to make Beatrice and Benedick, who seem to
despise each other and who spend their time trading insults, fall in
love. Claudio, deceived by Don John, rejects Hero at their marriage
service. She faints and her family pretend she is dead. Angered by this
treatment of Hero, Beatrice demands Benedick kill Claudio. Don
John's trickery comes to light, however, through the bungling incompetence of Dogberry and Verges, and Claudio and Hero marry, as do
Beatrice and Benedick. Don John flees but is apprehended.

The basic pattern of romantic comedy is that love creates discord
in society. We can see this at the beginning of this play: the troubles of
war are over and the characters have time to relax, and so their
thoughts turn to amusement and love. In *Twelfth Night* the characters
begin to act foolishly the moment they fall in love; their emotions are at
odds with the masks they would or should present to the world. In *Much
Ado* this is apparent in the Beatrice-and-Benedick subplot: they both
affect to disdain love, but then find themselves falling in love. The
scenes in which they appear are funny because they start to behave in a
way that previously they would have regarded as exaggerated, emotional and foolish. But the main plot goes off in another direction, a
direction which is also in evidence in *The Merchant of Venice*. There is very
little presentation of Hero and Claudio as comic and amusing figures.
What happens instead is that their falling in love provides the villain
Don John with an opportunity to indulge his resentment, hatred and
pure malice. The complications in the main plot are a result of love, but
only in the sense that the lovers abandon caution and reserve and make
themselves vulnerable. In *Twelfth Night* we laugh at characters caught up
in romantic dilemmas, as we do with Beatrice and Benedick in this play,
but the major emphasis in *Much Ado* is not on love in tension with social
restraint, but on love being threatened by something malevolent, and
the obvious malevolent, anti-comic force is the villainy of Don John. A
similar pattern is in evidence in *The Merchant of Venice*: Bassanio needs to

borrow money to visit Belmont, where he hopes to win the lady Portia in marriage. Antonio helps him out, even though he has to borrow the money from Shylock to do so, but then Antonio finds his life threatened by Shylock who seeks revenge for the wrongs he has previously suffered.

What we can say, then, is that so far there appear to be two basic patterns to Shakespeare's romantic comedies. The more light-hearted plays works on the basis of presenting characters in love acting irrationally in a sane and civilised society which finds love emotional and extreme. The darker plays, however, uncover two kinds of irrationality in society: there is the amiable irrationality of people in love, but also a more disturbing form of irrationality of people who seem to take a delight in destroying happiness or in hurting others. The plays present both attractive instincts and mean and cruel instincts in people.

What happens in *Much Ado* is that the villainy of Don John ruins the marriage plans of Hero and Claudio and, for a while, poisons the atmosphere in Leonato's house. Indeed, the presence of Don John can make us wonder why this play can still be regarded as a comedy. It is true that the problems are resolved and that the play ends happily, and that there are very funny scenes with Dogberry as well as the witty, comic scenes of Beatrice and Benedick, but all these elements might seem at odds with the issue at the heart of the plot. Part of the task in analysing *Much Ado* must therefore be to see why it is valid to talk about it as an essentially light-hearted comedy. If we cannot appreciate that, we fail to capture the true tone of the play: there is a tendency in studying and writing about *Much Ado* to make it seem a very serious play, but when we read it or see it on the stage it comes across mainly as a very light and happy play. What helps create this impression is the structure and staging of *Much Ado*. The rapid succession of events in the play means that darker scenes yield quickly to more frivolous scenes, and therefore a serious mood is not allowed to become dominant. In addition, what we see on the stage in the lighter scenes – things such as dancing, singing, and a very visual form of comedy in which we see characters acting in a somewhat ridiculous manner – establishes an atmosphere of fun rather than of gloom.

2   *Look at the first two or three scenes, trying to achieve a sense of what is happening in this particular play*

We are not actually going to analyse any scenes here. The section on *Twelfth Night* provides a model of how an analysis can be constructed, and all we want to do here is remind you of what you should be trying to do with the early scenes from a play. You should be attempting to sum them up in a fairly simple way, trying to relate them to the pattern you have already established. It should soon become apparent that this is the relaxed world of comedy. Much of the talk is of love, so you will realise that *Much Ado* is a romantic comedy, and you should be able to point to examples of characters acting in a slightly foolish way as the idea of love enters their lives. In Don John, however, you will come across a character whose attitude and behaviour are unreasonable but far from attractive, as he begins to plot against the lovers. So far, though, the atmosphere is predominantly happy and carefree.

3   *Choose a scene from Act II, and try to clarify your impression of what this play is about and how it is developing*

What happens in Act II is that at a masked ball Don John tells Claudio that Don Pedro is wooing Hero for himself, but Claudio soon discovers that this is not true. To while away the time before Hero and Claudio's wedding, Don Pedro thinks up a scheme to deceive Beatrice and Benedick into falling in love. Benedick is the first victim of the ploy and starts acting foolishly as a lover. At the same time Don John plans his trick to deceive Claudio into believing that Hero is unfaithful.

Throughout this book we have suggested that you select a scene at this stage and analyse it so as to establish a firmer sense of the issues in the play in question. You might be most drawn to the scene (II.ii) in which Don John prepares his plan, and this would certainly be a good scene to look at as it is obviously crucial to the development of the plot, and would also allow you to form a clearer impression of the nature of the force that the lovers are up against. You might notice how Don John intends to act the part of a dependable friend but beneath the surface is a scheming villain. As always, however, your criticism will only stand up as criticism if you can point to the specific details in the scene which illustrate the point.

Looking at the scene with Don John will, then, enable you to crystallise an impression of how the play is focusing on concealed, mean and cruel instincts in people, instincts which certainly seem far from comic. But this is not the only scene in Act II, although much of the other material might strike you as trivial and inconsequential. The other characters seem to be doing little more than playing games, and it might appear hard to think of anything that can be said about the trick that is played on Beatrice (in Act III) and Benedick. It is amusing on the stage, but might just seem light relief which is at odds with the true subject of the play.

There are two points to take into account here. The first is the way the trick itself is staged. As with the gulling of Malvolio in *Twelfth Night*, part of the comic effect lies in the fact that we know Beatrice and Benedick are being set up and we laugh at their almost instant change from witty, carefree people into serious lovers. Such laughter is not 'light relief' in a comedy but is crucial to its significance as a play that celebrates the irrational force of love. The second point about the behaviour of Don Pedro generally and the prank played on Beatrice and Benedick is the silliness of such behaviour. The characters have some time to waste and so act in a foolish way. But when a lot of scenes are devoted to presenting such behaviour we have something substantial to set against the villainy of Don John. The play might contain a sense of the viciousness that can be inherent in a person, but it devotes far more attention to the attractive folly of other characters. And in some ways there is not much difference between what Don John is doing and what Don Pedro is doing: Don Pedro contrives a plot to catch Beatrice and Benedick; Don John contrives a plot to catch Hero and Claudio. Rather than presenting a picture of people acting sensibly, the play creates an impression of people playing games. They seem to have an instinctive need to act absurdly, and in this Don John is in some ways not so much a villain as a fool as he puts so much of his energy into the destruction of happiness. The play thus presents a comprehensive impression of the folly of people who, both in attractive and in unpleasant ways, act irrationally. It is the standard vision of a comic play of the folly of human beings.

The other thing to pick up in all these scenes is the idea of deception. Don John suggests to Claudio that Don Pedro's behaviour is false, that he is wooing Hero for himself. Don Pedro then arranges the double deception of Benedick and Beatrice, and Don John prepares to deceive Claudio. In each instance, things are not as they might appear. Each trick again brings up the idea of the truth behind the surface appearance of things, and of how, as all the incidents in the play show, the moment we scratch the surface we see the folly of humankind. People rarely act reasonably for long but always veer off to some extreme. This is true of all the comedies, but, whereas *Twelfth Night* concentrates on the attractive side of folly, *Much Ado About Nothing* presents both the attractive and the unattractive faces of folly.

4   *Choose a scene from Act III to see how it develops the issues you have identified so far, and now begin to pay more attention to the principal characters in the play*

As you turn to Act III, it is always productive to start looking more closely at one or more of the central characters. Claudio is a good figure to select. Initially he might appear rather bland, a token figure of the lover surrounded by more colourful characters, but if you look more closely at his behaviour in a scene from Act III you might realise that he is a far from pleasant person. Again, it is essential that you do not just sum up his character in this kind of general way but look closely at, and refer to, those incidents and speeches that reveal his personality. Look at how, in scene ii, he is quite ready to believe that Hero has been unfaithful to him, and how quickly he is prepared to take his revenge by shaming her in church. Again, then, as with Don John, we are seeing unpleasant and disturbing instincts in a character. The surprise, of course, is that we find such traces of vindictiveness, rather than amiable irrationality, in the lover Claudio. *Much Ado* is a comic play, but at such moments it has a gritty edge, touching on a lack of feeling in people which is not amusing. Claudio's unpleasantness is, in fact, rather more disturbing than the outright villainy of Don John.

The more general point we can make, however, is that as always the wider tension of the play is reflected in the tension at the heart of every central character. The play concentrates on the attractive and unattractive instincts in people which disrupt the social order. Claudio is caught between his role as lover and bridegroom and his own spiteful instincts as an uncaring youth. The way Beatrice and Benedick fit into the wider pattern of the play is that they move in the opposite direction from Claudio: initially they pride themselves on being caustic and cynical people who have no time for such social conventions as marriage, but as the play goes on what we have suspected all along becomes increasingly obvious: that their wit is a sort of defensive barrier, a way of protecting vulnerable, generous feelings. What the play focuses on all the time, then, and what it embodies in the characters, are the extremes of foolish behaviour, setting humane and attractive instincts against inhumane and cruel instincts. The same idea of extreme behaviour is evident again, and presented in very broad and simple comic terms, in the roles played by and characters of Dogberry and Verges. They are the bungling, incompetent leaders of the watch who none the less manage to uncover Don John's villainy. Their jobs make them the custodians of law and order, the people who should maintain peace and stability in day-to-day life, but they are just amiable fools. Here, perhaps more clearly and simply than anywhere else in the play, we see how precarious social order is – given, that is, that the world is full of people who are all, in their own way, a little mad.

5   *Choose a scene from Act IV and attempt to build upon everything you have established so far*

As you look at Acts III and IV of a comedy you should be trying to convey a sense of what can be seen happening on the stage. In *Much Ado* the characters, even Don John, are pretending, hiding, playing games and playing tricks. Look at specific examples, and as you describe them you will be capturing a sense of how the characters behave more like rather silly children than like responsible adults. Such scenes obviously convey an impression of people's foolishness. As well as looking at the action you should also look at specific speeches, as this will add a great deal of precision to your critical case. As we have stressed all along, however, you can expect to see the themes you have been discussing in evidence in any speech you turn to. To demonstrate the point, here is part of the first substantial speech in Act IV. Claudio, rejecting Hero, says to her father Leonata,

> Give not this rotten orange to your friend;
> She's but the sign and semblance of her honour.
> Behold how like a maid she blushes here.
> O, what authority and show of truth
> Can cunning sin cover itself withal!
>
> (IV.i.31–5)

If you remember, the speeches we looked at from *Twelfth Night* consistently set civil virtues against undisciplined behaviour, and that seemed to be the wider tension and theme of the play. Here the tension is different: on the one hand is a repeated idea of what can be seen on the surface ('the sign and semblance', 'how like a maid'), while on the other there is a constant suggestion of something rotten beneath ('this rotten orange', 'cunning sin'). This is not just the way in which

Claudio chooses to condemn Hero but an idea which appears else-where in the play: the idea is the difference between how things appear in society and the disturbing truth beneath.

It seems a far from comic idea, but again we return to the fact that the sombre reading that might be produced by an analysis of the play does not accord with the far happier impression that the play makes on the stage. This is because when we see the play we are aware that there are far more scenes which show that if we scratch beneath the surface we discover the harmless folly of people. The overall vision of the play is not one that focuses on the rottenness of people (although there is a sufficient sense of this to make the play somewhat disturbing) but rather the vision is one which concentrates on the foolishness of people. The result is that such villainy as there is in the play is defused; it is contained within a comic world and contained within a comic vision of the world.

We can see this more clearly if we look at the sequence of the scenes. Act III ends with Dogberry and Verges put in charge of exam-ining Don John's villainous comrades who have been caught by the watch. Then follows the serious and solemn ritual of the church scene (IV.i) in which Claudio rejects Hero. The pain and suffering Don John's evil has produced are real enough, but the church scene is immediately followed by another scene with Dogberry and Verges, where comic incompetence asserts itself as more than a match for villainy. It is an example of Shakespeare's careful planning of his scenes in the play so that the darker elements are not allowed to undermine the logic of romantic comedy with its emphasis on laughter at the folly of people's irrational behaviour.

6   *Choose a scene from near the end of the play which shows how the issues are resolved, and which will enable you to draw together the threads of your critical analysis*

The play ends, of course, with marriage. Marriage is the institution which reconciles the demands of society and the nature of indivi-duals. There is a suggestion that Claudio's shortcomings were a result of his immaturity but now he is a fit person to marry. The good characters are thus brought into a circle of happiness, but the evil Don John is excluded. As always, however, although the neatness of the ending of a comedy is pleasing, it is the disorder of the central stages of the play that we remember. The ideal state of affairs is always a well-ordered society, but people always, in both attractive and disturbing ways, disrupt order. In one way there is no difference between the characters, as the comic dramatist views all behaviour as foolish, but the good characters do have something positive to contribute in that love will actually enrich society. Comedy may view people as unsteady and unreasonable but it also values and celebrates the kind and humane instincts in people, seeing what such feelings can contribute to the social order. The good qualities of Benedick and Beatrice in *Much Ago* are therefore important. As characters in the play they amuse us, but we must see the value of what they represent.

Much of what can be said about *Much Ado About Nothing* also applies to *The Merchant of Venice*. As we said earlier, it is again love that triggers off the complications in this play and again we find an anti-comic force in the dramatically powerful figure of Shylock. But there are other things that we have to take account of as well. At the centre of the play is not so much the folly of love as a concern with the relationship between moral values and money in society. The main plot turns on a legal contract between Shylock and Antonio who offers his own life as security for a loan. The contract in one way represents the legislative order which is imposed on humanity's conduct of its affairs. We could say that the contract is a symbol of social order in the society of the play. When Antonio cannot meet his obligations and repay Shylock, the latter presses for the cruellest enforcement of the contract, demanding a pound of Antonio's flesh, but he is opposed by Portia, who pleads for mercy in the situation. There is nothing wrong with the contract: its terms are extreme, but it is a perfectly proper legal and social document. The case made by Portia, however, indicates the need to infuse love, generosity and more humane feelings into society's ways of conducting its affairs, that society will be enriched if it accepts the spirit rather than the letter of the law and seeks to accommodate the follies and weaknesses of people. What complicates our response to *The Merchant of Venice*, and makes it a darker play than *Much Ado*, is that the issues it raises about the relationship between money, the law, justice and mercy go beyond its comic framework and disrupt its seemingly harmonious ending. To this extent *The Merchant of Venice* has much in common with Shakespeare's problem comedies which we discuss in the following section.

THE PROBLEM COMEDIES

What we have seen so far is how comedies look at the irrational nature of people. They acknowledge foolish and romantic instincts, but can also acknowledge mean and spiteful instincts. But the romantic comedies only touch lightly on these crueller instincts. The next step on would be a play that gave far greater prominence to unpleasant instincts in people, or a play where society felt itself so threatened by people's foolish and irresponsible behaviour that it decided to assert itself and stamp out anti-social behaviour. This is what we find in Shakespeare's 'problem' or 'dark' comedies: *Troilus and Cressida, All's Well That Ends Well,* and *Measure for Measure.* They are disturbing, rather than amusing, plays, where the serious elements in the plot seem to outweigh the light-hearted elements. They concentrate on the darker elements in human nature: deceit, treachery, lack of humane feeling, and lust. *Troilus and Cressida* tells the story of how Troilus wins Cressida's love but how, when she is forced to leave Troy, she betrays him for one of the Greeks besieging the city. In *All's Well That Ends Well* Helena falls in love with Bertram, is married to him as a reward for curing the King, but he deserts her. They are only reunited after she tricks him into getting her pregnant. *Measure for Measure* shows how Angelo attempts to use his power as the Duke's deputy to seduce Isabella, whose brother is under sentence of death for fornication. The problems are only resolved when the Duke returns, and the play ends with marriage. The plays are comedies in so far as no one dies at the end, but the situations are potentially tragic, and in each case we are confronted with the darker side of human behaviour.

If you are studying one of these plays you should try to see how it follows the standard pattern of romantic comedy in that the characters fall in love and the irrational passion of love creates discord in society. As always, there is a tension between the social role the people should play and the way their romantic instincts make them behave. But, whereas the pure romantic comedies are set in a make-believe world where no problem is allowed to become too serious, the problem comedies are set in a more realistic world where the young lovers come into serious conflict with those in positions of power. Indeed, they seem to live in societies which have in a sense legislated against folly and which will not countenance reckless behaviour. Consequently, there is always the threat that the lovers will be punished, even killed, if they do not conform to society's laws.

The plays, then, set social order against love, as do the romantic comedies, but the lovers live in a harsh and inflexible society. This leads us on to another characteristic of these plays, which is that they contain a much more eloquent defence of love, and of the importance of humane, generous and charitable feelings, than is the case in the pure romantic comedies. In the romantic comedies love is not really under threat, so nobody needs to defend it (the only exception is *The Merchant of Venice*, which comes close to being a problem comedy: Venice is seen as a materialistic society dominated by a concern with money and wealth, Shylock is a real threat, and Portia has to speak in defence of charitable feelings). In the problem comedies characters have to speak up in defence of feelings in a world which is in danger of becoming dominated by a cold and unfeeling ethic of socially acceptable behaviour. There is, though, another level of complication in these plays: there is not just abuse of power by the state but individual abuse of personal power. The plays present characters motivated not by love but by sexual lust who are prepared to manipulate, exploit and mistreat people. A pure notion of love is therefore under threat both from the power of the state and from individuals who are vicious and cruel.

Plays which deal with issues such as love, sex and power cannot be anything other than difficult, but the method of analysis described in this book might help you see your way through them. Perhaps what you need to cling on to more than anything else is the idea of the well-ordered and healthy society. All the complications and unpleasant elements in the plays will then begin to make sense in terms of baser instincts in people and an excessive authoritarianism in the state that together represent a kind of sickness that poisons society. The plays will provide ample examples of what is unattractive, disturbing and bullying in life, but you will also need to look for the positive vision, associated with love, that is set against this. These controlling ideas, which are the kind of ideas we have used throughout this book, are the foundation of the following very brief comments on *Measure for Measure*.

The plot of *Measure for Measure* concerns Angelo, who is put in charge of reinforcing the laws of Vienna when the Duke suddenly leaves. He sentences Claudio to death for getting his betrothed, Juliet, pregnant. Isabella, Claudio's sister and a novice nun, pleads for mercy, and Angelo agrees if she will exchange her virginity for her brother's life. She refuses, and rejects Claudio as her brother when he presses her to give way. The Duke, disguised as a friar, arranges for Mariana, Angelo's former lover, to take Isabella's place in bed, and on his official return sentences Angelo to death. He is saved by the pleas of Mariana and Isabella. Angelo marries Mariana and the Duke proposes to Isabella.

What we can see here is how there is an intention to clamp down on sexual laxity in society. This is not going to create a well-ordered society, but a cruel and repressive society, as is illustrated by the fact that Claudio is sentenced to death. Love here, then, is under threat. But there is more to it than this, for Angelo, the chief law-enforcer, reveals his own twisted and perverted lust in his offer to Isabella. The state abuses its power and Angelo abuses his personal power. We can identify, therefore, the nature of the issue in this play: a vicious inhumanity found both in the state and in individuals, a bullying disregard for people.

What the play has to set against this is a notion of humane and considerate behaviour, but what makes the play so effective is the way in which it presents a picture to us of the characters caught in the middle, the characters, particularly Isabella, caught in impossible dilemmas. The play, however, ends comically, for an answer is found in the exercise of mercy by the Duke. This ending might strike us as artificial, but really that does not matter, for that only makes us aware of the gap between how neatly problems can be solved on the stage as opposed to live, where issues of power and sex, which are closely related, always remain problems. We feel at the end that this is too artificial a solution, whereas the ending of, say, *Twelfth Night*, seems not only neat but also appropriate. But the whole point about the problem comedies is that they allow the problems of real life – particularly sexual problems – to intrude their way uncomfortably into the artificial form of comedy.

THE ROMANCES

In all Shakespeare's plays we see life thrown into disarray. This is again the basic pattern in Shakespeare's final comic plays, the 'romances': *Pericles, Cymbeline, The Winter's Tale* and *The Tempest*. If you are studying one of these plays, though, do not be surprised if you cannot immediately see this pattern in the plot. Indeed, you might find it very hard to trace any kind of plot at all. Even students who have studied several of Shakespeare's plays often find the romances bafflingly difficult to follow, let alone understand. This is because they are such stylised and artificial plays, set entirely in make-believe worlds of improbable coincidences and unpredictable events. With Shakespeare's other plays every reader has a vague idea of what kind of problems the characters are experiencing, but it is quite common to read or see one of the romances and to have no idea at all of what is happening.

Because they are such strange plays, the main aim of this section is to provide some basic ideas about them. We hope to convey an idea of what the romances are about, and attempt to explain and justify their unusual form. The first thing to grasp is that all four romances employ a broadly similar plot. In all of them evil disrupts the life of a noble family. Years of separation then follow before the members of the family are reunited in forgiveness and reconciliation. In *Pericles*, the hero is forced to flee the tyranny of the evil Antiochus, loses his wife and child, but is miraculously reunited with them after many years. In *Cymbeline*, Imogen is parted from her husband, Posthumus, who is unjustly banished by her father, Cymbeline; at the end of the play she is reunited with them both. In *The Winter's Tale*, Leontes's sexual jealously leads to the loss of his son, his wife Hermione, and their newborn daughter Perdita. Sixteen years later Perdita is reunited with her father and also with her mother, Hermione, who, improbably, is brought back to life. *The Tempest*, however, deals only with the final stages of this pattern of events, taking place on an island where Prospero, a deposed duke, uses his magic to regain his lost dukedom from his brother. Again, though, the play ends on a note of reconciliation and forgiveness.

This is what happens in the plays. To move forward we need an idea of the significance of what happens. In each play an action takes place near the beginning that throws life into disarray. As in all plays, then, an idea of order is set against the disorder that can disrupt life. And the idea, or ideal, or order in these plays is very simple: it is an idea of families living together in peace and harmony. This is what is conveyed at the end of the plays when we see order being restored as parents are reunited with their children, husbands with their wives, brothers with brothers, and young lovers with their families. What is set against this are forces of evil that challenge and disrupt such harmony.

The ideas being dramatised, then, are the common themes of Shakespeare's plays. As always, Shakespeare is looking at unruly forces (in both humanity and nature) that wreck people's lives, although, as these are comedies, order is always restored at the end. What is really puzzling about these plays, however, is the very odd manner in which Shakespeare presents his themes. In his other plays we are offered a fairly credible impression of the way in which life can become chaotic, but in the romances both the incidents and the characters are often bizarre rather than convincing. In *The Tempest*, for example, one of the central characters, Caliban, is the son of a witch, and is closer to a savage than a man. In *The Winter's Tale* a character is chased off stage by a bear and eaten: the incident presents an impression of a chaotic world where life is constantly threatened by arbitrary, unruly forces, but it is an odd way of dramatising the idea. Equally odd, and unrealistic, is the prominence given to magic in the romances, and the endings of the plays are peculiar in that suddenly, as if by magic, and sometimes directly as a result of magic, all the problems, even death, are eliminated and order is restored.

There are two points that might help you understand the logic and nature of these plays. The first is that Shakespeare has, in a sense, simplified his plays. The romances present a stylised conflict between an idea and impression of disorder and an idea and impression of order. In all his earlier plays Shakespeare explores the issues through the experiences of complex characters, but in these plays there is no longer the same kind of realistic or convincing characterisation: it is as if Shakespeare looks through the characters, who are representative types rather than realistic figures, and focuses more directly on the underlying issue of the tension between the desirability of order and the inevitability of disorder. It could be argued that the romances are not difficult plays, simply unconventional plays. They dispense with plausible characters and plausible plots so that the main focus can be on the themes and issues involved.

The second, related, point to grasp is how Shakespeare dramatises the issues, given that he is no longer exploring the themes through the experiences of complex characters involved in reasonably credible situations. In the romances, neither the characters nor the events are realistic. The plays take place in make-believe or mythical worlds. Some of the earlier comedies, particularly *A Midsummer Night's Dream*, feature a romantic make-believe world which is presented as an alternative to the real world. The romances, however, take place entirely in an unreal world. And the story told is incredible and unrealistic. The thing about such stories in such settings, however, is that like myths, folk tales, legends and fables, they focus on large questions about human life and human nature. A realistic play, or even a vaguely realistic play, focuses on particular individuals and their problems; a non-realistic play forces us to think about the whole nature of life and the problems humanity encounters.

We can see this in the typical scenes that we find in a romance. Every scene has a slightly unreal quality, such as we might find in a fairy story or folk tale. As in fairy stories, there are characters who vividly represent evil qualities and also characters who represent good qualities, and the incidents they are involved in have a similar bold and simple quality. What is not so simple about such scenes, however, is the significance of such incidents, what they add up to, for the scenes are designed to raise basic questions about the tussle between disorderly and orderly forces in life. In a realistic play the focus is on how credible characters cope in credible situations, and in particular on how they relate to society. The romances, however, are not concerned with social questions in this way. What they are concerned with is the whole idea of the remoteness of the ideal of order in life and the fact that life is disorderly and beyond humanity's control. In the typical scenes of romance the characters are constantly overtaken by sudden events: they are subject both to the disorderly forces of nature and to their own unruly passions. What is set against this is a vision of a perfectly ordered world, a world where people and nature are magically under control and in harmony, but it is a vision that is manifestly unreal, a point which is made clear to us in the make-believe elements in the staging.

These ideas about the general characteristics of Shakespeare's romances should help you as you start to look at an individual romance. You need (a) to have an idea of the issues of the play in terms of content: how an idea of order is being set against an impression of disorder. But that only establishes the common links with Shakespeare's other plays, so what you also need is (b) a sense of the form Shakespeare employs in the play, and the implications of choosing to dramatise his ideas in this way: how the method of presenting a non-realistic story, with representative characters in stylised scenes, forces us to consider the thematic questions at the heart of the plays. Such a method allows Shakespeare the freedom to explore question about life and human nature in a new and exploratory way. Just how might become clearer as we look very briefly at two of the romances in the light of these ideas.

In *The Winter's Tale* Leontes accuses his wife Hermione of adultery. He sends to the Oracle at Delphos for guidance, but refuses to accept the

Oracle's judgement that she is innocent. He is punished by the death of his son, itself quickly followed by the news of Hermione's death. Leontes repents, but his order that his daughter Perdita be abandoned to chance has already been carried out. She is found by shepherds, and, years later, is reunited with her father, and also with her mother, whom we discover did not die after all. The first part of the play focuses on Leontes's evil jealousy; the second half of the play restores order. In terms of content, we see how the unruly nature of human beings can create discord, and we also see the unruly force of nature that can overtake life. Throughout the play there is a sense of the precariousness of existence. What is set against this, however, is an ideal vision of how life should be, a vision of a desirable order associated with love and harmony in a family.

The themes, then, are familiar themes in Shakespeare's plays. What is unfamiliar is the unusual form of the play. One aspect of this is that, while the first half of the play resembles a tragedy, the second half is like a romantic comedy. In the first half, as in tragedy, Leontes's evil jealousy wreaks havoc; in the second half we see how, as in romantic comedy, love, in this instance the love of Perdita and Florizel, creates problems, but then how these problems, and the problems created by Leontes's jealousy, are overcome at the end. The question we have to ask is why Shakespeare chooses to dramatise his themes of evil and love in this stylised and artificial way. Why does he not present them in a realistic way as in *Othello* or *Much Ado About Nothing*, two other plays which also deal with love and jealousy? The answer has to be that this stylised method of presenting his material emphasises the issues involved of evil, sex and love, and how these things interrelate creating disorder or order in life. Shakespeare does not pursue complexity of character but the complexity of the themes themselves.

Every scene along the way embodies the wider issues of the play. This is, of course, always the case in Shakespeare's plays, but in the romances the underlying significance is brought to the surface, as the incidents do not attempt to imitate real life but are contrived to embody the wider themes of the play. We can see this in the use of the Oracle at Delphos: it suggests an idea of a divine order in life. This is set against Leontes's unmotivated jealousy. Both the Oracle and Leontes's jealousy are presented unrealistically: the effect is that we do not become involved in the play at the level of character, but think more about the concepts embodied in the action. We are not asked to think about why Leontes becomes jealous, but rather are asked to see how unstable human nature is, how evil instincts suddenly blast all ideas of peace and harmony in life.

To study a romance, then, you approach it as you approach any play. You need to start with some general ideas about the characteristic pattern of all the romances. The next step is that you should try to see the significance of individual scenes within this larger framework. This is, however, probably the biggest difficulty of all in studying these plays: it should be simple to see the significance of scenes, how they fit into the broader pattern, as they are always overtly dramatising the broader issues of the play. But because the scenes lack the usual kind of character interest they can prove hard to respond to and interpret. As always, however, you must strive to see how the scenes embody and explore the broader themes of the play. A typically bizarre and difficult scene is one at the end of *The Winter's Tale* where a statue of Hermione, Leontes's dead wife, is magically brought back to life. As Leontes and Perdita watch the statue, it moves. The statue is, however, only an illusion: Hermione has been alive all along, and the scene ends with joyous reunion. The significance that can be found in the scene is that it sets the perfect order of a work of art against the waste and decay of life. Yet life, with all its shortcomings, is obviously preferable to a dead work of art. The incident, then, makes us think about the disorder, decay and waste of life, and the remoteness of any ideal of perfect order in this world. But the scene also raises questions about how life, for all its faults, none the less has much to be said for it: the statue is cold and inhuman, and by implication a perfect world would be cold and inhuman. The messy, imperfect world (where Hermione has aged and time shows its marks) seems preferable even though people might always long for a better world. It is such questions about human existence that the scenes in a romance explore. Time after time, a perfect world, usually the perfect world of art, is held up against the imperfect world of nature and life, forcing us to think about the whole question of order and disorder in life.

We can see this again in *The Tempest*. Prospero, the deposed Duke of Milan, uses his magic powers to shipwreck his enemies onto a magic island. On the island there is an evil force in the shape of Caliban. Having failed in his attempt to rape the Duke's daughter Miranda, Caliban persuades the shipwrecked Stephano and Trinculo to try and murder Prospero. The scenes involving these three characters are comic in effect because Stephano and Trinculo are drunk most of the time and also extremely foolish. Meanwhile, on another part of the island, Sebastian and Antonio, Prospero's brother who usurped the dukedom, plot to kill Alonso, King of Naples. What we see both in the comic scenes involving Caliban and the drunken Stephano and Trinculo and in the murder plot against Alonso are those foolish instincts and violent forces in people that create discord in life. Set against this is a concept of order, seen in Prospero's magic control of human beings and nature through his spirit Ariel, and the innocent love of Miranda and Ferdinand, Alonso's son.

The Tempest is, then, like *The Winter's Tale*, concerned with the familiar theme of order and disorder in life, focusing on the question of evil instincts and good instincts in people and the endless struggle between the two. What is distinctive about *The Tempest* is the degree to which this theme is brought to life by the staging of the play, and in particular by its use of music and spectacle. In order to come to terms with *The Tempest* it is necessary to see how these two related elements work in the play. A brief example of each might help.

Throughout *The Tempest* music is used as a touchstone for the revelation of character, and a constant contrast is drawn between those evil characters who hear only discordant noises and those good characters who hear the harmony of the sweet sounds that fill the island. But music is also used as part of the action as well. In Act I, scene ii, Ferdinand is led on stage by Ariel's music, impelled against his will to follow it as it calms his grief at his father's supposed death. It is a vivid example of the way music is used to suggest an ideal of order as life is transformed, its pain and death left behind. At the same time we are aware how human nature pulls against such an ideal state of harmony, for no sooner does the music stop than Ferdinand falls in love with Miranda, but then seeks to draw his sword against Prospero. In just a short sequence of actions the play shifts between ideas of order and disorder, death and love, calm and violence. The same ideas are simultaneously being developed and explored in the language, especially the imagery, of this scene, but our point here is that the action on stage presents and realises these ideas in a very forceful way, a way which the audience in the theatre cannot avoid responding to. All Shakespeare's plays exploit to the full the visual impression that can be created on the stage, but the staging in *The Tempest* is particularly striking.

The most elaborate piece of staging in the play occurs in Act IV, scene i, where we see Prospero conjure up his spirits, who perform a play to celebrate the betrothal of Ferdinand and Miranda. The spirits take the shape of three goddesses, and then some nymphs and reapers appear. Their singing and dancing suggests the idea of a perfect union in which love and nature, humanity and heaven are at one. It is, however, only an illusion of such perfect order, a point which is made dramatically when Prospero, recalling Caliban's murderous plot against him, suddenly brings the spectacle to an end. The spirits vanish and we are made aware of the gap between the artificial world of order conjured up by Prospero's art and the unruliness of life. As in *The Winter's Tale*, we are forced to consider whether life, for all its problems, nevertheless has more substance and is much more acceptable to us than the perfect but illusory world controlled by Prospero's magic with its lack of freedom.

What we have described in this section is how to establish the foundations and broad direction of your analysis of a romance. You have to have an idea of the informing pattern, and you have to be able to see how scenes function in, and what they contribute to, a play. This work on scenes will take time, but if you keep on looking at and thinking about scenes you should be able to see how they reflect the larger concerns of a play. When you have begun to establish this more precise sense of what the play is about, you will then need to start looking more closely at scenes and speeches. What you will have to remember here is that you are not going to find the usual sort of character interest. Indeed, what you will find is that what the characters talk about are the issues at the heart of the play. Just as the scenes as a whole are always pointing to the larger issues, so the dialogue of the plays does not just raise the broader themes indirectly but always focuses directly on all the issues involved. It is again something that should make the plays easy to understand, as the themes are always so central, but many readers find it difficult to absorb the material when there are not conventional characters to hang on to and when the texture of the speeches is so dense with imagery.

When you are confronted by difficult speeches, the only practical answer is to hold on firmly to your simple ideas of what the play is about, and use these ideas to steer you through difficult waters. This is, of course, the point we have maintained throughout this book. Don't allow a play to baffle you. Establish your simple controlling ideas, and interpret the evidence in the light of your controlling ideas. You will find that this enables you to make coherent sense of a play and move towards a genuine appreciation of what the play is about and how it brings its themes to life on the stage. But, in addition, what will also help you is if you have good exam and essay-writing techniques. It is these skills we look at in the next two chapters. These will not only enable you to make full use of your work on the text, they will also help you take on more advanced critical ideas, something we discuss after the two essay-writing chapters.

5

Discussing an extract from a Shakespeare play

Examinations

THIS chapter and the next are primarily concerned with how to answer
essay and exam questions on Shakespeare. Obviously everything we
have said earlier about how to analyse a play is relevant to this: you
will not have anything substantial to say about a play unless you have
read and studied it carefully and accumulated some material and ideas.
How to make use of and how to present what you know are, however,
additional skills, and it is these issues of knowing what you are doing,
and how to organise your material, when writing an essay or other
kind of examination answer, that we focus on in these chapters.

Examination papers on Shakespeare usually feature three kinds of
questions. The first kind, commonly referred to as a context question,
consists of a short extract from a play, usually a single speech, followed
by a number of specific questions about this passage. The second kind
of question presents a longer extract from a play, perhaps about fifty
lines, and asks you to write an essay in which you discuss this passage
and relate it to the play as a whole. It is these two kinds of questions
that we consider in this chapter. The third kind is the traditional essay
question, where you are asked to discuss a statement about a play or
asked to look at a particular aspect of a play. We deal with traditional
essays in the next chapter.

Whatever kind of question is set, however, its purpose is not only
to test your understanding of a play and your response to it, but also to
test your ability to express your response and understanding. You
should always try to remember that the way in which you present your
response – which covers both the overall organisation of your answer
and the quality of your writing – is every bit as important as the quality

of your ideas. This does not mean that you have to be a gifted writer in order to do well in examinations. What it does mean, however, is that you have to see what the question is about, and then write clearly and sensibly on that topic. Part of this involves making proper use of paragraphs and writing in grammatical sentences: if you ignore paragraphing your answer as a whole inevitably will be poorly organised, while if you fail to write in grammatical sentences what you say will not make sense. It might seem insulting that we should start by reminding you of such obvious points, but you would be amazed at how many examination candidates ruin their chances because they do not follow the basic rules about how to write. Rather than rushing, trying to write as much as possible, it is much better to pause at the end of each sentence and make sure that it makes sense and that it says clearly what you want to say. Examiners cannot reward you for what you are trying to say or might have meant: they can only award marks for what you actually say in your examination paper.

If this insistence on thinking and writing clearly sounds daunting, it might redress the balance, and also help you write well, if we point out that examination questions on Shakespeare, as on any literary text, are never really difficult, and that answering a question is relatively easy if you know what you are doing. The major reason why many examination candidates produce badly written answers is that they fail to see how straightforward the questions are, and therefore fail to see how straightforwardly they can be answered. Instead of thinking, a lot of candidates plunge in blindly, hoping that their answers make some kind of sense, but such answers rarely do. If, however, you can see what a question is getting at, if you can see the logic behind it and also have some positive ideas about the material that might be included in your answer, then you should be well placed to write a clear and sensible essay. It is the aim of this and the next chapter to point out the thinking behind the various kinds of Shakespeare examination questions, and to show you how you can set about answering questions in a systematic and effective way.

Context questions

Once more unto the breach, dear friends, once more;
Or close the wall up with our English dead.
In peace there's nothing so becomes a man
As modest stillness and humility;

But when the blast of war blows in our ears,
Then imitate the action of the tiger:
Stiffen the sinews, summon up the blood,
Disguise fair nature with hard-favour'd rage;
Then lend the eye a terrible aspect;
Let it pry through the portage of the head
Like the brass cannon; let the brow o'erwhelm it
As fearfully as doth a galled rock
O'erhang and jutty his confounded base,
Swill'd with the wild and wasteful ocean.
Now set the teeth and stretch the nostril wide;
Hold hard the breath, and bend up every spirit
To his full height. On, on, you noblest English,
Whose blood is fet from fathers of war-proof . . . .
(*Henry V*, iii.i.1–18)

(i)   *By whom, and in what circumstances, is this passage spoken?*
(ii)   *Explain l.18: 'Whose blood is fet from fathers of war-proof'.*
(iii) *What is the dramatic significance of the subject matter of this passage?*
(iv)   *What can we learn, from this passage, of the speaker's character?*
(v)   *What do you consider to be the interest and importance of the way in which the passage is expressed?*

This is the sort of passage that you might be set in a context question, and the questions that follow are also typical, although it is unlikely that you would be asked as many questions as this. In a three-hour examination, where you have to answer four questions, you might have to discuss two context passages (making up one question), so you have about twenty minutes to answer this one. Use the available time sensibly, and don't write too much or you won't leave yourself enough time for the other questions.

The particular questions about a passage will vary, but the logic behind the set question, and the sequence in which they appear, is usually the same. The first two questions here are testing whether you know the play and whether you have a basic comprehension of the meaning of the words. They are straightforward, factual questions which you should answer briefly and clearly. For question (i) all you have to know is who is speaking at this point and what is happening at this stage of the play. All you would need to say in an answer is that the speaker is Henry V at the siege of Harfleur; Henry has come to France to establish his right to the throne and this is the first battle scene of the play, in which we see Henry urging his men on. Keep to the main point: you are not required to produce a summary of the whole play. The question is just testing your factual knowledge. The same is true of the second question, which is seeing whether you have read the play closely, looking at the footnotes that explain difficult words and phrases. It is not testing your intelligence or critical ability but whether you have studied the play carefully and conscientiously. The initial questions, then, are not very demanding: anybody who has read and reread the play should experience no difficulty at all in answering them.

It is the subsequent questions, however, that will begin to distinguish those who have read and understood the play from those who have merely read it, and, accordingly, these are likely to carry more marks. The central question on a context passage, the question here about 'the dramatic significance of the subject matter of the passage', almost invariably asks you to comment on the broader significance of the extract. A lot of students, however, fail to understand what the question is asking them to do here and so they just tell the story of the play, saying where this episode fits in the plot. Clearly this is wrong: in order to answer question (iii) you have to move beyond the story-telling that is sufficient to answer question (i) and see how the larger issues of the play are embodied in the passage presented. In other words you have to see how the passage ties in with the larger themes of the play.

The answer to a question such as question (iii) here, then, will always be that the dramatic significance of the passage is that it reflects and reveals the broader themes of the play. This gives you a starting-point, and a direction for your answer, but what you have to do in your answer is to show that the passage *does* reflect and reveal the broader themes. You can be confident that it always will: the examiners won't set some peculiar or unrepresentative passage, but a passage which embodies in a fairly direct way the larger concerns of the play. This is because the question is designed to test whether you know what the play as a whole is about and whether you can see how the broader themes of the play are reflected in particular speeches.

In tackling question (iii), or any similar question, deal first with what is being said in the passage and then try to show how it relates to the play as a whole. Just how simple and straightforward this is might become clearer as we look at this extract from *Henry V*. Henry is telling his men to raise their fighting spirits and adopt their fiercest manner in the battle at hand. All thoughts of peace, he tells them, should be replaced by bloody thoughts if they are to win and to prove themselves valiant and noble Englishmen. It is a rallying speech, meant to spur his men on to take Harfleur. As we now go on to discuss how this passage relates to the play as a whole, it should be evident that we are employing the ideas about the desirability of order and the inevitability of disorder that we have used throughout this book, but that in addition we are also employing ideas about the themes and issues that are distinctive in *Henry V* which we would have become aware of in studying the play. It is necessary to have this sense of the specific themes in the play in order to answer the question adequately.

The subject matter of this speech is war. It offers a vivid sense of how war affects men and turns them into something like animals bent on savage destruction. This whole issue of war is something that is central in the play: war is an extreme example of the destructive disorder that can consume life. The speech, then, is about disorder in life. At the same time there is a contrast with an ideal of civilised behaviour in peace when people behave rationally and quietly. The dramatic significance of the passage, then, is that it deals with themes of war and peace which are central in the play. But if you have studied *Henry V* you would know that the play is also concerned with kingship, and this passage is one relation of a larger issue in the play of the difficult role of a king, who must lead and encourage his men, persuading them that bloodshed and the loss of their own lives is heroic and in the national interest. You might well be able to point to other larger issues of the play which are embodied in this passage, but there is no single correct answer. What matters is that you provide your own impression of how the larger concerns of the play are reflected and revealed here.

Question (iv) asks you to discuss Henry's character. Remember always to read the questions carefully: this question directs you to deal exclusively with what we can learn *from this passage* of the speaker's character. Many candidates might embark on a long character sketch of Henry here, but this is not what is required. The problem you might encounter, however, in trying to establish some ideas about a character from a short speech, is that you might feel that your comments are flimsy. Here, for example, you might feel that you could manage to say something about what an inspiring leader Henry is, but then be left with nothing else to say. The answer to this is that, although you have got to concentrate on the passage, you can use your wider ideas about the play and about Shakespeare's presentation of characters to shape the impression you receive from the extract. What we mean by this is that the main characters in Shakespeare's plays are not only caught up in a conflict but also experience this conflict within themselves: they are pulled between reasonable and unreasonable, between orderly and disorderly conduct. It should always be possible to detect some such conflict in the presentation of any major character.

In this passage you might want to talk about how Henry shows himself to be a great leader and how this is revealed in his attitude to his men: they are 'dear friends', valued comrades rather than mere soldiers. Again, you might want to argue that Henry's language throughout implies the strong, firm leadership necessary for a king, that it is full of commands and orders. But the language also reveals the horror of war as, for example, in the comparison with the action of the tiger, suggesting the fierce, bestial quality war brings out in men. And this complicates our response to Henry, making us question his actions as we see him whipping up the fervour of his troops. There are thus tensions at the heart of Henry's presentation here which suggest two different views of his character, one as a heroic figure, the other as a man intent only on victory almost regardless of the human cost. More simply, we see a contrast between the heroic ideals Henry speaks of and the ugly reality of what he wants his men to do. As with all Shakespeare's major characters, what gives us a way of talking about Henry is to see how he is presented in terms of a clash between reasonable and unreasonable behaviour, how he is caught between conflicting impulses. This idea of a conflict in a character is one that applies everywhere in Shakespeare, but the important thing in answering a context question on character is to show how the actual speech presented for analysis reveals this conflict within the character's language.

The sequence in any set of context questions is that they move from factual questions, through questions which ask you to relate the passage to the play as a whole, to questions, such as (iv) and (v) here, which ask you to focus more closely on the words on the page. What should be clear by now is that you need to employ your larger ideas about the play to answer the more difficult, non-factual questions. This is also the case as you turn to question (v), a question about 'the way in which the passage is expressed'. The last context question is usually a question about the language of the passage, and this unnerves a great many candidates. A lot of candidates realise that they are writing in very vague terms, often saying no more than that the language of the extract is very poetic and powerful, but, while they know what they are saying is inadequate, they cannot see a way of improving their comments. What you need, therefore, is a sense of the direction in which your answer can move and an idea of the sort of things worth saying, and again what provides these is if you tell yourself that the large themes of the play are evident in the smallest details of the verse.

In answering a context question on the language of a passage, the most important thing to look at is the words used. Make a little go a long way: don't try to analyse everything, but focus on a few details and then spell out as clearly as possible why this word or detail was included. Your controlling idea has got to be that the words chosen vividly bring to life the themes and larger issues of the play. But you must always establish this connection, stating clearly what larger themes the words you look at reveal. In this extract from *Henry V*, for example, you should be able to spot vivid words and phrases that suggest the horror of war (for example, 'summon up the blood', 'lend the eye a terrible aspect'), and also words and phrases that suggest peace and stability (for example, 'stillness', and 'peace' itself). In any extract from any play there will be this kind of tension between opposed images, and these will reflect the broader tension of the play. What you are doing in effect is listing opposed images, but by showing how central they are in the passage you will illustrate the power of the speech in bringing to life the themes of the play.

Looking at the language of a passage, then, involves using your larger, interpretative framework of ideas to help you organise your impression of what is happening with the words on the page. What you should be able to spot in any passage is how ideas of order and disorder are in conflict, but don't just talk in these general terms. You do need to be precise, spelling out how the particular words chosen reflect the larger issues of the play. What most candidates find most difficult, however, is knowing what to say about the pattern of the verse in the extract. Sometimes the question will ask you to comment specifically on the rhythm of the speech. The key to talking about such issues is to tell yourself that the verse will reflect what the speaker says at this particular moment of the play. Here, for example, Henry is urging his men on to victory in the middle of battle: the verse, therefore, is vigorous, full of commands. In a long speech such as this, however, you can expect to find the same sort of tension in the pattern of the verse as can be seen in both Henry's character and in the language of the play: in other words, you can expect to find some lines that are orderly and others that are disorderly. In line 4, for example, Henry talks about 'modest stillness and humility': the rhythm of the line is therefore calm and even: in line 14, however, he talks about 'the wild and wasteful ocean': the rhythm of the line therefore is wild and uneven. What we are saying here is that the meaning of the words will tell you what to say about the rhythm.

Talking about the verse involves nothing more than an appreciation of how the rhythm and movement of the lines matches the sense of the words. Lying behind this, however, should be your awareness that the tensions you find in the verse of an extract reflect the larger tensions in the play. You will not be able to make sense of and justify the details and local features unless you also have a sense of the broad pattern of the play. This is true of questions (iii), (iv) and (v) as a whole. Answering all these questions involves being able to see the larger pattern of the play in the particular passage presented for comment, and then using your broad impressions of the play to shape your closer analysis of the passage.

Put like that, it might sound difficult, so we will conclude this section by repeating our main points as simply as possible. Context questions for the most part ask you to make a number of very straightforward connections, primarily in the areas of theme, character, and language, between the specific passage and the play as a whole. The main points to bear in mind are the following.

(i) The first couple of questions are likely to be factual questions which demand nothing more than a knowledge of what happens in the play.

(ii) The subsequent questions ask you to spot the larger concerns in the passage set. But don't start discussing the whole play: show how the issues are embodied and expressed in the extract.

(iii) Images of order and disorder are likely to be apparent in any passage, but you also need to know what specific themes are dealt with in the play in question so that you can search for these in the passage.

(iv) Your main task is to look closely at the passage, seeing *where* and *how* it expresses, embodies, reflects and reveals the broader issues of the play.

Writing about a longer extract

Part of the secret of answering a context question well is feeling confident. For this you need a clear sense of what the play as a whole is about. If you have a good overall grasp of a play your answers on the context question will have an air of authority as you establish connections between the specific extract and your larger sense of the play. The earlier chapters of this book have obviously been concerned with showing you how to achieve just this kind of firm, clear understanding of a play. If you have this sort of simple but clear understanding of a play, and also appreciate what you are expected to do in answering context questions, then tackling a longer extract from a play should not prove too difficult. This is because you are being asked to do essentially the same thing as in a context question: you are being asked to say how the particular extract reflects and reveals the larger concerns of the play. The difference is that a context question provides you with a lot of signposts about what you are meant to be looking for whereas with a longer extract you are given less specific directions, and in addition you have to face all the problems associated with organising and presenting a longer essay.

We shall offer some advice on this in a moment, but it might also help if first we say something about the logic behind this second kind of question where you are confronted with a longish passage, perhaps even a short scene, which you are asked to discuss and relate to the play as a whole. This kind of question (which usually counts as a single full question) has become increasingly popular as a standard question on examination papers. The reason for this is that examiners are attempting to help candidates to produce better answers. The temptation in answering a traditional essay question is either to lapse into story-telling or to talk about the play in very broad and general terms. The long-extract question, however, forces you to pay close attention to the text. The hope is that candidates will produce less general answers, that they will produce answers which actually examine the evidence of the play itself. But this doesn't always happen. The most common fault in answering such questions is that candidates all but ignore the passage and just launch into a general essay about the play. Sometimes, however, students talk at great length about the passage, but fail to see its broader significance. What you should be attempting to do in your answers on long-extract questions is to focus on the words of the passage, but at the same time you should also be trying to see how the passage reflects and reveals the larger concerns of the play. In a word, you should be attempting to show how the text itself provides the best evidence of what the play is about.

Here is a typical example of this kind of question:

Write an essay on the significance of the following passage, saying, briefly, what importance it has in the development of the plot, and commenting on such matters as the revelation of character, the use of language, verse and stage action and the development of the play's themes. Relate your answer, where appropriate, to other parts of the play.

What is likely to disturb you here is that you are asked to write about so many things. You must, however, answer the question set. A general essay about the play won't do: you have got to write about the things that the questions directs you to write about. In fact the question is really very helpful: if you worked systematically through the things it lists, attempting to cover every point, the examiner immediately would start rewarding you for relevance and for genuinely attempting to answer the question set. It is worth remembering that a relevant answer, however clumsily written, will always gain more marks than an essay which fails to answer the question that has been set.

The problem, however, is that a relevant answer might come close to being just a sequence of unconnected points. Obviously you need to try to achieve some overall shape and direction in your answer. What will help pull all the separate points together is if you have a central thesis or idea running through your answer. The question set will, in fact, often help you achieve just this if, as here, it begins by directing you to talk about 'the significance of the passage'. The best way of starting your answer is to establish a very clear sense of how the passage selected reflects and reveals the larger thematic concerns and issues in the play. And it always will: the examiners will have selected a passage which embodies many of the wider issues in the play. What you have to do is to spell out as clearly as possible what larger themes you can see in the particular extract chosen.

This provides you with your opening paragraph: you have focused on the passage itself, but you have also established a view of the broader significance of the passage. This will then provide you with a constant point of reference as you build up your case in the succeeding paragraphs. Everything you look at subsequently can be interpreted in the light of the controlling ideas you have established at the outset. The result will be that you can examine every aspect of the passage, but at the same time your controlling ideas will give your essay as a whole a sense of direction and coherence. What we are talking about here is really the approach we have illustrated in the earlier chapters of the book, where, with each play, we started by establishing a clear sense of what the play was about, and then looked at plot, characters, language, themes and staging in the light of our controlling ideas.

What you should be attempting to produce overall is an essay which builds in a sequence of clear paragraphs. So, after a paragraph that establishes the general picture, you need a separate paragraph for each point mentioned in the question. If the question is more vague (perhaps asking you to discuss the play working mainly, but not exclusively, from the passage), the things to talk about are the plot, staging, characters, language and verse. You could have a separate paragraph on the themes, but in a sense you are talking about the themes all the time. If you follow this format it will mean that you will produce an essay of about six to eight substantial paragraphs, and that is a sensible number to aim at. Each paragraph should focus on a separate aspect of the play, explaining how it is presented in the passage, but also referring to other scenes where appropriate. But remember that each paragraph is a step in your essay, a step in a developing argument. Your initial paragraph establishes some controlling ideas; these help shape your impressions in your second paragraph, so that by the end of this paragraph your controlling ideas are becoming a lot more concrete. Every subsequent paragraph should add to the argument in this kind of way, so that by the end you will have examined the passage from all sorts of angles, but in addition, in the process of doing so, you will have steadily established a very full and clear sense of what the play is about and how it dramatises its issues.

These ideas about a method of answering 'extract' questions should become easier to understand as we look at the following passage from *Macbeth*. In our comments on the extract we concentrate on *how to understand* the issues implicit in a passage, and, in addition, on *how to present* an answer in the form of a coherent essay.

MACBETH This is a sorry sight. [*Looking on his hands.*]
LADY MACBETH A foolish thought to say a sorry sight.
MACBETH There's one did laugh in's sleep, and one cried 'Murder!'
    That they did wake each other. I stood and heard them;
    But they did say their prayers, and address'd them
    Again to sleep.
LADY MACBETH There are two lodg'd together.
MACBETH One cried 'God bless us', and 'Amen' the other,
    As they had seen me with these hangman's hands.
    List'ning their fear, I could not say 'Amen'

When they did say 'God bless us!'

LADY MACBETH Consider it not so deeply.

MACBETH But wherefore could not I pronounce 'Amen'?
I had most need of blessing, and 'Amen'
Stuck in my throat.

LADY MACBETH These deeds must not be thought
After these ways: so, it will make us mad.

MACBETH Methought I heard a voice cry 'Sleep no more;
Macbeth does murder sleep' – the innocent sleep,
Sleep that knits up the ravell'd sleave of care,
The death of each day's life, sore labour's bath,
Balm of hurt minds, great nature's second course,
Chief nourisher in life's feast.

LADY MACBETH What do you mean?

MACBETH Still it cried 'Sleep no more' to all the house;
'Glamis hath murder'd sleep; and therefore Cawdor
Shall sleep no more – Macbeth shall sleep no more.'

LADY MACBETH Who was it that thus cried? Why, worthy Thane,
You do unbend your noble strength to think
So brainsickly of things. Go get some water
And wash this filthy witness from your hand.
Why did you bring these daggers from the place?
They must lie there. Go carry them, and smear
The sleepy grooms with blood.

MACBETH I'll go no more:
I am afraid to think what I have done;
Look on't again I dare not.

LADY MACBETH Infirm of purpose!
Give me the daggers. The sleeping and the dead
Are but as pictures; 'tis the eye of childhood
That fears a painted devil. If he do bleed,
I'll gild the faces of the grooms withal,
For it must seem their guilt.

(II.ii.20–57)

Macbeth has just murdered Duncan, King of Scotland. It is night. Lady Macbeth has been awaiting Macbeth's return and the passage focuses on their response to what has happened. What you need to do at the outset is establish how the broader concerns of the play are reflected in this scene. The most obvious thing that you might notice is that the talk is of murder. Murder is a shocking example of human-kind's capacity for evil behaviour. The passage, then, is dealing with the issue of evil as a disruptive force in life, a theme which is central in the play. At this point Macbeth has only just started on his orgy of destruction. The murder of Duncan will throw the state into chaos, and the world of the play will become nightmarish as Macbeth, attempting to make his own position as King secure, engages in more bloody acts of murder. The scene, then, not only focuses on the question of evil behaviour, but also touches on the whole idea of life collapsing into barbarity and chaos, and the remoteness of any ideal of a well-ordered state. What is probably of most interest in this extract is the response of the two characters to the events that have taken place, but this is something that you can look at subsequently. What you need to identify at the outset is the subject matter of the passage, and how this is a reflection of the broader theme of the play of the disruptive force of evil in life. It is that idea which can become the controlling idea for your whole essay: it will guide your interpretation of everything else you discuss, but as you look at further details you will be able to add to your ideas about the nature and problem of evil.

Sometimes the question will suggest a sequence of things to look at, but where it doesn't our inclination would be to turn next to the staging of the scene, as this will offer a bold, visual impression of the issues involved. The obvious thing to discuss here is the stage direction, where Macbeth looks at his blood-stained hands, stained with the blood of the rightful King. The impression that comes across is of a man staring at the signs of his own evil nature, almost in a daze, mesmerised by the sight. This force of evil is so overwhelming and dangerous that it seems to stagger even Macbeth himself. The consequence of looking at this particular detail, then, is that it begins to add to our understanding of the theme in the play. In our first paragraph we merely talked about evil as an almost abstract theme, but now we are beginning to see how evil is presented as an uncontrollable and gruesome force. You are encouraged, in this kind of question, to refer to other relevant scenes, and you might therefore at this point want to refer to other episodes in the play where the spectacle on the stage is gruesome and bloody. If you do this, however, you must refer to specific scenes, to other details which also create a strong visual impression of how the force of evil can be seen in life.

Another thing you could comment on in the staging is the fact that the scene, as with so many scenes in the play, takes place at night. Again, however, there is no point in mentioning the detail unless you can relate it to some wider ideas about the play. The explanation is quite simple: we are being exposed to dark, nightmarish forces that undermine the stability of life. But you have to spell out, in this kind of way, the larger significance of the detail. Try to appreciate how straightforward our approach has been in looking at the staging of the scene. We did not attempt to comment on too much. We just picked out a couple of specific details, and found a way of talking about them in the light of our controlling idea of evil disrupting life. If you follow this kind of approach, however, the result will be that as you reach the end of the second paragraph of your essay you will not only have commented on specific aspects of the scene but added considerably to your initial statement of what the play is about and how it dramatises its concerns.

If now you were to turn to the characters, you might want to comment on how Macbeth is terrified at his own act, but also baffled by it. This is another way in which evil is presented in the play, as a force which is so vicious and unreasonable that it defies all understanding. We have though, throughout this book, made the point that the principal characters experience a conflict within themselves, and as Macbeth talks about the murder, examining his own inability to say 'Amen', we can see that he is caught between a sense of how people should behave and a force which drives him to act in a different way. There is a sense of a man who, because he still has some notion of civilised behaviour, cannot understand what is happening to him and why he has acted in a certain way. In talking about this, in talking about how Macbeth is caught between rational and irrational impulses, you again would be adding to the sense your essay conveys of what the concerns of the play are and how they are dramatised. Lady Macbeth, in contrast to Macbeth, seems unmoved; she feels that he is over-reacting. But here you might want to refer to other scenes in the play, such as the scene where Lady Macbeth sleepwalks, in order to make the point that her appearance of calm is only an appearance, that she too is disturbed by the murders, and that she too, like Macbeth, is caught between an idea of reasonable behaviour and the force of irrational instincts.

As you can see, we are using a fairly simple argument as we progress through our answer, and it is almost invariably the case that an essay will prove most effective if the controlling ideas, and the structure of the essay as a whole, are simple. The reason for this is that you won't get tied up in knots trying to control your argument, and can put all your effort into focusing on the details of the scene to show how the play actually brings its themes to life. In the very act of doing that, however, in selecting and explaining the details Shakespeare has included in the scene, your essay almost effortlessly will become more complex as you create a fuller sense of the issues involved and how they are presented. By the end of the third paragraph, having looked at the general picture, at the staging and at the characters, you might well be surprised at how much you have managed to say about the specific passage and about the play as a whole.

It is at this point that you can turn to the language of the extract. As we have said before, many candidates feel nervous talking about the language of a play, but by this stage of your essay details should be becoming easier to explain, as you are establishing a clear framework in which they can be understood. You do, however, still need to proceed in a methodical way. There's no point in looking at the passage as a whole hoping that inspiration will suddenly strike. It's much better to pick out a particular word or phrase, which you can then try to relate to, and interpret in the light of the ideas you are presenting about the play. Really, you should be able to make something of any word that catches your attention; here, for example, we noticed the fact that Macbeth uses the word 'sleep' several times. The ideas that are presented are of two men who wake from their sleep, say their prayers, and return to sleep, and then, a little later on, Macbeth hearing a voice that says 'Sleep no more; / Macbeth does murder sleep'. If you can't make sense of such details use the order/disorder formula that we have used throughout this book. Sleep is clearly for the innocent, who can rest quietly, but Macbeth can never rest peacefully again, he will forever be tormented for his crimes. Now, you could go on from here to connect this with other ideas in the passage and the play as a whole about a dark and disturbing night-time world, and the whole idea of torments in the mind. All of these are ways in which the issues in the play are dramatised and made vivid. Or you could look more closely at the sleep images in this passage, for example the way in which sleep is referred to as

> Balm of hurt minds, great nature's second course,
> Chief nourisher in life's feast.

These images might seem difficult to understand, but the key to interpreting them is to use your controlling framework of ideas. Macbeth will sleep no more. Sleep seems part of the natural order of life, and here it is associated with nature and food. The idea that comes across is that evil is disrupting the whole pattern of nature, that evil is a terrible appetite as opposed to this sense of sleep as something that nourishes. What we are doing, then, in looking at the words Shakespeare uses, is using our controlling ideas as a key to interpreting them, but in the very act of interpreting them, we are adding to our sense of the ideas in the play and how the play expresses the themes. As always, don't try to comment on too much: if you can pursue a couple of the images in a passage, relating them to your ideas about the play as a whole, then you will have provided a vivid illustration of how the language of the passage works. The key to the whole thing is that in any passage you will find a lot of words that suggest an idea of order and also words, probably far more words, that suggest a disruption of order.

The words used are one thing to talk about, the general pattern of the verse is another. The clue to talking about the diction and structure of the speeches is to remember that the characters will be speaking in a way that reflects their personalities and actions at this stage of the play. So, Macbeth's speeches, in structure, are wandering and confused. By contrast, Lady Macbeth's speeches are harsh and abrupt. Similarly, while the rhythm of Macbeth's speech is wandering, unsettled, the rhythm of Lady Macbeth's lines is abrupt, strident. The point, quite simply, is that Shakespeare makes the characters speak in a way that is appropriate to them and their situation, but, if we can show that this is the case, then this enables us to add yet another comment on how the play creates the impression it does, and how the writing dramatises the issues. Again, if you take just one or two small examples, this will make the point far more effectively than a large general comment. Here, for example, you might take Macbeth's second speech and argue that because it repeats the words 'they did' it gives the impression of Macbeth's mind going over and over the events; Lady Macbeth, however, repeats the word 'Go', she takes charge, issues orders, as if she were untroubled by the murder. As throughout, however, try to relate such comments to your controlling ideas, how Macbeth's language itself conveys a powerful impression of the way evil disrupts rational behaviour and rational thought to which Lady Macbeth still attempts to cling here.

We have now provided an outline of how you can tackle this kind of question. You might want to add a concluding paragraph which almost inevitably would have to say how astonishingly rich the texture of the extract is, as it embodies, explores and reveals the issues of the play in so many ways. Although we have concentrated on a scene from *Macbeth*, we do hope that it is apparent that the same kind of approach could be adopted to discuss any passage from any play. The things to bear in mind are as follows:

(i)   Your essay is likely to prove most effective if it has a simple overall structure, looking at a different aspect of the play in each paragraph.
(ii) Use the opening paragraph to set up your controlling ideas.
(iii) In each subsequent paragraph, focus on specific details, but interpret them in the light of your controlling ideas.
(iv) Don't try to discuss too much. It is better to do justice to a couple of details in a paragraph, showing how they illustrate and bring to life the wider concerns of the play, than to list a host of details which you don't bother to justify or to explain.
(v)   Remember that each paragraph is a step in an argument. As you examine each detail, you are adding to the general sense of the play that is conveyed in your essay and also adding to the sense of how the play dramatises its issues.

What you say about any passage is, of course, up to you, but what you say is likely to appear most impressive if you present your ideas in the kind of clear and logical way described above. Indeed, the examiner will be looking for two things as he or she marks your answer. He or she will be interested in the quality of your ideas and the quality of your response to and understanding of the play; what this means is that you must have read and studied the play thoroughly so that you know what is important in the passage and how to analyse it. But the examiner will also be looking at how you organise, control and present your material. There is, therefore, everything to be said for making the effort to produce a clear, logical and well-organised essay.

6

Writing an essay

Essay writing

AN essay is a piece of writing where you put forward an argument
about how you see a particular issue or topic in a play. It should be the
place where all your hard work on the text pays off, but often students
find it difficult to organise their thoughts and to organise their material
in a clear, logical way. One reason for this lies in the mistaken assumption that an essay has to be a very long, elaborate piece of writing, full
of complicated sentences, where you try to make complex points that
you don't fully understand. It is much more sensible to take a practical
view of essay writing, and see that it is far more important to put your
views across clearly than to get tangled up, not really knowing what
you are saying or where your essay is going next. What follows here
are some basic guidelines which should help you avoid the common
errors of essay writing and also help you argue your case in a logical
way. Far too many candidates go into examinations with the mistaken
belief that a good essay is the result of a mixture of luck and inspiration. The truth, however, is that you can learn the skills necessary for
producing a good essay. And these skills are simple and straightforward. Above all else, what you need for an essay is a clear idea of what
you are trying to do and a clear idea of how to present your material
in an effective and convincing way. This means thinking both about
the question and also about your answer.

The question

Answer the question set

The basic rule of all good essay writing is **answer the question
set**. The question will direct you towards a significant and interesting

part or aspect of the play, and it is this particular issue you have to discuss. The logic behind this is straightforward: the examiner assumes that you have read and thought about the play as a whole and also looked in detail at various aspects of the play. A general essay about the play as a whole would not really test you; the examiner wants to see if you really do know the play, whether you can use what you know to focus on and answer a question that you have not considered previously.

The most common fault in examination essays is irrelevance: candidates are set a question they did not expect and simply write their prepared answers. Some might bend the question to suit their material, but many examination candidates all but ignore the question. The examiner will understand why candidates are doing this – after all, he or she has taken similar examinations, and knows the feelings of panic that can overtake all of us in an examination room – but the examiner cannot give any credit for irrelevant work. Sometimes you might feel that you have a lot of information and material on one topic, but very little on the topic specified in the question. At such times it is especially important to remember that you must answer the question set. Even if you stumble along, trying to make a little go a long way, the examiner will reward you if you are genuinely attempting to answer the question. This problem of irrelevance can occur even when candidates have prepared the topic in the question. There might be, for example, a question about 'evil in *Macbeth*'. Most examination candidates would have some prepared material on this, but many would just pour out all their prepared material without bothering to look at precisely what the question is asking them to discuss. You must remember that an essay is presenting an argument: it is important that you keep on referring to material in the text, but you must also be using these examples to build an argument that answers the question set.

Understanding the question

Essay writing becomes a lot easier if you know what sorts of questions are usually set and if you can see the implications of the various kinds of question. A glance at old examination papers will soon reveal that there are only a limited number of types of questions that can be asked about any particular play. Sometimes questions can look difficult or different because of their wording, but try to look through the wording and grasp what essentially you are being asked to do. Almost invariably, what a question will be asking you to do is to discuss a topic which you will be familiar with if you have studied the play carefully and in detail.

The most common kinds of essay questions on Shakespeare are either questions about a play's characters or questions about a play's themes or questions about a play's technique. In every case you will be asked to analyse and discuss a specified topic or question or statement. You must realise that you are being asked to present an argument. Let us assume that a question has been set about the central character in a play. The question will not be asking you to talk about his or her character generally or to list the things he or she does in the play; the question will be asking you to argue a case about this character. In your answer it is important that you refer to the play in detail, but you must also be building an argument from the evidence you consider. An essay answer must always argue a case. This always involves going beyond merely describing, or telling the story of, what happens in a play. Indeed, after irrelevance, story-telling is the most common fault in examination answers. It is also the easiest to make. Far too often students make the mistake of thinking they are answering the question and saying something significant when they just describe the events or characters in a scene. You have to remember that if you refer to a scene in a play, you then have to comment on the scene. You have to say what kind of significance you can see in the scene, extract or detail that you have referred to. If you don't comment, you are failing to build an argument.

This whole business of building an argument does become somewhat easier, however, if you can see the implications involved in the questions set. We shall look first at *questions about characters*: you may be asked to discuss one of the main characters, showing how they are presented and discussing the significance of what they say and do. Or you may be asked to discuss the dramatic role of a character, saying, for example, what part they play in the plot, their effect on other characters and on the audience, analysing their individual interest but also what purpose they serve in the play. Or you may be asked to discuss the dramatic function of a character, meaning that you are expected to concentrate more on how their actions and speeches serve to bring out the themes of the play. In each case, however, you have to move beyond an analysis of the personalities of the characters to a sense of how they are being used by the dramatist and how they illuminate what the play is about and how it works. This is the main point to grasp with questions about characters: you have to focus on the characters themselves, but your answer must be informed by a sense of the broader issues inherent in the play. You are never interested in characters just as characters: you are interested in them because of the way in which they reflect, reveal and embody the broader concerns of the play.

Questions about themes always ask you to discuss a particular topic or issue in a play. Again, as with questions about character, the thing to bear in mind is that, although you are asked to focus on a specific topic, your answer must be informed by a sense of the broader issues in the play. If you were asked, for example, to look at a play's 'treatment and presentation of the theme of love', your comments might amount to nothing more than general chit-chat unless you could see that the play's presentation of love is a particular way of focusing a consideration of its broader themes. Similarly, if you were asked to discuss 'the theme of nature' in a play, your comments might lack any sense of direction unless you could see that nature was a particular example of the whole problem of order and disorder in life.

Thematic questions often consist of a statement about the play followed by the word 'discuss'. The statement will often point to a tension in the play, but, if it does not, then you must stop and think and remind yourself that plays always deal with conflicts and problems, and that any theme specified will reflect the broader conflict found in the play in some way. The earlier chapters of this book have tried to show how there is a tension at the very heart of drama between the messy reality of life and simple ideals, that there is always a tension between the reality of disorder and the idea of order. In concentrating on a theme you need to be aware of how it relates to and dramatises just such a wider tension. But remember that, although you are having to use your larger sense of the play to answer the question – telling yourself, for example, that the play contrasts an ideal of love with the complex reality of love in a disordered world – you must concentrate on the specified topic, showing how and where in specific incidents this theme is in evidence. At the same time you have to comment on the significance of the details you look at, saying how they bring this tension to life. Writing about a theme in a play, then, is a case of using what you know about the play as a whole to get hold of the significance of the particular theme mentioned, and then concentrating on the theme but showing how the details reflect the broader tension of the play.

Questions about technique can either focus on something precise, such as the imagery in a play, or something much larger, such as whether a play is a tragedy or not. You might be asked, however, to discuss whether a play is successful in the way in which it combines various elements (for example, the question might draw attention to the way in which a certain play mixes an improbable story with realistic characters). Such questions might appear frightening, because they seem abstract: they don't appear as appealing as talking about the people in a play, or talking about something solid such as the themes or issues in a play. But the point is, again, that exactly the same logic informs questions about technique as informs questions about characters or themes. You are being asked to look at a certain aspect of the play, or being asked to look at the play from a certain angle, but the broader conflicts and tensions at the heart of the play should be evident in, and shape your response to, the aspect you are considering. Take imagery, for example: you could list every image in a play, and your answer could have got nowhere at all. But use the idea that there is a tension in the play between how things should be and the reality of how things are, and you immediately have a way of explaining and justifying the imagery in the play.

The point is that you need a sense of what the play as a whole is about to answer a question. You can't explain whether a play is a tragedy or not unless you have a clear idea of the play's broader significance, and you can't explain why the play is presented in the way Shakespeare chose, unless you have a clear idea of what the play as a whole is doing. You then have a framework for your comments and your analysis of details. It is the same with all questions. To answer on a character, on themes, or on technique, you need a larger sense of the play to inform and organise your comments on the specific issue. But you must answer on the character, issue, or topic specified in the question, finding the larger pattern of the play in the particular examples, incidents or details you refer to.

What the examiner wants to see

The examiner wants to see a clear, well-set-out answer which refers to the text a lot. He or she wants to see an essay with a strong, clear central argument closely illustrated and substantiated from relevant scenes or speeches in the play. We might also add that examiners are not looking for a single, right answer and do not have a perfect model answer in their minds as they read your essay. Candidates sometimes worry about whether they will be saying the kind of things that please examiners. To worry about this shows a fundamental misconception of the whole nature of essay writing and of what examiners are looking for in essays. Examiners are not interested in whether you take one view or another view of the text. What they are interested in is how effectively you organise, present and argue the case you are offering. They are likely to award poor marks to the answer which is full of strong opinions, but only because such an answer will usually just be offering opinions about the text rather than examining the evidence of the words on the page. What the examiner wants to see is how good you are at presenting a convincing argument: this involves being able to see the issues in the play, being able to discuss the text in detail, and being able to develop a broader argument about the play.

Your answer

Abstract discussion of the nature of examination questions, such as we have presented up to this point, can make the whole problem of writing an essay seem more frightening rather than less so. At the moment, if you have followed this chapter so far, it might seem to you that in your essays you have got to achieve a very difficult balance between an awareness of the play as a whole, attention to details of the play, and developing an argument. It is a difficult balance to achieve, but in a moment we are going to suggest how you can use the format of an essay to its full potential, making the essay itself work for you so that you can guarantee that you will produce, at the least, a competent essay. The main secret of constructing an essay is that, the simpler the structure of your essay is, the more effective your essay as a whole is likely to be.

Before we turn to the actual format of an essay, however, we want to make just a brief comment about the mass of knowledge that you might have accumulated about a play before an examination. It might well be that you cannot use all this material in the exam. Don't be tempted into writing down everything you know about a play. Having masses and masses of details and ideas won't gain you any marks at all, unless they are relevant to the question. So you might have to sacrifice a lot of your prepared material. But it isn't being wasted: your detailed study of the text will have given you a clear sense of the play and it is this which informs and shapes your response to the question set. It's the obvious point that the more you have read the play, and the more familiar you are with it, the better equipped you will be to answer any question about the play.

We now have got, then, as far as answering the essay question. You have selected the question you want to answer, and have thought about it very carefully. You are aware that an examination question always asks you to do more than just describe something, that it always asks you to consider some problem: your essay won't have an argument, it won't have an issue to discuss, unless you can see how there is a problem involved in the question. It might well be that you have the answer to the problem in the question, and if you do this will give you an idea of where your essay as a whole is going to go, but it doesn't matter if you don't know the answer yet: that will emerge in your essay as you build your argument. The important thing is to see what problem is being raised in the question.

You can help crystallise and define the problem as you write your **first paragraph**. The best use you can make of the opening paragraph of an essay is to identify the problem. An opening paragraph need not be very long, perhaps no more than a dozen lines, but it has to focus on the issue at the heart of the question. There's no point in revealing the answer at this stage: after all, the whole purpose of your essay is that it is going to explore a problem, and finally arrive at some conclusions, so all the opening paragraph needs to do is to identify and state the problem. In effect, you are saying, 'This is the problem, but as yet I don't know the answer. As I turn to examining the text, an answer should begin to become clear.' Your opening paragraph, then, defines the area you are going to explore and the problems it involves.

In passing we might refer to a very common fault in essays. Students often begin their essays with two introductory paragraphs. They write an opening paragraph which rambles round the question a bit, and then, probably half-aware that this first paragraph has not achieved very much, write a second paragraph which again drifts round the question. This kind of double opening to an essay is a very clear indication that the person writing the essay does not know what he or she is doing. They have rambled at the outset, and the chances are that the whole essay is going to ramble on in the same way, becoming confused and going out of control. If, on the other hand, you start with a disciplined first paragraph, which says 'This is the problem to be considered', then your essay probably will answer the question both efficiently and effectively.

Your essay as yet, however, has not attempted to supply an answer. It is at this point, as you begin the **second paragraph**, that you can start to make the format of your essay help you produce a good answer. The only place to find the answer is in the evidence of the text, so turn to a particular scene or speech in the play. It must, of course, be a scene or speech which is relevant to the question, but this shouldn't prove too difficult to find: if it's a question about a character, it obviously has to be a scene which features that character. Refer to the incident, or quote part of a speech, and then begin to discuss and analyse what you can see happening in this section of the play. If you are talking about a theme, for example, you might, at this stage, be interested in establishing a basic idea of how the theme is in evidence in the play, and again you do this by focusing on a specific scene or speech. But how do you know what to say about this extract you have chosen? Well, the last chapter showed you. Obviously you don't discuss as much as in a context question or extract question since there your whole answer is concerned with one passage, but these provide you with models of how to draw larger ideas out of the evidence of the text. Concentrate on one or two details and really work on these instead of trying to cover everything. If you follow the same pattern of briefly summarising the incident or speech you have chosen, and then analysing and discussing its dramatic significance, you will have something solid to say. More important, your analysis of the extract will have begun to establish certain things: in a way, you will have begun to answer the question. But it is important that you answer the question explicitly as well as in this implicit way, so end your paragraph with a very definite conclusion – it might run over several sentences – which establishes what you have discovered so far about the problem you are looking at and how it presents itself in the play.

Can you see how an essay format like this is not only simple, but how it guarantees that you do all the things you should be doing in an essay? It starts by identifying a problem, so immediately it has an implicit sense of the larger significance of the play; it then focuses on the details of the play, and extrapolates a broader argument from the details of the play. In addition, however, by ending every paragraph very definitely with a running conclusion you can be sure that you are developing an argument and answer to the question as you go along, and that you are firmly in control of that argument.

As you reach the end of the second paragraph you will have established the first step in your argument and answer. It is essential that you make proper use of paragraphs in writing an essay. Each paragraph is an additional step in your argument. At the end of each paragraph your examination of the evidence in that paragraph should have advanced your answer to a point beyond the stage evident at the end of the previous paragraph. If you do not write in paragraphs in an examination essay, your answer will lack coherence and just turn into a string of points or quotations from the text. If you find yourself occasionally writing very short paragraphs of five or six lines, or just one long sentence, something is going wrong in your answer. The point you are making is unlikely to be supported by textual evidence, or you are likely to be just referring to an incident in the text and not discussing it; an essay should build in paragraphs which are fairly equal in length.

By the time you start the **third paragraph** your essay has used the text to start building an answer. But clearly there is more to the issue than you have discussed so far. And your third paragraph can virtually begin by saying this. Then turn to another scene or speech in the play, discuss and analyse it, and again end the paragraph with a very clear conclusion. What your conclusion in effect will be saying is, 'I have now established this point about the play. When I add this on to what I established at the end of the second paragraph, I feel confident in saying this about the question as a whole.'

The technique the whole time is to be working directly from the play, proving a lot from very specific examples and details in the text. **Subsequent paragraphs** can follow the same format, each one advancing to another point, each one looking at further evidence from the text, and analysing the evidence of the text to advance your argument. Such a format might seem too mechanical, but it is much better to produce a systematic answer than to produce a confused, illogical answer. In addition, however, because the format of the essay is predetermined and designed to help you produce a good answer, you are not likely to have too many problems with controlling your material. You can therefore put all your effort into making your answer a good answer. It is a fact that a simple format such as this can support a very complex and sophisticated response to a play, whereas a confused and untidy format can only produce a confused and untidy response to a play.

What we are suggesting, then, is that you try using this format of an opening paragraph which defines the problem, followed by, perhaps, six paragraphs each of which turns to the text, examines it, and arrives at a running conclusion. You have to be aware of how each paragraph must advance on the previous paragraph. As you deliberately force yourself to write a clear conclusion to each paragraph you will inevitably find that you are answering the question and seeing all the larger issues in the play as revealed in the specific incidents you discuss. Six central paragraphs should be enough to allow you to go into the problem thoroughly, and to establish a clear answer. At the end you will need a **concluding paragraph** which pulls all the aspects of the problem together, but this is really only a resumé of what you have established along the way. It is, then, a method of essay writing that makes use of the essay format itself to lead you to answer, and a method in which an answer emerges naturally and gradually from the evidence of the text itself.

There are, we should hasten to add, many other ways of organising and presenting an essay, and obviously you do not need to use the method we recommend here. But you do need to be aware that *how* you present what you know about a play is as important as what you know, and therefore you must find a method which you feel happy with and which enables you to present your views clearly, logically and intelligently. It might be that you can see a certain appeal in the method we recommend, but don't like the idea of sticking rigidly to such a format. That's a perfectly reasonable response: your essay can complicate itself in all sorts of ways, but there is a lot to be said for having a basic shape underlying your essay, such as the shape we have described above.

There are just two points we want to add about establishing connections between the text and your ideas about the text. The first point is that any ideas you have about the play are absolutely worthless unless you can indicate how the evidence of the play itself supports what you think. It is always a warning sign to the examiner (and it should be to the candidate) when a paragraph begins 'In my opinion . . . .' What this usually indicates is that the candidate is going to offer some totally unsubstantiated views about the play. Quite simply, then, if you have a point to make you must show how and where the text suggests the idea. (It is again the case that the method of essay writing we have described provides a very easy way of guaranteeing that you always work from the evidence of the text.) The other point about the relationship between the text and your ideas about the text is the whole problem of how to make use of quotations in an answer. It often appears to the examiner that candidates put in all the quotations they know to fill up space. If you quote you must always discuss the quotation. You must discuss what the quotation says, suggests and reveals. You have got to move from the quotation to broader ideas that you can extract from the quotation, and this is the balance you are after in the essay as a whole: looking at the details of the text, but always using your examination of the text to establish a larger case and to answer the larger question about the plays.

There are two common ways of misusing quotations. The first is to insert words or phrases from the play into your own sentences, interlacing the text with your answer as you write to give the impression that you do know the play very well. If you do this, you will pass over the text and never actually discuss it. The second, much more common, error is to end a paragraph with a quotation. Usually this is introduced by the words 'This is illustrated in the following quotation', and then the candidate goes on to quote five or six lines, without any comment afterwards as if to say that the lines are self-explanatory. The quotation might well be relevant, but if you do not discuss the specific words used you will not be able to show how it adds to your argument. A brief example might help. Let us assume you are writing an essay on the theme of evil in *Macbeth*. Your first paragraph need say no more than that evil, as in all the tragedies, is at the centre of the play, but that it is only as we examine the play itself that we can appreciate the nature and force of evil in this work. In your second paragraph you have decided to look at the first scene and say how from the very start of the play an evil atmosphere is created by the witches's appearance. You sum up the scene briefly, saying what happens, and then focus on the final two lines of the scene:

Fair is foul, and foul is fair:
Hover through the fog and filthy air.
(I.i.10–11)

Instead of just saying the witches's words create an impression of evil, focus on the words themselves. The first line here is a sort of riddle in which we can see a confusion between values that are usually or should be separate: 'fair' implies goodness, light, 'foul' implies something ugly, dark. So the first line suggests how evil involves a confusion and reversal of values. The second line suggests a sort of contamination of nature: the air is 'filthy', as if heavy with evil. There is, too, the word 'fog', which adds to our impression of evil as something that envelops and encloses people. Now, you might see these lines differently, but the point we want to make is that from just a couple of lines you can build a substantial paragraph provided you discuss the text. Following your analysis you can then draw your conclusion about how the theme of evil is being presented and explored, how one aspect of it involves a confusion of values in a disordering of nature. What you say is up to you, but, if you connect your analysis with your larger ideas, then your argument will hold together. Originally we had planned that this chapter should end with a discussion of the sorts of questions that are often set on the histories, tragedies and comedies, but the earlier chapters have already indicated the likely areas of interest, and also offered some suggestions about what sort of material you might want to include in an answer. There seemed little point in returning to the themes of the plays and the method of analysing them, particularly as this would divert attention from the main issue that we want to get across here. This is that an examination question can be answered in a systematic way. When you are preparing for an examination you obviously study and learn about the texts. What you also need to do is to think about, practise and learn how to write essays. Don't think of each essay as a chore, or as another attempt to try and make sense of a book. Instead, think of each essay as another step in learning and practising the skills of essay-writing. As you learn more about how to write essays you will discover that you can make more confident responses to the books you are studying, but you will also discover that the essay can serve as a very useful medium for working out your own thoughts and response to a text.

It might help if we conclude by reminding you of the main points we have made:

(i) The main rule of essay writing is to keep the overall structure of your essay simple.

(ii) Remember that you are always examining a problem, and your answer must therefore develop an argument.

(iii) The first paragraph should define the problem you are going to examine.

(iv) Subsequent paragraphs need to look closely at the evidence of the text, establishing an answer from specific incidents and details in the play.

(v) An essay needs to develop an argument, and each paragraph should be thought of as a step in an argument, advancing the case beyond the point reached at the end of the previous paragraph.

(vi) Each step in the argument must develop from the actual evidence of the text.

When you look at a scene or a speech, you are looking for its significance in the larger context of the play. If you focus on the details of the text and then move out from the details to larger conclusions, you will be doing everything that you are expected to do in an essay. You will be revealing your grasp of the play as a whole, you will be demonstrating your ability to look closely at, respond to, and interpret the details of the text, and you will be showing your powers of developing a larger argument. That is an impressive list of achievements, but the point we are making is that a clear, logical method of essay writing can help you achieve all this without too much difficulty.

Having a good essay-writing technique will give you confidence and help structure your thinking. In particular, it will give you the confidence to move on in your work to more complex ideas and to begin to explore new approaches to Shakespeare and criticism. This is the subject of the next five chapters. Their purpose is to introduce some of the new ideas and new ways of thinking that have swept through literary criticism in recent years, especially as they have affected the study of Shakespeare.

Part Two

7

New approaches to Shakespeare

So far in this book we have been looking at how you can construct
your own reading of a Shakespeare play: how, by working with a set of
simple ideas centring on the notions of order and disorder, it is possible
to make sense quickly of both the overall significance of a play and also
the details that give substance to its particular themes and ideas. At the
heart of the method lies the strategy of moving from a broad sense of
the play to looking closely at a short extract which is then interpreted
in the light of your broad ideas. The logic of this method is that we
move from a very general idea of what the play is about towards a
more complex view built on the evidence of a sequence of extracts.
That is worth stressing. Your view of a play should change as you work
on it. Indeed, your final view of a text may well be very different from
that with which you started.

What may also change your view about a particular play is the
sort of criticism you read. That might seem an odd point to make in a
book about how to build your own analysis of a text, but it is almost
inevitable that you will come across a great deal of criticism of the play
you are studying. Such criticism may take the form of notes from a
teacher, or it may be the introduction to the edition you are using, or a
collection of essays on the play or even the notes to a production of a
play. One of the advantages of having worked out your own view is
that you are in a much better position to cope with such critical discussion and can relate it to your personal reading of the text. At the same
time, by reading or listening to the views of others, you will be able to
assess your own critical performance and think about your ideas. If you
do this, what you may find is that you start to change your critical
position. Gradually – sometimes suddenly – you may find yourself
thinking about the overall significance of the play, or even of what is
central or important in it, in a different way.

It is at this stage that the whole activity of criticism begins to get rather more complicated. At this point you have moved beyond the stage of seeing a single path through a text, the stage we have described in this book, and become aware that there are various possibilities, various options open to you. This can prove unnerving: the most common response is to feel a slight sense of inadequacy, as if there are others (published critics, people in your group who always seem to get a good mark), who are looking at the issue in a more sophisticated way, spotting more subtle patterns of significance and meaning than you have been able to spot. There are two points we could make in relation to this. One is that published criticism needn't intimidate you; as we hope to show below, it falls into particular patterns, follows certain assumptions, and often arrives at predictable results. The second point is that it is possible to offer some sense of what it is that, at a more sophisticated level, you should be looking for in a text, and this is the main thing we concentrate on in this and the following chapters. That is, we shall be looking at the kind of things that critics today look for and say about Shakespeare – and how you can, following the kind of analysis of scenes method we have laid out in this book, be fairly confident that you are looking for (and finding) the things that people today consider to be of most importance in Shakespeare's plays.

Let's start by thinking about criticism itself. When we were at school and university, we assumed that all published criticism came along with a certain objective authority; that, alongside our own stumbling efforts to make sense of things, essays and books on Shakespeare were produced by people who really knew what they were doing and always had something worthwhile to say. What we have discovered since is that critics aren't 'know-it-alls' in this kind of way; they are fallible, they always operate from very clear positions and perspectives, and always bring their own individual prejudices to bear upon the texts. What we have also come to realise, however, is that although critics are different, most critics writing at a certain time seem to hold similar views, that they tend to bring the same assumptions to texts. What this means is that, for all their differences, critics around twenty to thirty years ago used to work from the same basis; and, in the same way, critics today tend to have shared views, shared assumptions. We discuss contemporary criticism below, but first let's look at what critics used to think.

Essentially what critics used to argue (when we say 'used to' we mean, roughly speaking, criticism from around 1900 to the early 1970s;

included here are famous names in Shakespeare criticism such as A.C. Bradley, Wilson Knight, L.C. Knights, the introductions to editions of the plays, essays in the old Casebooks [but not the New Casebooks], study guides, etc.) was that Shakespeare's plays present a coherent vision of life, that they offer us a picture of human behaviour that is true for all times and all people. Accompanying this stress on the coherence of the plays and their universality was the idea of the plays as putting forward a clear set of moral values that we could recognise, a moral message about the right way to act. This approach is probably the one we are most familiar with from school; it most often focuses on the characters in the play and asks us to consider such questions as the nature of Macbeth's evil or the relationship between love and folly in the comedies. In the case of *King Lear*, for example, the old man suffers, but in the process learns a great deal about humanity's potential for evil; the negative vision – of evil – is more than compensated for by the sense that Lear, as tragic hero, in giving voice to his feelings, offers us a sense of human potential. In an odd way, therefore, a Shakespeare play becomes something like a huge parable, an enormous positive story about human experience. We might add that *King Lear* is one of the most successful plays for teaching in schools and colleges because it can be fitted in rather neatly to this positive view. *Hamlet*, by contrast, has often left examination candidates feeling a lot more puzzled. This is because, although we can stress Hamlet's humanity, his intelligence, the power of his analytic speeches, somehow there is too much material in the play that won't quite fit in with the positive reading of events. Plays that the approach *does* work with are the more straightforward comedies – plays like *A Midsummer Night's Dream, Much Ado About Nothing, As You Like It* – plays where things go awry in the central stages, but plays which end with a, seemingly universal, message about marriage, self-control, moderation as the answers to most of the problems in life. It is an overall approach, therefore, that sees Shakespeare exploring complicated topics but always within a framework that makes sense of the world. In larger terms, we might say that traditionally critics have emphasised the extent to which Shakespeare seems to endorse an ordered view of society, with a stress on harmony and concord in which everything has a place and role.

Today, by contrast, critics have moved from seeing the plays as offering this kind of coherent vision about life to stressing the way they question everything, the way they break down confident assumptions we might have about the social order or gender or language. The movement has been from an emphasis on how the plays affirm values to how they are subversive, how they undermine any idea that the social order is natural or just. Instead of an emphasis on harmony and concord there is a stress on the way the plays foreground a clash of ideas, on how in their discord they seem to anticipate the Civil War that was to come in 1642 between the Puritans led by Cromwell and Charles I. It is an approach that shifts the debate away from the moral to the social and the political; where before critics saw the plays as confirming the need for order, now the stress has shifted to how the plays are radical and subversive, how they question all ideas and values.

In order to illustrate this shift in critical emphasis let's look briefly at a speech from *Richard II*. If you have read the play you may remember that towards the end Richard, after he has been deposed by Bolingbroke, delivers a soliloquy in which he says he has been trying to work out in his mind where he stands in the world now he is no longer king and has nothing left:

> Thus play I in one person many people
> And none contented. Sometimes am I king;
> Then treasons make me wish myself a beggar,
> And so I am. Then crushing penury
> Persuades me I was better when a king;
> Then am I king'd again; and by and by
> Think that I am unking'd by Bolingbroke,
> And straight am nothing. But whate'er I be,
> Nor I, nor any man that but man is,
> With nothing shall be pleas'd till he be eas'd
> With being nothing.
>
> (v.v.31–41)

If we were to look at this extract from a traditional perspective, what might we say about it? We can start with what it tells us about Richard himself. We can see that Richard is trying to come to terms with the world, but above all we can see his suffering: he speaks of not being able to find a role and how he seems caught between being a beggar and a king but how, in the end, he will only be at ease by being nothing. We have a sense of a man, then, struggling to find an identity in a world that offers few comforts: if he is a beggar he has to endure 'penury', poverty; if he is king he suffers by being betrayed. But from this suffering Richard seems to have gained an insight into the meaning of life, how it is that true peace only comes once we have left behind this earth and are dead. It is the kind of insight the tragic hero commonly achieves in his suffering, an insight into the workings of the universe. In other words a traditional reading of the speech would see it largely in terms of the character of the tragic hero and how, in tragedy, suffering leads to the recognition of some higher laws governing people's lives or some higher moral values than those which have brought about his downfall. It is an approach that, while it may admit that the hero has brought his suffering upon himself by his flawed nature, nevertheless sees much to admire in his ability to battle on against adversity and to reach some kind of higher understanding of life.

What would a more recent approach have to say about the speech? A more recent approach would be very much less concerned with Richard's individual plight and feelings, less concerned with analysing his character and drawing out large statements about human life. It would, that is, look beyond seeing the play in terms of individual characters and their experiences as it would also look beyond the notion that the political order of society depends upon specific individuals, that politics is just a matter of what kings say. Instead, a more recent approach would focus on those areas that traditional criticism does not see or does not mention or does not recognise as important. There is first, and most obviously, the way the speech talks about only 'man', the way it assumes that only man's experience in the world is worth discussing, as if only men mattered in any account of the world. The speech marginalises women but also, by repeating the word 'man', emphasises how insignificant a role women have in the thinking of the play. The second area a more recent approach might take up would be to look at the way the speech, despite its claim to be examining how things are in the world, doesn't really examine the social order but instead reinforces it by having as its key terms king and beggar. Richard flies between two opposites in his role-playing, but those opposites are really just the top and bottom of the existing hierarchy: what the speech does, therefore, is not question the existing power structure but replicate it, with rich set against poor, king set against beggar, and man set over woman. What a non-traditional approach to the speech would stress, then, is the way in which its language serves to perpetuate a certain kind of social structure built on certain notions about gender and class. A point that might occur to you to ask here is what is Shakespeare's stance: is he questioning conventional ways of seeing things or, as appears to be the case, is he showing a trust in these traditional ways of organising experience, with fixed hierarchies and oppositions? But the very fact of wondering where Shakespeare stood is something that belongs to the old way of looking at the text. Modern criticism has moved from identifying the author's view to examining the full range of social, political ideas and values found in the text; it has moved from identifying the 'meaning' of the play with the author to seeing how texts are always plural, how they are full of clashing ideas that have their origin not in the writer but in culture, in all the circumstances that the play is part of.

We have tried in the paragraph above to illustrate some of the differences between the traditional approaches to Shakespeare and the new approaches, that, whereas traditional criticism looked at character and the moral order of society, what the new approaches show is how these very terms – such as character, author, man, moral order, society – are no longer regarded as trustworthy or acceptable pointers for talking about experience. Why should this be? What has happened in the sixties, seventies and eighties, to undermine the credibility of such terms? Of course, we still can, if we wish, use such terms, and as our first (traditional) analysis suggests, it is still possible to read the speech in the light of conventional ideas about characters and the suffering of the tragic hero, but nevertheless it is becoming increasingly old-fashioned to do so. Why? If we think about it, the answer has got to be connected with the sort of social change that has taken place in the recent past that has undermined an old order; more specifically, it has to be connected with the kind of social revolution that has challenged all kinds of ideas about society, gender roles, sexual behaviour, about how we dress, talk, about money, marriage, music, literature, television. Think about the totally different attitude to marriage, divorce and co-habitation that now influences people's behaviour, and how the old morality seems more like a trick of history, a Victorian hangover, than a universal rule. The most obvious sign of this social revolution is the women's movement which has challenged nearly every aspect of conventional society. Of course, the struggle for equality by women began long before the 1960s, but it is since then that perhaps the greatest changes in women's lives have come about alongside changes in the whole social matrix.

The social revolution and social changes of the last thirty years have had an enormous influence, however, not simply on everyday living but on all kinds of thinking about society, so that alongside the social revolution there has also been a change in the way critics, philosophers, teachers, sociologists look at the past and the present. In brief, there has been a change in the sort of theories people apply in their thinking, a change which has encouraged people to stand apart from traditional assumptions and values and to re-examine them from new perspectives, questioning them and their implications. This change in thinking might best be described as a sort of profound scepticism about traditional values and ideas, and, in the face of economic and social difficulties, such as recession and mass unemployment, a scepticism about western capitalism and its ability to provide jobs, health services and education for the people.

How this revolution has affected literary criticism can be glimpsed in the example above from *Richard II*; the critical response has moved from sympathising with the figure in power to questioning the assumptions and values of the figure in power. Behind the contrast in approaches lie two very different attitudes to language which we need to spend a moment discussing. The whole issue of the way language works is something that has received a lot of attention in contemporary criticism. The reason for this is that language is central to any discussion we hold about society or literature. If you look back at what we have said about traditional criticism above, you should see that informing the discussion of Richard's speech is the idea that language expresses the character's personality: it gives us an insight into his or her mind and feelings, as if it were a sort of window on to his or her inner life. What we can set against this is the view of language as something artificial, as something that we use to order the world. This is a view of language which is most often associated with the critical movement known as structuralism. Essentially what structuralism says is that language is not a window into people's inner life but that language is a structure or a system that we learn. Richard's discourse – discourse means the specific vocabulary which serves specific institutions or interests, such as kingship or patriarchy – is something that we are now likely to step back from, seeing it as the language of a certain class and gender, rather than a language expressing some sort of 'universal' truth.

Why critics were attracted by structuralism in the early seventies was that it offered a way of talking about language and society that coincided with the new scepticism we have described above; it offered a way of questioning ideas that had previously been taken for granted. Suddenly it could be seen that language was not a matter of truth or something that expressed what people felt: it was something they learned and with it they learned all kinds of assumptions. What previously had been presented as 'natural' was now seen to be the effect of what the language said it was; and more and more it came to be seen that instead of *us* speaking *language*, it was a case that *language* speaks *us*, that language constitutes us as the human, political and grammatical subjects we are.

At this point, it may be a good idea if we add a few other items of information. Structuralism took most of its inspiration from the work of the Swiss linguist Ferdinand de Saussure. His important contribution was, first of all, to point out that language was a sign system or structure; second, Saussure drew a distinction between what he called the signifier – the word, the letters, the sound – and the signified, the concept referred to. What Saussure noted was that there was no reason why the letters that make up *king* should mean 'king'; there is nothing that connects the letters and the idea 'king' except convention. Or, to put it another way, there is nothing doggy about the word 'dog': there is no natural link between the letters and the four-legged animal we usually refer to as a 'dog'. Language is a system; words work by being different from each other rather than by possessing any innate meaning.

Such ideas may not seem very exciting, but their implications were pursued vigorously by literary critics. More to the point, no sooner was structuralism a live debating point than it was followed by poststructuralism. The difference, really, comes down to the idea of harmony. Structuralism sees language as a system, something that has order, it is a sort of code that transmits messages. By contrast poststructuralism emphasises the extent to which all meaning is unstable, arbitrary; that where structuralism saw convention operating to enable *dog* to mean 'dog', poststructuralism sees that the gap between *dog* and 'dog' points to the inherent instability of language, the way in which meaning may be plural, not fixed. It should be said that this notion of the instability of meaning is one that informs nearly all modern criticism. All modern criticism, that is to say, is broadly poststructuralist. In the next chapter we offer an analysis of *Richard II* and *Twelfth Night* that illustrates this crossover from structuralism to poststructuralism, but we would also want to stress, for example, that most recent feminist criticism is also poststructuralist. Indeed, most critics these days draw upon several strands from the new critical ideas, combining poststructuralist insights into the nature of language with other theoretically-informed positions.

Implicit in structuralism and poststructuralism is the same kind of questioning of society that is explicit in the women's movement.

Modern feminist criticism begins, like structuralism, in the 1970s and focuses especially on the question of gender, on how society represents women in stereotyped ways or how the language we use assigns particular roles or positions to women. In the case of Shakespeare, feminist criticism is most often concerned with the way the plays represent women and how the plays seem to support patriarchy, that is, male rule of society and the family. Much more than structuralism, feminism is a radical criticism which questions and challenges assumptions about women, about gender, about the family, and which questions, too, how criticism has talked about women and served to perpetuate mythical images of them. Feminist criticism has had a profound effect on Shakespeare studies and is one of the most important developments in new approaches to Shakespeare, and indeed to literary texts as a whole.

In chapter 9 we offer some broad tips on how to construct a feminist reading of Shakespeare's plays focusing on questions of gender and before that, in chapter 8, a structuralist/poststructuralist reading which is largely concerned with ideas of language. These make up two of the new areas we discuss. There is one other approach or area we take up and which is also the product of the social revolution discussed above. In looking at the speech from *Richard II* we commented on the way the speech reinforces rather than challenges the existing social hierarchy: Richard does not suggest that his deposition could lead to a new sort of social pattern; he speaks still in terms of rich and poor, powerful and weak, king and beggar. Traditional criticism had little time for such points, but for recent Shakespeare criticism the question of power – about how power is exercised in the state and about how it operates – has become one of the central issues explored. It has so because it leads on to questions of whether Shakespeare's plays are indeed deeply radical or whether they are essentially conservative in their ideology, in their beliefs, ideas and values. This is a topic that a good deal of criticism has been concerned with, especially what is called New Historicism and Cultural Materialism, both of which we look at in chapter 10. New Historicism and Cultural Materialism are the names given to a type of criticism that examines the wider political context of Shakespeare's plays, how they lock into the politics of the time.

These, then, are the three broad areas we will be looking at – language, gender and power – which will enable us to say more about the theories behind recent discussions of Shakespeare. Here we can perhaps stress the extent to which the new readings of Shakespeare, and especially New Historicism and Cultural Materialism, have also been concerned with setting the plays back in their historical and cultural contexts. The reason for this has to do with the way recent criticism has come to argue that Shakespeare is not a unique figure writing in the Renaissance but is part of a rich, often contradictory, social and historical period and that we cannot isolate his plays from other writings or events if we want to understand how they were produced by the age in which they were written. This might seem to resemble a traditional approach – looking at a text in its cultural context and in relation to other texts produced at the same time – but it is in fact a reflection of the changed social climate in which we live. It is not simply that there has been a rejection of the old order or a call for justice for women or a reappraisal of the question of sexual politics; it is rather that the whole political stance has changed. With the changes in society and the questioning of such ideas as the family, marriage, national identity, there has come a shift in the way history and culture are thought about and how Shakespeare's plays are to be regarded as caught up in the dilemmas and contradictions of their times just as we are in the difficult choices of ours.

What we are going to describe in the following chapters, therefore, is a critical revolution, a critical revolution that has come along in the last thirty years and which is still in process of change. This is an important point; criticism is part of a continuing debate which asks you to consider issues for yourself. But you may be wondering at this point why, after we have encouraged you to develop your own views, we now wish to encourage you to explore other avenues that in some cases cut across the earlier parts of this book. Several things need to be said here. First, the previous chapters of this book have been designed to get you to a certain level of competence where you can write a clear essay and work your way through a Shakespeare play with ease. Once you can do that you are ready to move up a level and take on some new ideas. Second, all critics operate in the context of their time, building on what already exists; you, too, need to operate with your finger on the pulse of what is going on around you, but as you look at the new approaches you will inevitably add to and modify them. Third, the new approaches are not rigid, they present opportunities to look again at Shakespeare's plays from some rewarding angles. Finally, the basic method of working from small extracts from the text is still the same, enabling you to open up all sorts of questions and all sorts of aspects of the texts that were closed off before simply because critics could not see them.

8

Structuralism,
poststructuralism and
deconstruction

Richard II

1   *Look at a scene from Act I*

WE have decided to look again at *Richard II*, with a particular emphasis on the differences between our discussion of the play here and our initial discussion of it in chapter 2. At that point we were largely interested in describing the basic moves to make with a text. Here we want to look at the way to build a reading that focuses on the issue of language in the play and how the play might be said, in some senses, to be about language. This, very broadly, can be called a structuralist approach: some structuralist criticism is very technical and concerned with the general principles that operate in literature, but for our purposes we can take structuralism to mean looking at a text to see how it thematises the issue of language, how the problems of interpreting language become the text's main concern. As we will see, however, much more is involved than just language.

Our starting-point is exactly the same plot summary we used in our earlier discussion of the play. Richard banishes Bolingbroke and then confiscates his lands to help finance a war in Ireland. Bolingbroke consequently invades England and deposes Richard; he then ascends the throne as Henry IV. Almost immediately Richard is murdered, and the play ends with Bolingbroke's troubled awareness that Richard had to be murdered to make his own position as King secure.

The basic pattern of the play, we said in our first analysis, is a king overthrown by rebels; underlying this pattern is the implicit idea of a gap between a notion of order, of how things might be in a well-ordered state, and the reality of how things are. In chapter 2 we went on to explore this idea of the elusiveness of order and some of the implications it has for the way we look at the figures of Bolingbroke and Richard. In this second analysis we are interested in moving on from this critical view to an exploration of the role of language in the play. In particular, we want to look at speeches where the characters talk about words, talk about how they frame and control experience through language. Of course, in order to do this you have to find relevant examples. At first this might appear difficult, but it is often the case that once you start looking for a particular line of examples they begin appearing everywhere. Don't be put off, however, if you cannot find anything in the first scene or so of a play. We, in fact, found nothing we could focus on in *Richard II* until Act I scene iii where Richard banishes Bolingbroke and his opponent Mowbray whom he has accused of treason.

The scene begins with Bolingbroke and Mowbray about to engage in a trial by combat to establish which of them is telling the truth. Richard stops the fight before it has begun, banishing Mowbray for life and Bolingbroke for ten years, which he then reduces to six out of sympathy for Bolingbroke's father, Gaunt. We are not told why Richard treats the men differently; what we see is how powerful Richard is, something reinforced by Bolingbroke's reaction to his reduced sentence:

> How long a time lies in one little word!
> Four lagging winters and four wanton springs
> End in a word: such is the breath of kings.
> (I.iii.213–15)

Obviously we have chosen this quotation because it highlights an issue dealing with language in the play; very simply, the word 'word' caught our eye, letting us know that there would be sufficient material here to make a large point, a general point about the play. Bolingbroke's comment clearly draws attention to the power of Richard's words as king and how he seems able to change time merely by speaking. It is as if Richard has power to order the world by his very breath: winter and spring are said to end in a word, as if Richard's words have control over the seasons. Now, you might want to put these points rather differently, but, however you see Bolingbroke's comment, remember that the object is to achieve an analysis of the play built around ideas to do with language. This means that we must step back, we must try to extrapolate an idea that will offer us a larger purchase on the play. Here, for example, we can state that at the start of the play attention is drawn to the apparent power of language to change and shape the world, to control time and men's fates. There is something impressive about Richard's language, perhaps something almost god-like. Certainly Bolingbroke seems awe-struck by it. The point we might make is that power is often expressed through language, and that the reverse is also true: that language is power. Bolingbroke at this point is effectively silenced in that he is sent into exile, banished from both England and the stage. He has no alternative other than to defer to the words of the King.

In order to move on we now need to find another scene where the issue of language comes up. It is worth stressing that your strategy in building an analysis can be as simple as finding a sequence of short extracts to talk about that focus on the topic of the language. Earlier in this book we selected scenes and speeches that represented significant steps and developments in the plot of a play. Your focus here is narrower: sometimes a substantial speech, but often just a few lines that touch on the issue of language. All the time you should be trying to open up your ideas to see what more you can say about the topic, exploring what you see as its interest and implications. We've started with a clear point about language as power – we need to look at another scene to see how this idea develops, where we are led to.

2   *Look at a scene from Act II*

Act II begins with the death of Gaunt, Bolingbroke's father. He has sent for Richard so that he can give him his dying advice, but Richard has plans to seize Gaunt's lands in order to pay for his Irish wars. The result is a series of clashes between the two in which Gaunt attacks Richard's rule. But much of their dialogue to start with turns on a series of puns to do with illness and Gaunt's name:

> RICHARD What comfort, man? How is't with aged Gaunt?
> GAUNT O, how that name befits my composition!
>   Old Gaunt indeed; and gaunt in being old . . .
>   The pleasure that some fathers feed upon
>   Is my strict fast – I mean my children's looks;
>   And therein fasting hast thou made me gaunt.

> Gaunt am I for the grave, gaunt as a grave
> Whose hollow womb inherits naught but bones.
> RICHARD Can sick men play so nicely with their names?
>
> (II.i.72–84)

At first sight this seems a hard passage to talk about since it doesn't immediately offer us any obvious clues to what to say. We can see Gaunt is punning on his name and making jokes about how his name, which means thin or haggard, is appropriate to his ill condition, but that is all. At this point it is very difficult to see any connection between the triviality of this and the weight of the previous passage considered, where Richard's words had, for Bolingbroke, terrible, almost life-destroying consequences. If we think about it, however, we should be able to see how the extract is drawing attention to something very important about words, and that is how they can have more than one meaning. Gaunt puns on his name and then keeps punning on it as he goes through its associations: he is 'gaunt' because he is old, because he is thin and ready for the grave. But as well as this point we can make two others: first, that this time it is Richard who is surprised by the power of words; second, that what Gaunt's speech highlights is also the question of names.

What we need to do at this stage is stand back and see where we have arrived. Our first example from Act I was about how language seems able to change and alter things; the word, as spoken by Richard, carried authority. His word was his word, his final decree and could not be challenged, though the astute reader might make the point that his words don't perhaps carry all that much authority, for no sooner has he passed sentence on Bolingbroke than he changes his mind and cuts four years off the sentence. That, obviously, is a point we will have to return to, but what we can say in relation to this second passage is that, unlike the first speech, it offers us a very direct sense of the unsteadiness of words. Words don't mean just one thing; words don't define and control experience in as neat a way as that. Words are unsteady, with multiple meanings.

What we can say, then, is that the play so far seems to be offering us two different ideas about language: one view is that it is all-powerful and can change the world, the other is that it is slippery and elusive. It is at this point that a traditional critic might try to resolve this clash of ideas by, for example, arguing that just as Richard is running the country down by his unfitness to be king, so language is starting to break up. In other words, the traditional critic would brush aside any larger issue that the play might be beginning to speculate upon – for example, the play might be going to ask some difficult questions about the relationship between language and power. Instead, the traditional critic would close the issue down, making the language images serve nothing more than a simple purpose of illustrating Richard and his character flaws. Potentially interesting possibilities in a play are, thus, often ignored in a traditional reading, the kind of reading that tries to organise the world on the basis of the potential and capabilities of individuals. However, contemporary criticism is not really interested in creating this sort of coherent pattern out of texts; rather, what a structuralist or, more accurately, a poststructuralist critic might argue is that here we have a sort of contradiction in the text, that it dramatises a conflict between two different views of language and so challenges us to think about them – and, moreover, as we shall see, that this questioning attitude towards language forces us to ask fundamental questions about the whole construction and exercise of power in political life.

In the course of the previous paragraph we slipped from the word structuralist to the word poststructuralist. Before we proceed any further we need to explain our terms a little more. As we noted in the previous chapter, poststructuralist criticism is a general term for all the recent critical developments that followed structuralism and accepted and built on the basic insight of structuralism about language, that language is a highly conventional system of codes. No sooner had structuralism arrived in the seventies, than poststructuralist criticism developed, employing ideas from feminism, Marxism, psychoanalysis and other disciplines and theories to re-examine the whole approach to literary studies. All the approaches we will be discussing in the following chapters can be loosely grouped under the poststructuralist umbrella. One of the most distinct differences between structuralism and poststructuralism, we might add, is that structuralism, in its pure form, might well stop short at just a technical analysis of the operations in a text, at just looking at its structure and patterns. But structuralism became poststructuralism at that point where critics began to realise that a close look at the language of a text has implications. The moment the critic looks at how people use words to order experience, an awareness follows that there is a constructed quality – constructed through language – to our entire sense of the world. And at that point there follows a desire to analyse and dissect all the values, the ideologies, the political convictions we usually live by.

This impulse to analyse the constructedness of language and of what we mean by it expresses itself in feminist criticism, in Marxist criticism, in New Historicism and Cultural Materialism as well as in psychoanalytic criticism. But it expresses itself most clearly of all in deconstruction, another form of poststructuralist criticism. Like structuralism, deconstruction is a criticism that focuses on language and meaning, but where structuralism sees language being organised into meaning, deconstruction focuses on the warring forces of meaning in the text, on its contradictions, on its plurality and how this undermines any single, stable 'meaning'. Put another way, we can describe deconstruction as a probing of all statements, exposing their flimsiness and depriving us of all points of reference and definitions. We can say deconstruction takes statements apart, undoing them, opening up the gaps which a traditional reading glosses over or ignores in its pursuit of a unified meaning for the text.

How does this apply to *Richard II?* We have already seen how in the first passage Richard's word was law, although as we noted above the astute reader might also spot that Richard's words are quick to change when he reduces Bolingbroke's sentence. There is, then, a trace in Richard's language of a sort of instability, that his words can be altered at will. But then Gaunt adds a whole new dimension to this when he plays with the different meanings of his name, deconstructing it through a series of puns. Indeed, Gaunt is a sort of deconstructionist critic. He might think of himself, of course, as John of Gaunt, as a noble lord who has a fixed place in the political hierarchy as Richard's uncle, as a man who through his words can give solid advice to the king about how to rule the country, as a man who can name the world, label it and control it. It is Gaunt, after all, who delivers the famous 'This royal throne of kings. . . . This blessed plot, this earth, this realm, this England' speech just before he sees Richard in this scene. But the moment Gaunt plays with his name, the moment he begins to undo its supplementary meanings and unweave its threads, then the whole fabric of the play starts to come undone, the whole political structure starts to collapse and spin out of control. Gaunt's word-games sow confusion and throw the play into a different mode: what was seemingly stable and ordered is seen to be built on the shifting sands of language. To this extent we might well argue that, ironically, Gaunt, the epitome of English nobility and patriotism, is the figure in the play who begins the process of deposing England's monarch, that Richard is safe until Gaunt undermines the platform on which Richard's authority stands, that words name things as they are. By deconstructing his own name Gaunt deconstructs the whole idea that anything can be named, fixed, certain, including the idea of kingship and Richard as king.

We have spent some time on the question of the relationship between structuralism, poststructuralism, deconstruction, language and politics because it does inform a lot of critical thinking these days. Almost without exception modern critics accept the poststructuralist idea that language is unstable and that texts are plural in their meanings, criss-crossed by all kinds of contradictions, uncertainties, warring ideas. From now on, however, we will be saying less about such theoretical issues and simply applying some of the points. The main ones that have come out of our discussion of *Richard II* so far is that the play seems to be built on opposing views of language and words, and in particular on the conflict between the notion that language can be fixed and the idea, implicit in Gaunt's speech, of the radical instability of language, and especially names. What we want to do now is explore further examples of this problem.

3   Look at a scene from Act III

After Gaunt dies Richard seizes his lands which ought to go to the banished Bolingbroke. The result of Richard's action is rebellion by the nobles and Bolingbroke who returns from banishment to claim his rights. When challenged in ii.iii by York about his rebellion, Bolingbroke says that while he was banished under one name – Duke of Hereford – he now comes back under another, his title as Duke of Lancaster, inherited from his father. It is an interesting illustration and confirmation of much of what we have been saying so far. The constitution of the state, the smooth running of political and social life depends upon everybody having their place, having a name and position in the system. Bolingbroke's action is rather clever. He is not acting as an individual. In a sense, he is not even rebelling against the King. Instead, he has simply assumed his role, his name in the state – the role he acquires through inheritance – and therefore returns. But at the same time he is cynically challenging the authority of the King's words, for like his father, Gaunt, he is prepared to shift and slide with words, to play with and question even the label of a name. Like his father, we might argue, Bolingbroke is a type of deconstructionist, forcing out the links between words, equivocating with their meanings. But Bolingbroke takes the process one stage further. Gaunt explores the puns in his name, but uses only one name. Bolingbroke, in contrast, equivocates with his titles of Hereford and Lancaster, being now one, now the other. Like Humpty Dumpty, we might suggest, Bolingbroke in effect says that words mean what he says they mean, that he is who he is or wants to be. Once we grasp this we see how dangerously subversive Bolingbroke's strategy is and how it unfixes the political order Richard depends upon.

All of this is thrown into even sharper relief when Richard returns from Ireland to be greeted by news of Bolingbroke's rebellion. At first Richard remains confident that his appearance will see off the rebels, but when he learns that all his forces have already deserted him he sinks into despair:

> . . . of comfort no man speak.
> Let's talk of graves, of worms, and epitaphs;
> Make dust our paper, and with rainy eyes
> Write sorrow on the bosom of the earth.
> Let's choose executors and talk of wills
>
> (III.ii.144–8)

It is fairly easy to spot a number of images here that refer to language in its written form: Richard mentions epitaphs, paper, wills and writing. What we can say about these is that, as well as offering us different ideas about spoken language to think about, the play is also aware of the issue of written language, of how there is more than one form of language. There is, however, something special about writing that differentiates it from spoken language, and that is the fact that it is tangible, solid. Writing can also, of course, be read and seen; it can be read and seen at a date after it was written and so preserve an apparently exact record. Above all, writing is an attempt to fix meaning, to delimit and control significance to those marks that are put on paper or stone. Richard lists here a sequence of written texts that can be handled, seen, passed on and used to order things, including death. To that extent we can talk about the way in which his speech, for all its sense of despair and defeat, still clings to a notion of order and control. If Richard is to be deposed, if he is to be unkinged, his language remains cast in the mode of political authority: to make a will is to determine the future, to decide who shall rule.

On another level, though, what Richard is also talking about are ways of making sense of the play's events by casting them into a written form, by casting them into the shape of a tragedy. Indeed, we might see Richard here as a figure seeking to give the events of the play a tragic rather than political meaning, to rewrite what is happening in terms of sorrow, graves and death rather than the language of names and titles used by Gaunt and Bolingbroke. Where their discourse registers the instability of language and how titles, names, words do not possess any inherent, fixed meaning, ironically Richard's discourse clings to the notion that meaning can be written down and limited. The irony is that it was Richard, of course, who by seizing Bolingbroke's inheritance undermined the idea of a fixed register of laws. No less than Bolingbroke, Richard wants words to mean what he says they mean, but unlike Bolingbroke he continues to live under the illusion that writing can guarantee order. The larger point we can draw from this, however, is how the text takes up and explores the central role language has in the politics of the play as we see the characters on stage wrestling for control both of the meaning of the events but also for control of language itself. It is as if the whole play is turning into an analysis of the importance of language to politics and the state. At the same time we cannot help but be aware of how the play is cast as a struggle to control language, a struggle that involves the different forms of language being set against one another as Bolingbroke and Richard vie for the crown.

4   Look at a scene from Act IV

In Act IV scene i Richard is deposed by Bolingbroke. We could look at a speech from the opening of the scene where the nobles quarrel about who is telling the truth about what happened in Richard's reign and whether the King was involved in the murder of his uncle Gloucester. This is again another aspect of language that the play foregrounds at this point, the question of the relationship between language and truth. However, we prefer to focus on Richard's deposition speech since it is obviously a highly dramatic moment on stage:

> With mine own tears I wash away my balm,
> With mine own hands I give away my crown,
> With mine own tongue deny my sacred state,

> With mine own breath release all duteous oaths;
> All pomp and majesty I do forswear;
> My manors, rents, revenues, I forgo;
> My acts, decrees and statutes, I deny.
> God pardon all oaths that are broke to me!
> God keep all vows unbroke are made to thee!
>
> (IV.i.207–15)

Richard is here giving up all the signs that make him king – the holy balm, the crown, his property, but above all we cannot help but notice the emphasis placed on oaths. Richard himself says he releases all oaths sworn to him, so he alone can do so. The significance we can attach to this is that here Richard is undoing the order that marks him out as king, but especially undoing the language that binds his subjects to him. The paradox is that although he is being deposed he still has power in his breath to dissolve ties, as if there were something special about the language of the king. This is a point we noted in the first extract when we looked at Bolingbroke's comment on how the breath of kings can change time. And yet in the play Richard has not been able to command the nobles or even his army to do as he orders: his words have not stopped the rebellion. This contradiction between the apparent power of language and its lack of effect on the deeds of men is not something we need to resolve; indeed, the play, we might argue, has gone out of its way to open up this gap in the system of language so that we become aware of the disjunction between words and the world, between rhetoric and actions, between signifier and signified, with Richard as a site where these disjunctions take place. More simply, what we can say is that the play seems to offer us two views of Richard's language, as something powerful and yet unable to hold men in loyalty. It is as if the play is juxtaposing two views about the issue so that we are unsure whether language really is a way of shaping the world or whether language is just a matter of words that have no consequences on people's actions. In this the play has raised not only questions about power, but has proved to be intensely aware of the role of language in the very constitution of power.

5   Look at a scene from Act V

But the matter seems to go deeper than just examining the language of kingship. There is a more fundamental examination of the very nature of language itself. We can see this in the final Act where Richard delivers a long soliloquy in prison about his plight in a world where he is alone. In trying to puzzle out his position as deposed king Richard finds his thoughts constantly contradicting one another, and it is this problem he puts into words in the soliloquy:

> I have been studying how I may compare
> This prison where I live unto the world;
> And, for because the world is populous
> And here is not a creature but myself,
> I cannot do it. Yet I'll hammer it out.
> My brain I'll prove the female to my soul,
> My soul the father; and these two beget
> A generation of still-breeding thoughts,
> And these same thoughts people this little world,
> In humours like the people of this world,
> For no thought is contented. The better sort,
> As thoughts of things divine, are intermix'd
> With scruples, and do set the word itself
> Against the word,
> As thus: 'Come, little ones'; and then again,
> 'It is as hard to come as for a camel
> To thread the postern of a small needle's eye'.
>
> (v.v.1–17)

This is a hard speech to get hold of, but we can begin our analysis by noting how, like the previous speech we looked at, it is part of the debate in the play about the word of kings. As with the previous speech, we can see how a gap has opened up between Richard's words and the world, how his words are no longer able to fit the world into an orderly pattern. In very specific terms Richard says he is unable to draw a comparison between his prison and the world: in an orderly system it ought to be possible to construct an analogy between places, but now Richard is aware only of differences. But the matter goes beyond this question of analogy and correspondence, as Richard's phrase about setting 'the word itself/Against the word' suggests. In order to grasp the force of this we need to think back here to Gaunt's punning on his name, on how he set the word 'Gaunt' against the pun of 'gaunt'. In doing this Gaunt set off a pattern in the play that deconstructed the word of kings, but also in the process initiated a more fundamental debate as if the world is a sort of chaos in which words struggle to control it. We can glimpse something of that debate in Richard's image of the world being filled with people who are never content but riven by humours, by elemental forces which defeat all attempts to order it.

There is, though, another level to Richard's speech. The speech, we might say, is not just about the gap between the word and the world. What it seems to do, rather, is to foreground the very issue of ordering and control we seek through language, and in particular the mechanisms of language. Here we can be more specific still and note how the speech focuses on two aspects of the mechanics of language: one is the idea of comparison, of how we use language to try and forge links between things – in this case Richard's prison and the world – but how that very act seems to draw attention to the unlikeness of the things compared. Then, second, there is the way we use written texts – in this case the Bible with its holy 'word' – to construct order only to find this riven by contradiction. It is, however, not only these mechanisms that the play foregrounds, for throughout the text there are references to wills, stories, names, lies, accusations, pledges, oaths, indeed the whole system of language which enables people to communicate but which entangles them in complex problems of meaning.

Let's take stock! We have come a long way very quickly. We suggested that the play might be said to be about language. Then we looked at how Bolingbroke's comment on Richard's 'word' draws attention to the connection between language and power, but how that connection becomes complicated by Gaunt's deconstructive punning on his name. With Gaunt's speech the relationship between words and the world, the king and the subject is thrown into confusion, a confusion Bolingbroke further exploits in his use of the names Hereford and Lancaster. The play, though, does not throw out the idea of the relationship between power and language: as we saw, Richard's deposition speech paradoxically invests his words with a force that Bolingbroke's speeches lack; and Richard's prison soliloquy serves to focus in a very fundamental way the question of the relationship between language and our ordering of the world.

But probably the most important point to grasp is that we have not made the play an introverted examination of language for its own sake. On the contrary, we have tried to show how examining what the play says about language forces us into a consideration of the whole role of language in bringing us into existence as members of society, the whole role of language in creating social and political order. At the same time we have tried to get across how the play shows us the fragility of the social and political order, for as the words multiply so the attempt to order life becomes more and more complicated. In this way we are left with an acute sense of the political implications of language.

Twelfth Night

We have looked at *Richard II* as a play that is intensely concerned with the role of language in political and social ordering. In particular, we have looked at how the play thematises the issue of language and how that issue is central to the fundamental debate in the play about how we understand and construct the world we live in. An important question is whether these issues are just to be found in *Richard II* as a play that happens to deal with a king who seems to prefer words to action. The answer, as you might expect, is that the question of language is central in Shakespeare and indeed central in all Shakespearean criticism, that the issues we discussed in *Richard II*, but with different emphases and different dimensions, are always being referred to in Shakespeare. In order to illustrate this we are going to look briefly at *Twelfth Night* to see how it thematises language. Again, as with *Richard II*, we want to draw out the fuller implications of this concern with language, how the debate about language is really a much more fundamental debate about the whole structure and existence of the social world, but in this case seen from a comic perspective.

We looked at *Twelfth Night* in chapter 4 as a comedy. In this chapter we are still looking at it as a comedy, but focusing on how it handles the issue of language. In the case of the comedies it should not be too hard to find references to language in one form or another. Language and language games figure prominently in the comedies: lovers are always writing sonnets or singing songs; fools are always punning or wilfully misunderstanding what is said; there is always a sort of excess in the comedies, which registers itself in the exuberance of the language and action on stage; there is always a tone of fantasy or playfulness which catches the audience up in the mood of enjoying what is said. Often, however, set against this exuberant playfulness is another attitude to language characterised by figures who oppose fun and love, figures who believe in the strict letter of the law, its written rules and regulations.

These general remarks are meant as pointers to the way the theme of language is set up in the comedies: we can often find a sort of contrast between those who revel in the play of language and those who use it to regulate behaviour. Each particular play will handle this contrast differently, but it is helpful to have this kind of basic pattern in your thinking as you turn to the text. At the same time, as we noted with *Richard II*, as we look at the text and begin to analyse its implications, we can expect that this simple pattern of binary opposites will turn into something much more unsettling and subversive, something much more questioning of the whole social construct.

We can start our analysis of *Twelfth Night*, as we did with *Richard II*, with a summary of the play. Orsino, Duke of Illyria, is in love with Olivia, but she has vowed not to marry for seven years because her brother has died recently. Viola is shipwrecked off Illyria and, believing her twin brother Sebastian has drowned, assumes a boy's disguise. Under the name 'Cesario' Viola becomes Orsino's page and acts as his emissary to Olivia. Viola herself is in love with Orsino. The complications arise when Olivia falls in love with Viola in her guise as 'Cesario'. Other characters include Sir Toby Belch, a relative of Olivia's, his foolish friend Sir Andrew Aguecheek, a clown Feste, and Olivia's killjoy steward Malvolio. Sir Toby and his cronies leave a letter for Malvolio, apparently written by Olivia, which encourages him to believe she loves him. Malvolio makes a fool of himself in his advances to her. The main plot, however, concerns the tangled triangle of Viola, Orsino and Olivia. This is further complicated when Viola's supposedly dead brother Sebastian arrives in Illyria. Olivia believes he is Cesario and they become betrothed. Total confusion arises, however, when Olivia confronts Viola, believing her to be Sebastian. The problems are solved when Sebastian reappears. Orsino marries Viola, Olivia marries Sebastian, and even Sir Toby marries Maria, Olivia's gentlewoman. Only Malvolio and Sir Andrew are left outside this circle of happiness.

The basic pattern of the play, we argued in chapter 4, is that sane and rational behaviour is disrupted by people falling in love, but the plot summary also reveals how much confusion there really is in the play and how a good deal of it is generated by the letter-trick against Malvolio. Obviously this is something we will have to look at in our analysis of the issue of language in the play.

1   Look at a scene from Act I

The way to start an analysis of the play, however, is by choosing a passage for analysis – and, in this instance, a passage or speech that makes some reference to the existence and nature of words. We have chosen this extract from scene four of the first act, where Orsino is about to send Viola to woo Olivia for him. To grasp the speech you have to remember that Viola is disguised as a boy, Cesario, and that Orsino wants Cesario, to whom he has confessed his love for Olivia, to persuade Olivia to listen to his proposal. Olivia has pledged to lock herself away in mourning for her dead brother for seven years, and so Orsino advises Cesario to use all his verbal skills to win Olivia over. Orsino believes Cesario will succeed because of his 'small pipe', his small voice which Olivia will pay attention to because it is like a woman's voice and will therefore chime in with Olivia's thinking:

DUKE   Cesario,
    Thou know'st no less but all; I have unclasp'd
    To thee the book even of my secret soul.
    Therefore, good youth, address thy gait unto her;
    Be not denied access, stand at her doors,
    And tell them there thy fixed foot shall grow
    Till thou have audience.
VIOLA   Sure, my noble lord,
    If she be so abandon'd to her sorrow
    As it is spoke, she never will admit me.
DUKE Be clamorous and leap all civil bounds,
    Rather than make unprofited return.
VIOLA Say I do speak with her, my lord, what then?
DUKE O, then unfold the passion of my love,
    Surprise her with discourse of my dear faith!
    It shall become thee well to act my woes:
    She will attend it better in thy youth
    Than in a nuncio's of more grave aspect.
VIOLA I think not so, my lord.
DUKE   Dear lad, believe it,
    For they shall yet belie thy happy years
    That say thou art a man: Diana's lip
    Is not more smooth and rubious; thy small pipe
    Is as the maiden's organ, shrill and sound,
    And all is semblative a woman's part.
                              (I.iv.11–33)

Initially your response to this extract may be that it is just concerned with setting up the ironies of the plot, and certainly this aspect is important: the fact that Orsino praises Cesario for his resemblance to being a young woman ties in with the play's exploration of how people see themselves and others when in love. But the passage is also filled with references to language. We mentioned some of these above, but we can spell out the list here: Orsino speaks of the book of his soul; he advises Viola to be clamorous, to shout; he refers to the discourse of his faith, his very language of love; and then at the end he talks about how well suited Cesario is to deliver the love-message, for he has smooth lips and a small voice. All these images foreground the idea of language, or rather they present two ideas of language. Orsino speaks of his soul as a book, and then later he speaks of how Cesario is to unfold his discourse of faith, as if unfolding a letter or reading from a text. From this we might conclude Orsino's love is itself bookish, something written or learnt, a text that he has read and whose rules he is following. Set against this is the stress put on Cesario as an oral messenger: he is to be clamorous, shrill, to act and speak love, to overthrow restraint.

What we can say so far, therefore, is that at the start of the play there seems to be a contrast between the emphasis Orsino puts on his love as if it were a piece of holy text and the performance Cesario is to give as a speaker of love. Clearly Orsino has failed to convince Olivia by his own words. In addition, his first messenger has been turned back. He recognises he needs Cesario's voice to win Olivia. What we might draw out from this is that the play seems to set writing against speech in some way that we have yet to define.

2   *Look at a scene from Act II*

In Act II scene iii we find Sir Toby and Sir Andrew drunkenly enjoying themselves. Feste, the clown, enters and they get him to sing a love-song for sixpence, after which they comment:

> SIR ANDREW A mellifluous voice, as I am a true knight.
> SIR TOBY A contagious breath.
> SIR ANDREW Very sweet and contagious, i'faith.
>
> (II.iii.52–4)

We have to imagine here how Feste has just sung the song 'O mistress mine': on stage it can be a powerful moment with its message of how 'Youth's a stuff will not endure'. What Sir Andrew and Sir Toby praise about the song, however, is not its message but its delivery, the oral performance by Feste with his mellifluous voice and sweet breath. What is important about the song is not, then, so much its ideas as its medium: as with Cesario in Act I, the emphasis falls upon the persuasive powers of words and sounds, of the voice – it is 'mellifluous', sweet, but also 'contagious', as if dangerously catching like a sickness. To suggest that the voice is both sweet and catching is obviously contradictory: it is a hint, but no more than that, of something powerfully seductive but subversive of social order. But singing is also part of the spirit of fun and revelry that Sir Toby and Sir Andrew stand for, a spirit that is checked when they themselves sing, for their efforts provoke the arrival of Malvolio, the kill-joy, who berates them for their unruly behaviour.

After Malvolio leaves, Maria comes up with her plan to take revenge by planting a letter to fool him into believing Olivia loves him. We'll look at Malvolio's reading of the letter in a minute: it is obviously central to the play's comic effect on stage. First, however, we need to stand back and think how the letter fits into what we have established so far. Why should Malvolio be duped by a letter? At the level of character we can talk about the appeal to his vanity, but the letter also fits in with the hostility Malvolio shows to the singing and joking of Sir Toby's crew. Malvolio, the Puritan, is all too ready to put his faith in the written word while being the enemy of linguistic revelry, to songs and jokes and witty conversation. We noted a similar sort of opposition in the first act between Orsino's account of his love as something serious and his depiction of Cesario as his oral messenger. Underlying the play, then, there seems to be an opposition not just between spoken and written language, but between the sort of seriousness that is attached to written language and the spirit of enjoyment and wit that attaches to oral language.

At this point we have taken our concern with language in *Twelfth Night* as far as we can without crossing over into other approaches involving history and politics. In order to get hold of the conflict in the play, we need to contextualise it in a number of ways so that we can see what really lies behind the debate about language, texts, noise and revelry that is going on in the text. It should be fairly clear by now that Malvolio is not just a kill-joy but a Puritan, a figure of strict discipline and severe moral faith opposed to all entertainment, to all unregulated behaviour. What we can also see in Malvolio is the voice of the Puritan opposition to the theatre which was eventually to triumph in 1642 when the public theatres were closed at the start of the Civil War. For the Puritans the theatre represented not merely a challenge to the moral order of society but a dangerous place of sin, full of idolatrous images where men disguised themselves as women and acted out fantasies of the corrupt imagination. In this sense Malvolio is part of a growing authoritarianism in Elizabethan England, which not only saw the introduction of censorship and licensing of the theatres, but a whole series of measures that restricted people's freedom and choices. There were, for example, the sumptuary laws setting out statutes about what people could wear (sumptuary means the regulating of expense, and the laws therefore limited the amount that could be spent on dress); there were the regular readings in church of the Homilies – sermons – on obedience; there were laws about the eating of fish; Elizabeth's minister Walsingham ran a complex and far-reaching spy system; but just as dangerous from another angle, Elizabeth organised popular festivities around the court calendar, so that celebrations came less and less to be about people letting off steam or enjoying a day off work and more and more about having to celebrate the Queen's accession or a visit by her. Malvolio might be a Puritan, but Elizabeth, as ruler of the country, was also involved in regulating public behaviour.

Malvolio, then, is a site for all these anxieties about the growing restriction as well as regulation of behaviour through the letter of the law. Those anxieties are labelled as a type of Puritanism in the play, but go beyond the simple idea of someone opposed to fun and become a much deeper worry about the way in which the Tudor state was developing. We often assume that as history progresses, so things get better, that life improves for people. But in the case of Elizabethan England there is evidence that, as we approach 1600, the approximate date of *Twelfth Night*, there is a movement towards a much more rigid state apparatus restricting what people could do or say. The clash between Malvolio and the other figures embodies a struggle not just about freedom to enjoy yourself but a struggle about control of those aspects of culture – singing, noise-making, jokes, tricks, puns – where words take on a life outside the letter of the law and indeed threaten to undermine it. This is something, however, we can look at in Malvolio's discovery of the letter in II.v even though this means we are taking another scene from Act II

3   Look at another scene from Act II

In II.v Malvolio picks up the planted letter and sets about trying to make sense of it. The letter is addressed to an 'unknown belov'd'; it contains a four-line poem which ends 'M.O.A.I. doth sway my life'. Malvolio seizes on this riddle and begins to unravel it in his own favour:

> And the end – what should that alphabetical position portend? If I could make that resemble something in me. Softly! M.O.A.I. . . .
> M – Malvolio; M – why, that begins my name.
>
> (II.v.108–11, 115–16)

Malvolio is clearly intent on interpreting the letter in his own interest; he reads into it what he wants to find. This hugely funny moment on stage, however, opens up a number of issues that go well beyond satire on Malvolio's vanity and sense of self-importance. There is, first of all, the way the trick serves to highlight the whole arbitrary nature of meaning and language, but especially how it serves to undermine the idea that written language is somehow more stable or serious or respectable than spoken language. Malvolio finds a text in the garden and makes it mean what he wants it to mean. What, though, makes the trick subversive, and why the revelry of the others is more than just fun, has to do with its anarchic quality. The letter-trick – and some critics still waste their time trying to fill out the initials to make sense – not only attacks the idea of Puritans as being somehow specially gifted in interpreting texts, and in particular the Bible, but clearly hints at the erotic nature of their religious zeal. And, second, and perhaps even more anarchic, the letter trick not only attacks the idea of interpretation but the very notion that meaning somehow lies in the signs we make on paper, that there is a 'meaning' to be had from language, from laws, from letters, from homilies, treatises, religion, texts – indeed, any form of cultural production.

The far-reaching political implications of such a proposition – that meaning is something we read into the texts we make, not something inherent in them – become evident if we think about the sumptuary laws of dress imposed on Elizabethans. Going with such laws were ideas of propriety, but also of gender, of what a woman should wear, what a man should look like. It is no accident that the trick letter instructs Malvolio to dress in yellow stockings and cross-garters, to transgress decorum and put himself on display. The letter subverts both social and legal restraint by exposing the arbitrary nature of conventional sexual codes and how they are constructed to satisfy the desires of those who read and write them. On the surface the letter trick makes a fool of Malvolio and turns him into a theatrical spectacle, a player in a play, but what it also does is deconstruct the logic behind legislation and how it serves to cover over anarchic desires which threaten not simply social behaviour but the artificial rules that formulate sexual roles.

4   *Look at a scene from Act IV*

The anarchy let loose in Act III is pushed on a stage further in Act IV when Malvolio is locked up as if mad. Then, in Act IV scene ii, Feste pretends to be the priest Sir Topas come to dispossess Malvolio of his devils – he has been locked up as if he is a possessed demoniac. The scene is part of the carnival chaos called into being by the revellers, but it also has disturbing echoes of the frequent trials of demoniacs – people possessed by the devil – during the sixteenth and seventeenth centuries. It is, then, no wonder that critics have sometimes felt uneasy about the humour of the scene and about what sort of attitude we are supposed to take towards the tormenting of Malvolio. That tormenting takes the form both of physical confinement but also verbal taunts and tricks designed, it seems, to drive Malvolio mad. At one point in the scene Feste, the main tormentor, plays both himself and Sir Topas, and holds a conversation between Sir Topas and himself discussing Malvolio's condition:

> FESTE Advise you what you say: the minister is here. [*Speaking as Sir Topas*] Malvolio, Malvolio, thy wits the heavens restore! Endeavour thyself to sleep, and leave thy vain bibble-babble.
> MALVOLIO Sir Topas!
> FESTE Maintain no words with him, good fellow. – Who, I, sir? Not I, sir. God buy you, good Sir Topas. – Marry, amen. – I will, sir, I will.
> MALVOLIO Fool, fool, fool, I say!
> FESTE Alas, sir, be patient. What say you, sir? I am shent for speaking to you.
>
> (IV.ii.91–100)

Feste as Sir Topas tells himself not to have any conversation with Malvolio, and then tells Malvolio he has been advised not to talk to him. At once very funny and very cruel, the trick Feste plays on Malvolio is his own piece of revenge against Malvolio for suggesting that Olivia should get rid of Feste because he is past his best. But Feste's trick is a virtuoso demonstration that he is not, that his verbal skills and games are just as powerful as they used to be, stronger even than the letter-trick Maria played on Malvolio.

We can see that Feste's trick is part of the spirit of comedy and carnival that Malvolio opposes, that spirit of playfulness, singing, joking which the Puritan seeks to end. It is as if throughout the play there is a struggle going on about who is to control language and society, the deadly serious Malvolio with his trust in the written word, or those who trick and taunt him with their language games. Indeed, it might be said that the central issues the play deals with do not really concern the main characters; while they are playing their love games, the battle against Malvolio is being fought by those people who have most to lose if he wins and imposes rules and regulations on their lives and words. But the play is not quite as simple as this. The tormenting of Malvolio starts to raise a number of unsettling questions not just about the spirit of comedy with its need for victims but about the way in which the language of carnival and festivity replicates and imitates the language of order. If we stand back from the play a little and think about the tricks played on Malvolio – the letter trick, Feste's role-playing – it is not that we are necessarily asked to feel sorry for Malvolio but rather that it is unclear where the dividing line between comic anarchy and disciplinary punishment is to be drawn. Having set up oppositions between festive liberty and kill-joy regulation, it is as if the play has deconstructed these oppositions and blurred the boundary lines, unsettling our sense of what is comic and what is not, of whether there can be any sort of balance between liberty and order. The world cannot, we recognise, be run along the lines promoted by Sir Toby Belch and his crew; nor can it be conducted through Malvolio's scheme of things, but there seems no language available in the play to resolve the debate between the parties. Nor is it entirely clear what each side stands for by this stage of the play, with Malvolio the image of comedy and Feste the image of punishment.

5   *Look at a scene from Act V*

Despite the complications of Act IV a resolution of sorts is reached in Act V. Here Cesario is revealed to be Viola and is married to Orsino; her brother Sebastian is married to Olivia. At the same time Malvolio is released from his confinement and the trick explained to him:

OLIVIA Alas, Malvolio, this is not my writing,
Though, I confess, much like the character;
But out of question 'tis Maria's hand.
And now I do bethink me, it was she
First told me thou wast mad; then cam'st in smiling,
And in such forms which here were presuppos'd
Upon thee in the letter. Prithee, be content;
This practice hath most shrewdly pass'd upon thee,
But, when we know the grounds and authors of it,
Thou shalt be both the plaintiff and the judge
Of thine own cause.

(v.i.332–42)

Olivia's explanation that Maria forged the letter that deceived Malvolio and then told Olivia that Malvolio had gone mad picks up the two images of language that have been at odds throughout the play, the written and the spoken. But what Olivia's speech confirms is that neither of these forms is reliable or trustworthy; just as Feste can imitate Sir Topas in speech, so Maria can imitate Olivia's writing character. The play, then, does not simply endorse the oral world of comedy over the rigid letter of the law, but instead offers us a perspective which reveals them both to be deceptive. To that extent neither of them can offer us any assurance about how social order can be maintained or changed: for a moment the play hints at the idea that social and political ordering may be nothing more than an elaborate fiction, a convenient forgery or trick designed to give us a sense that there is something solid behind the world of words we live in and through.

This might seem an uncomfortable ending for a comedy, and indeed there is something unnerving about the end of the play. Malvolio, when he discovers the author of the trick as Feste, leaves the stage, pledging to be revenged on the whole company. It is a threat that was to be executed in 1642 when the Puritans were able to silence the revelry of the theatres and put an end to its tricks and disguises. That ending of the theatres is perhaps implicit in the sense we get throughout the play of an irreconcilable gap between the letter of the law and the spirit of comedy, but more darkly it is there in that blurring of boundaries at moments in the play when we are unsure where we stand or what is comic any more.

The reading we have constructed of *Twelfth Night* has deliberately moved beyond just looking at language and deliberately moved beyond just seeing the play in terms of a simple opposition between speech and writing, revelry and regulation. What, as we said at the beginning, we have tried to do is draw out the implications of the debate about language in the play, and how it ties up with larger political and social issues. This is not to undervalue the exuberance of the play's speeches, its songs, energy, wit, humour, fun, irony, all those things that language gives us in the theatre. It is rather to give those things a point, a relevance: plays are only powerful politically because they are attractive and lively and engaging. But in analysing plays we also have to pay attention to their implications concerning how we use language to think about the world and construct it.

9

Feminist criticism

IN chapter 7 we stressed the important part feminism has played in changing thinking about society and how feminist criticism has had a major impact on literary criticism. We now want to fill out the picture with illustrations of how feminist criticism enables us to look at two of Shakespeare's plays in a new light. In the case of one of those plays, *Romeo and Juliet*, what we will see is how it amounts to much more than an enticing love story, which is how most people tend to view it. In the case of *Much Ado About Nothing*, we should see how a Shakespeare comedy can be read in a way that uncovers some surprising dimensions.

Feminist criticism starts from one principal point, that is a recognition of the patriarchal structure of society, a recognition of how the world is organised by men to the advantage of men. Following on from this point and no less central to feminist criticism is a commitment to change women's position in society by challenging that male rule and the ways in which women are represented in all texts, be those texts Shakespeare's plays, films, judges' statements, advertising slogans or anything else that purports to speak on behalf of or about women. In that challenge feminist criticism not only goes on to question the way in which we construct gender and sexuality, but to question the relationship between gender and language and the whole social set-up. As the main figure of English literature, Shakespeare occupies a significant position in that set-up. He is taught in all schools, politicians quote from Shakespeare, he is felt to stand for something, for certain ideas and values. In these ways he has become a figure who has acquired a powerful cultural and even political significance. What feminists are interested in examining, and analysing, is how we think about and respond to this powerful image.

Having said that, it must be added that feminist criticism now includes a very wide variety of critical approaches so it is probably much more accurate to speak not of feminist criticism but instead of feminist criticisms in the plural. For instance, many feminists are particularly interested in the work of the French psychoanalyst Jacques Lacan and his theories about desire and the human subject. This interest in Lacan has to do with the way in which the conventional stereotyping of women has sought to suppress notions of female sexual desire. Linked in here also are questions of male anxiety about controlling women. These are issues we touch on below, as we also touch on questions of male bonding and female friendship. The main gist of our analysis, however, will be a focus on patriarchy, on male rule, and on the politics of the family and marriage.

Romeo and Juliet

1 *Look at a scene from Act I*

As usual, we can start with a summary of the play. The play begins with a brawl between the servants of two warring families, the Montagues and the Capulets. Romeo, the heir of the Montagues, is in love with Rosaline and goes uninvited to see her at a party at the Capulets. The Capulets have granted the Count Paris permission to woo their daughter Juliet, but she and Romeo fall in love at first sight and marry secretly. Meanwhile, Tybalt, a kinsman of Juliet's, has challenged Romeo to fight; in the event Romeo kills Tybalt and is banished. The news renders Juliet distraught; Romeo visits her and while they are in her bedroom consummating their marriage her parents are busy making arrangements to marry her to Paris in the hope it will ease her supposed grief for Tybalt. Juliet seeks help from Friar Lawrence who gives her a potion which will bring on a fake death. The intention is that Romeo will return from Matua and release her from the family vault after her funeral. Juliet takes the potion and is buried by her grieving family. Romeo, however, never gets the Friar's letter about the potion plot and believes Juliet is indeed dead. As he breaks into the vault to die with her he is challenged by Paris whom he kills. He then poisons himself. Juliet wakes and, finding Romeo's body, stabs herself. The families, roused by the watch, are told of the tragic story by Friar Lawrence.

One thing worth pointing out is how even a summary as bland as this has a considerable effect on how we think about the play. If you

look at the summary you should be able to make sense of it in terms of
the order/disorder idea we began with – how the brawling of the
family servants, for example, disrupts the social order of Verona and
how the love of Romeo and Juliet suggests to us that life is always more
complicated than the patterns we impose on it. But the summary itself
does little to highlight the issues we are interested in in this analysis –
how women are represented in the text, the question of patriarchy, the
politics of the family and marriage. What, then, our analysis has to do
is begin to highlight these issues so as to shift our understanding of the
text. As ever, the best way to do this is by looking at the text itself. We
decided to start with the conversation between Lady Capulet, the
Nurse and Juliet in Act I scene iii where Juliet is told to fall in love with
Count Paris since she is now old enough to be married:

> LADY CAPULET   Tell me, daughter Juliet,
>   How stands you dispositions to be married?
> JULIET It is an honour that I dream not of.
> NURSE An honour! Were not I thine only nurse,
>   I would say thou hadst suck'd wisdom from thy teat.
> LADY CAPULET Well, think of marriage now.
>   Younger than you,
>   Here in Verona, ladies of esteem,
>   Are made already mothers. By my count,
>   I was your mother much upon these years
>   That you are now a maid. Thus, then, in brief:
>   The valiant Paris seeks you for his love.
> NURSE A man, young lady! lady, such a man
>   As all the world – why, he's a man of wax.
> LADY CAPULET Verona's summer hath not such a flower.
> NURSE Nay, he's a flower; in faith, a very flower.
> LADY CAPULET What say you? Can you love the gentleman?
>   This night you shall behold him at our feast;
>   Read o'er the volume of young Paris' face
>   And find delight writ there with beauty's pen;
>   Examine every married lineament,
>   And see how one another lends content.
>
>   (I.iii.65–85)

We can start with a number of points. The scene is important for our
analysis precisely because it focuses on three female figures: mother,
daughter, nurse. Already certain stereotyped ideas can be spotted in the
way this group might be said to constitute the play's representation of
women and their roles in society: women are limited to being mothers,

daughters, or servants. It will be worth seeing to what extent this pattern is challenged by the text later on, but initially it looks like we are being offered a view of women which constructs them around certain roles, all of which serve the needs of men: the women do not exist in their own right but only in relation to the head of the Capulet household.

The dialogue in the scene is clearly about marriage and love, rather than choice and freedom. The intended marriage with Paris is obviously a matter of what Juliet's parents wish to arrange rather than a matter of affection or love. Juliet is being prompted or schooled by her mother into accepting Paris: she tells her that other girls of her age are already mothers, that she herself was married by Juliet's age, and that if she looks carefully at Paris she will see he is eminently made for marriage. The imagery of reading reinforces the point about Juliet being taught how to look at the 'valiant' Paris: she is being instructed how to read Paris. What is striking is the extent to which Paris and therefore men more generally are elevated by Lady Capulet's discourse; he is praised as valiant, his beauty is emphasised as well as his manliness. And yet we might hesitate at this point and wonder what, indeed, the text is up to. The Nurse's interjections seem to undercut Paris and make him sound a little absurd; Lady Capulet's praise seems highly artificial and bookish, as if she herself has learnt it or been taught it. How are we, then, to react to what they say?

There is, though, another issue here that we need to confront. It is, in fact, fairly easy to see that Lady Capulet, by trying to talk Juliet into an arranged marriage, is carrying out the work of patriarchy. She is persuading her daughter that marriage is the best thing for her and that she would do well to follow in her mother's footsteps. Built into this advice is the view that Paris and men generally are to be revered. Lady Capulet is very much the subdued wife figure and so we could read this scene as an example of the way patriarchy uses women and indeed language to promote and further itself, specifically through marriage and all its associated roles for women. That is one way of reading the scene. The complication arises, however, when we start to consider the effect of the scene. How do we feel about Lady Capulet's advice? What sort of response do we have to the rather silent figure of Juliet? Does the scene, in other words, endorse patriarchy or are we invited to take a critical view of what is happening? Where do our sympathies lie?

The question is important because it bears upon the whole issue of whether Shakespeare's plays simply replicate the patriarchal values of their times or whether they are more radical and challenging than this view suggests. Some feminists see Shakespeare as the patriarchal bard, a writer who merely reproduces the conservative ideology of his times in which women were for the most part regarded either as depraved or innocent and merely chattels to be exchanged between men. It is a view which sees Shakespeare's plays as part of the political oppression of women carried out by society. The alternative view to this is that which, while accepting that the plays do represent women in limited terms, argues that the plays do not endorse patriarchy but instead often take the woman's side; that we, as an audience, are encouraged to take sides and led to see the wrongs of patriarchy, wrongs which lead to death and tragedy for women.

This is an issue you will have to make up your own mind about. What we have attempted to do is to outline the debate between feminists about the texts and their political significance for women. Our position is that the plays are not, as it were, just mirrors depicting the worst of patriarchy without saying any more, but that they are radical texts that encourage us to reject patriarchy, or certainly its most obvious wrongs. In the scene above the audience is surely asked to sympathise with Juliet and to see that her mother is herself a victim of the system of arranged marriages. In order to support this proposition, however, we need to look at some other scenes.

2   Look at a scene from Act II

After the party at the Capulet's Romeo climbs into the orchard to see Juliet again. She comes to a window and they confess their love to one another. It is, however, Juliet who voices her love first, and it is she who makes the running in the scene. At one point she tells Romeo that it is only because it is night that she dare speak:

> Thou knowest the mask of night is on my face,
> Else would a maiden blush bepaint my cheek
> For that which thou hast heard me speak to-night.
> Fain would I dwell on form, fain, fain deny
> What I have spoke; but farewell compliment!
> Dost thou love me? I know thou wilt say ay,
> And I will take thy word; yet, if thou swear'st,
> Thou mayst prove false; at lovers' perjuries
> They say Jove laughs. O gentle Romeo,

If thou dost love, pronounce it faithfully,
Or, if thou think'st I am too quickly won,
I'll frown, and be perverse, and say thee nay,
So thou wilt woo; but else, not for the world.
In faith, fair Montague, I am too fond;
And therefore thou mayst think my haviour light,
But trust me, gentleman, I'll prove more true
Than those that have more cunning to be strange.

(II.ii.85–101)

Once again this seems a speech calculated to generate sympathy for Juliet's dilemma as she confesses her love and then worries about what Romeo will think. How do women utter their sexual desire in a society that expects them to blush like maidens all the time? The speech itself runs backwards and forwards between, on the one hand, Juliet's wish to convince Romeo of her love and her awareness of social constraint and form. In the fourth line she says she would like to dwell on form, she would like to stay within the bounds of conventional behaviour and deny her own words since that would convince him she is after all a proper maiden of honest integrity. At the same time she is aware of how fickle men's oaths are, so this adds to her dilemma. Then the speech turns again to the problem of how to convince him she is not 'light', that she is not lascivious and promiscuous just because she dare voice her love for him. What marks the speech, then, is how Juliet's desire is entangled in social form, in all the codes, values and ideas of society which pre-judges it as unmaidenly. All through the speech we see Juliet resisting the conventions which prevent her from articulating desire without guilt. We might add that this is not a problem the male characters have: Romeo begins the play in love with Rosaline, but then falls in love with Juliet. There is no question of him having to debate with his conscience either about his change of love or his sexual urges.

What we may also notice about the speech is how it constructs Romeo. There is first of all her distrust of him, that he will too readily swear he loves her. The audience may well agree at this moment since we have seen Romeo drop Rosaline and change to Juliet. Of course, his life is in danger at this point so we do get the sense of a mutual desire. But we also have to remember how much danger Juliet is in both from her family and from social opprobrium. Her youth is all part of this: in the first scene we looked at, her young age is stressed so that we have the sense of someone struggling, not only with first love but also with a society that she has just begun to resist. This comes through in the curious way she identifies Romeo with a number of names. He is identified as both Romeo and Montague and as a gentleman, as if Juliet is seeking to undo his links with the Montague family, or even with patriarchy itself. Earlier in the scene she asks Romeo to 'deny thy father', to deny, as it were, the bonds and limits and politics of the male institution.

What we gain in this scene, then, is a complex sense of Juliet resisting patriarchy but at the same time a sense of how the very forms and rules of society, including its rules about how women should behave and speak, prevent her from uttering her desire without guilt. It is Juliet's resistance to these rules that marks her out as heroic.

3 Look at a scene from Act III

At the start of Act III scene v Romeo and Juliet part after consummating their marriage. Almost immediately her mother enters to tell her she must marry Paris the following Thursday. Juliet refuses, giving as her reason that it is too soon after Tybalt's death. Then her father enters and explodes into violent anger at her excuse:

> . . . fettle your fine joints 'gainst Thursday next,
> To go with Paris to Saint Peter's Church,
> Or I will drag thee on a hurdle thither.
> Out, you green-sickness carrion! Out, you baggage!
> You tallow-face!
> LADY CAPULET Fie, fie! what, are you mad?
> JULIET Good father, I beseech you on my knees,
> Hear me with patience but to speak a word.
> CAPULET Hang thee, young baggage! disobedient wretch!
> I tell thee what – get thee to church a Thursday
> Or never after look me in the face.
> Speak not, reply not, do not answer me.
> My fingers itch. Wife, we scarce thought us blest
> That God had lent us but this only child.
> But now I see this one is one too much,
> And that we have a curse in having her.
> Out on her, hilding!
> NURSE   God in heaven bless her.
> You are to blame, my lord, to rate her so.
> CAPULET And why, my Lady Wisdom? hold your tongue,
> Good Prudence; smatter with your gossips, go.
>
> (III.v.153–71)

Capulet's speech leaves us with little room to doubt which side to take in the play. His violent anger and abuse of Juliet are vile – she is called names, humiliated, threatened, silenced, ignored, indeed, there is a whole series of verbal assaults used by Capulet in his bullying tirade. This is not, however, simply a matter of personal disappointment on Capulet's part. Instead, what the scene adds up to is a representation of the viciousness of patriarchy. With God-like power and gesture Capulet refuses to listen to the kneeling Juliet; similarly he silences the Nurse and ignores his wife's comment. What he requires, and what patriarchy requires, is absolute obedience built on passive silence and acceptance. Resistance is to be crushed in the most extreme fashion, particularly in the area of sexual conduct and marriage, for it is through marriage that patriarchy is able to maintain its grip on society. There is to Capulet's speech a violence so extreme, however, that it begins to suggest not control so much as insecurity at the possibility of rebellion, a rebellion which is associated, through the reference to a curse, with the idea of Eve's rebellion in Paradise.

The religious images Capulet uses, then, are one way in which he seeks to legitimate his authority: he associates himself with God, Juliet with Eve. His threat to turn his face away from her is equivalent to God's banishment of Eve from the garden, but we should not forget the terrifying social consequences withdrawal of Capulet's favour would have had in the sixteenth century for a young girl. The alternative to the family structure was poverty and begging. It is possible that some of Capulet's threats have perhaps lost some of their implications for us, but it is difficult to ignore the way in which patriarchy here is associated both with verbal violence and also physical threat: he speaks of dragging Juliet and of how his fingers itch, how he itches to get his hands on her. Interestingly Lady Capulet calls his behaviour mad, so prompting the audience to see its irrationality and undermining the attempt to establish its authority. There is, too, in the scene, just a hint of resistance in the three women, something which itself inflames Capulet further as he turns his anger on the Nurse. The purpose of that anger is to push the Nurse back into the stereotype of the gossip, a babbler who lacks wisdom and position in society.

Patriarchy in the play thus takes a number of forms. In its most literal sense it is embodied in the figure of Capulet, the violent male father. Spreading out from that we can argue it is figured in the violent feuding between the two families, the Capulets and the Montagues, but as we have seen in II.iii, patriarchy also runs through the discourse of the play, seeking to control and order women in all aspects of their lives. At the same time, the play does seem positively to ask the audience to recognise the evils of patriarchy and its destructiveness of women, a point we can take further in the next extract.

Before we move on, however, it may be worth exploring for a moment some of the tensions that lie behind patriarchy. One of the areas feminist criticism has been most interested in is psychoanalysis, and in particular the whole question of male fear and anxiety about women. Control of woman is necessary, it seems, because of the threat female sexuality poses not just to the social system – you cannot maintain primogeniture, the system of male inheritance, if you cannot guarantee who is the father of the child – but to manliness, to male notions of sexual identity. There is, in *Romeo and Juliet*, a great deal of macho display, of phallic manliness exhibited in public in the brawls and in the sword fights. Feminist critics have not been slow to identify this element in Shakespeare, the way in which males assert their manliness in public, and how that assertion is haunted by the fear of betrayal, that women will be unfaithful or disobedient. It is a fear, it is suggested, prompted by the physical difference between men and women, that men fear women's lack of a phallus and are exercised by the implicit threat of castration. This, it has to be said, is to simplify greatly what is a very complex debate. But even in this simplified form it should be evident that the analysis of patriarchal society by feminist criticism has profound implications for how we think about the human subject, gender and for the relationships we construct.

4   Look at a scene from Act IV

In IV.iii Juliet swallows the potion Friar Lawrence has given her to bring on a fake death. But before she drinks it she hesitates, tormented by doubts and misgivings about what will happen:

> What if it be a poison which the friar
> Subtly hath minist'red to have me dead,
> Lest in this marriage he should be dishonour'd,
> Because he married me before to Romeo?
> I fear it is; and yet methinks it should not,
> For he hath still been tried a holy man.
> How if, when I am laid into the tomb,
> I wake before the time that Romeo

Come to redeem me? There's a fearful point.
Shall I not then be stifled in the vault,
To whose foul mouth no healthsome air breathes in,
And there die strangled ere my Romeo comes?
(IV.iii.24–35)

In the speech Juliet begins to imagine what will happen to her if Romeo does not come: how she may die for want of air, or how, later in the speech, she might dash out her brains with a bone in her panic. It is a picture of horror, but a picture in which Juliet finds herself dependent on men she does not appear to trust. There is the Friar who may be out to poison her; there is Romeo who may not come, and (later) there is Tybalt whose bones may help her brain herself. Running through the speech is an association of men with death, with actions that will end Juliet's life because of her love for Romeo. It is a complex speech because as well as registering Juliet's terror at the thought of being buried alive, it also suggests the link between male love and death, how men's love for women leads to or desires their death. The juxtaposition of love and death throughout the play reinforces this association and highlights a further aspect of patriarchy. It would seem that patriarchy is tragic for women because they have to die.

At the same time we might notice in this speech how Juliet refers to Romeo as coming to 'redeem' her, like the figure of Christ raising the dead from hell. Once again this positions Romeo as spectacularly above Juliet in the hierarchy, as if he were some super-being. Her fear, therefore, mingles with her love for him so that we get a sense of her toiling in the contradictions of the male world she inhabits. There is, too, something bizarre about the plot of the play at this point: it is as if Juliet is required to die not just to escape her family but because she has challenged the whole structure by marrying Romeo. Like the Duchess of Malfi in Webster's play of that title, she seems to be destined to die not for reasons of fate or character but because of the culture that shapes her life and death.

5   *Look at a scene from Act V*

Juliet does not die as a result of the Friar's potion. She dies instead at her own hand in Act V after she discovers Romeo has died. There is an important difference between the two deaths, for while he dies deluded believing her to be dead, Juliet dies knowing the truth. This once again puts her in a heroic light and helps reinforce the audience's critical and political position: there is no mystery to her death, it is the result of certain social factors and the way in which society is constructed.

There is, though, something very odd about the last scene beyond this. Juliet is in the family vault. Paris comes bringing flowers; when he hears Romeo coming he hides and watches as the latter, with a crowbar, forces open the vault. He then challenges Romeo and is killed in the duel. Romeo then places him in the tomb: also present is the body of Tybalt. Finally, Romeo poisons himself. It is a macabre spectacle, and we cannot help but notice the pile of male bodies now surrounding Juliet that have fought over her and for her. Each in his different way has entangled her in the world of male violence and feud. Of course, Romeo loves her, but so, it seems, does Paris. The spectacle in the tomb serves to widen the play away from a simple love story that goes wrong to a series of questions about the way love functions in a society ruled by men who struggle for possession of a woman as well as a series of questions about how women can act to achieve their desires in a patriarchal culture that prohibits them from voicing their feelings or following their desires.

Romeo and Juliet is often seen as an early Shakespeare play celebrating romantic love that goes wrong. What we have tried to demonstrate is how a feminist approach can re-read the play to suggest that things don't just go wrong for no apparent reason. Nor does the play merely tell a story: rather, it offers a radical critique of patriarchy and the language and values that shape it, in particular male violence and the silencing of woman. Your reading will inevitably be different from ours, and you will choose different scenes and different aspects, but central to a feminist reading of the play will be a concern with how the structure and politics of society affect women. In terms of the play itself, that will involve looking not just at the action, but at the language of the text and how subject positions are defined as well as looking at the sort of resistance to patriarchy that is glimpsed.

Much Ado About Nothing

1 *Look at a scene from Act I*

Our analysis of *Much Ado About Nothing* once again looks at the play from a feminist perspective. We start with a review of the summary of the play we offered in chapter 4. *Much Ado* is a comedy. It begins with the happy return from war of Don Pedro and his retinue, who are to be entertained at Leonato's house. Claudio falls in love with Hero, Leonato's daughter, and gets Don Pedro to woo her for him. Don John, the villain of the play, hates Claudio and plots to wreck his marriage to Hero: he contrives to make Claudio think she is unfaithful. In the meantime the other characters contrive to make Beatrice and Benedick, who seem to despise each other and who spend their time trading insults, fall in love. Claudio, deceived by Don John, rejects Hero at their marriage service. She faints and her family pretend she is dead. Angered by this treatment of Hero, Beatrice demands Benedick kill Claudio. Don John's trickery comes to light, however, through the bungling incompetence of Dogberry and Verges, and Claudio and Hero marry, as do Beatrice and Benedick. Don John flees, but is apprehended.

You may notice how, as in *Romeo and Juliet*, the plot turns around marriage and the death of woman. Hero, of course, does not actually die, but nevertheless her fake death is sufficiently similar to that of Juliet's to suggest that the two plays share a common set of ideas and values. It is precisely this sharing of ideas and beliefs and values that the term ideology implies: how texts both explicitly and implicitly foster the dominant view and support the status quo. In the case of Shakespeare's plays, the status quo is male rule furthered by marriage. However, as we saw in *Romeo and Juliet*, that rule is interrogated by the resistance in the play of women and also by the way the play asks the audience to think about what they are seeing and to take sides. As we noted in our earlier discussion of *Much Ado*, while the play on stage seems very light, it has some dark edges which may lead us to question that surface lightness. We do not mean by this that we should try to turn *Much Ado* into *Romeo and Juliet*; rather, what we have to recognise is that it is precisely because comedies work so well on stage, sustaining a mood that all is well and that everything ends in harmony, that they are such powerful promoters of ideology. In turn this means it can seem all the more difficult to produce a political reading – and all feminist readings are political – since it seems to cut across the sense of the comedies as comic. In part this explains the notion of reading against the grain which modern theorists often talk about, reading the play, that is, against its conventional interpretation or presentation on stage. One of the exciting things about the new critical approaches, however, is that they can liberate new ideas so that we start to rethink some of our preconceptions about what a comedy might be or how it might work on stage. There is no reason why an audience should not laugh at a play yet also be challenged to reconsider the comic assumptions in the play – that marriage is a force for social harmony, that women can only be defined by their relationships to men, that there is anything 'natural' or inevitable above love between the sexes.

Some of that rethinking might well begin in *Much Ado* with the following exchange where Claudio is asking the Prince, Don Pedro, to woo Hero for him:

> CLAUDIO My liege, your Highness now may do me good.
> DON PEDRO My love is thine to teach; teach it but how,
>   And thou shalt see how apt it is to learn
>   Any hard lesson that may do thee good.
> CLAUDIO Hath Leonato any son, my lord?
> DON PEDRO No child but Hero; she's his only heir.
>   Dost thou affect her, Claudio?
> CLAUDIO O, my lord,
>   When you went onward on this ended action,
>   I look'd upon her with a soldier's eye,
>   That lik'd but had a rougher task in hand
>   Than to drive liking to the name of love;
>   But now I am return'd, and that war-thoughts
>   Have left their places vacant, in their rooms
>   Come thronging soft and delicate desires,
>   All prompting me how fair young Hero is,
>   Saying I lik'd her ere I went to wars.
> DON PEDRO Thou wilt be like a lover presently,
>   And tire the hearer with a book of words.
>   If thou dost love fair Hero, cherish it;
>   And I will break with her, and with her father,
>   And thou shalt have her. Was't not to this end
>   That thou began'st to twist so fine a story?
>
>   (I.i.252–73)

There is something more than a little offensive in the way that Claudio goes about asking the Prince to do him a favour. It's not just that he wants the Prince to woo Hero for him so that neither she nor Leonato can really refuse, but that he begins by making sure that Hero is her father's only heir. Claudio knows as well as the Princes that she would not inherit if Leonato had a son – male rule ensures that primogeniture operates to exclude women from economic independence. Throughout the exchange between the two figures on stage we also get a sense of how Hero is only defined in relation to men, especially her father, as if she had no existence outside those relationships. In the exchange we notice how she is simply described as 'fair'. It is an adjective that is used of her again in the scene which serves both to idealise her but also to construct her in the simplest of terms – beautiful and virtuous.

Complicating the exchange, however, is Claudio's relationship to the Prince. Don Pedro is to secure Hero for Claudio, but by so doing will bind Claudio to him. Paradoxically, the arranged marriage will result, it seems, in an even closer link between the Prince and Claudio – the Prince speaks of how willing his love is to learn to obey Claudio. The exchange, then, is not just about an arranged marriage in which Hero is to be won for Claudio, it is also about the sort of male bonding that exists between Claudio and the Prince, men who have returned from fighting together and who now go wooing together. Once we begin to see this sort of complication in the play, then we start to see why there is a nervousness about some of the scenes involving Beatrice and Benedick, with their witty challenges to the dominant social order.

2   Look at a scene from Act II

The kind of challenge posed by Beatrice in particular is evident in the following dialogue between her and Leonata – it is from the beginning of Act II where the conversation has turned to husbands:

> BEATRICE . . . Lord! I could not endure a husband with a beard on his face; I had rather lie in the woollen.
> LEONATO You may light on a husband that hath no beard.
> BEATRICE What should I do with him? Dress him in my apparel, and make him my waiting gentlewoman? He that hath a beard is more than a youth, and he that hath no beard is less than a man; and he that is more than a youth is not for me, and he that is less than a man I am not for him.
>
> (II.i.24–33)

Beatrice here wittily plays with the two categories of youth and man to suggest that both are inadequate and no match for her intelligence. To this extent she is a social renegade, but her suggestion that she might dress an unbearded youth in her clothes and turn him into a gentlewoman makes her into a sexual rebel who threatens the gender distinctions that keep men in control. Patriarchy needs to emphasise gender differences in order to justify the inequalities of society: Beatrice's joke

undermines those differences and so begins to question why, for
example, Leonato is in charge of the household when he is clearly less
competent than Beatrice. At the same time her playfulness signals her
refusal to take seriously one of the conventional signs of male virility
and manliness – a beard – which is also a refusal to see the world in
conventional terms. Those conventional terms are misogynistic, and it
is misogyny that Beatrice stands out against as she battles verbally with
Leonato.

The weapon Leonato uses in this war of words is a sexual joke
about 'lighting' on a man – that is, going to bed with a man. Jokes are
important to a feminist analysis because they are so often aimed at
women. Just above this extract Leonato calls Beatrice 'curst', that is a
shrew. It is another attempt, like the jokes, to reduce her to a stereotype: she is either the light woman or the shrew who will drive men
away. Beatrice's retort is that she does not need men in her conversation or life, and it is this which is the challenge of her speech. It is very
often assumed that Beatrice is secretly in love with Benedick or that
they have had an affair in the past, but there is a way of reading Beatrice's speech where we do not have to invest in that sort of history for
her; instead, we can see her as a woman who wishes to lead her own
life without conforming to the expectations of society about marriage or
about how she should talk. It is that independence which in the final
analysis is the most serious threat she offers to society and helps explain
why the Prince and the others plot to make her fall in love with Benedick.

3   Look at a scene from Act III

At the start of Act III Hero and Margaret deliberately allow themselves
to be overheard by Beatrice as they talk about Benedick's supposed
love for her. Beatrice believes them and, at the end of the scene, delivers a short speech pledging herself to Benedick:

> What fire is in mine ears? Can this be true?
> Stand I condemn'd for pride and scorn so much?
> Contempt, farewell! and maiden pride, adieu!
> No glory lives behind the back of such.
> And, Benedick, love on; I will requite thee,
> Taming my wild heart to thy loving hand;
> If thou dost love me, my kindness shall incite thee

To bind our loves in a holy band;
For others say thou dost deserve, and I
Believe it better than reportingly.

(III.i.107–16)

There are two points to be made here. First, the effect of the trick on Beatrice is to bring her into line with the dominant social order and position her in its gender divisions. The social outsider is brought inside and we see this in her language: she is now to abandon her 'maiden pride' – her pride as a woman which has been seen as shrewish behaviour – and to tame her wild heart to Benedick's hand. The image here is that of the wild animal or of the bird obedient to the falconer's control, so that what Beatrice is accepting is not just love but an inferior position in the hierarchy: she is tamed, repentant. Of course, we may want to argue that Beatrice is still in control here insofar as she makes the decision to marry Benedick, but that cannot disguise what has happened, the way the trick has turned Beatrice into a different kind of person, one subject to the bonds of marriage. While we may feel she has more choice than Hero whose marriage is arranged, a moment's reflection might lead us to see that Beatrice's match is no less arranged by patriarchy – significantly, it is Don Pedro who in II.i instigates the love plot against Benedick and who undertakes to teach Hero how to deceive Beatrice.

The second point to note about the above extract concerns Hero herself. Even as she is being used by patriarchy to plot against Beatrice, she is being plotted against by Don John for supposedly betraying Claudio. Hero, by duping Beatrice, is doing the work of patriarchy in overcoming the social and sexual renegade; paradoxically, at the same time, Hero's very passivity makes her the target of male anxiety and fear of being betrayed or cuckolded by the sexually loose woman. In order to see the significance of the trick on Beatrice, then, we have to combine it with the accusation against Hero and see how together they make up the double-bind of patriarchy: that women are dangerous when they are disobedient, but they are no less feared when they conform. In both cases women are being read from a male point of view which constructs them either as dangerous shrews or as sexually compliant. It is this kind of thinking that lies behind the plot against Hero in which she is made to appear as a whore. That plot only works, however, because the other male figures in the play already share Don John's values and assumptions: like him they believe all women are deceivers and sexually active with other men despite their appearance. This becomes plain in the play's central episode, the rejection of Hero by Claudio in the marriage scene.

4   Look at a scene from Act IV

The marriage scene in which Claudio accuses Hero of sleeping with another man the night before her wedding occupies the whole of Act IV and is made up of a series of powerful moments, including the actual rejection, Hero's swoon and her father's ready acceptance of her guilt and his terrifying cry, 'let her die' (IV.i.154), and, then, at the end of the scene, Beatrice's defence of her cousin. The rejection itself occurs almost immediately the marriage service starts:

> CLAUDIO Stand thee by, friar. Father, by your leave:
>   Will you with free and unconstrained soul
>   Give me this maid, your daughter?
> LEONATO As freely, son, as God did give her me.
> CLAUDIO And what have I to give you back those worth
>   May counterpoise this rich and precious gift?
> DON PEDRO Nothing. unless you render her again.
> CLAUDIO Sweet Prince, you learn me noble thankfulness.
>   There, Leonato, take her back again;
>   Give not this rotten orange to your friend;
>   She's but the sign and semblance of her honour.
>   Behold how like a maid she blushes here.
>   O, what authority and show of truth
>   Can cunning sin cover itself withal!
>
> (IV.i.22–35)

What we have not stressed so far, but needs emphasising here, is, first, Hero's innocence, and second, the effect of the play on the audience. The slander Don John has devised against Hero clearly convinces the males who surround her on stage, but more and more the audience finds itself not simply sympathising with Hero but outraged by the brutal dialogue. Claudio's comparison of Hero to a rotten orange degrades and humiliates her; it is the bitter side of his earlier idealisation of her as 'fair', suggesting at once something that has been handled and also that is morally and physically corrupt. Such extreme language leaves the audience in no doubt about the shallowness of patriarchy and its readiness to lash out if its power is challenged. Notice how the whole dialogue here is contained between the three men, the Prince, the father, and the husband-to-be. It is conducted as an exchange of goods in which what matters is the trust and bonding between the three men. Hero herself is not addressed so much as read: she is a sign to be interpreted by the men, who read her, indeed, in terms of simple binary oppositions. Either she is a maiden, the sign of honour, or a whore, the very emblem of sin, an Eve who tempts mankind to eat of her fruit. As in *Romeo and Juliet*, then, at the moment of crisis in the text we see how patriarchy to justify itself turns to the pattern of the fall in the garden of Eden and associates women with Eve, and men with Adam and God.

What we can also see here, however, is how, in this crisis, the text deconstructs the marriage service. Beneath the ritual and ceremony lies an exchange between men of a woman who serves as a token to bind men together in an honourable pact. What is so odd about the scene above is the way Claudio and Leonato address each other as father and son, and then the sycophantic words of Claudio to the Prince. On one level Hero is not needed in this male relationship: Leonato is not upset by what Claudio says, and Claudio does not see Hero's apparent crime as anything to do with her father. It is, therefore, no surprise that Leonato accepts what Claudio says and wishes Hero would die when she faints, an act he sees as a sign of her guilt rather than her innocence. This reversal of meaning is perhaps the most terrifying aspect of patriarchy: that which it judges one moment to be ideal, the next becomes evil; one moment it is innocent, the next guilty.

A noticeable feature of the action is the powerlessness of the other figures to intervene. The Friar does not come forward with his plan to pretend Hero is dead until the damage has been done. Beatrice tries valiantly to defend her cousin, but Leonato won't listen. At the end of the scene, however, Beatrice takes further action to help Hero by asking Benedick to kill Claudio. This might seem a weak gesture on Beatrice's part, that she has to turn to a man to help her, but this would be to misread the scene. Beatrice refuses to accept the valuation of Hero as a whore, instead affirming she is slandered. But power and authority in the play lie with Don Pedro, and ultimately, as the talk of war at the start of the play reminds us, it lies with violence. There is nothing Beatrice can do in such a system: she cannot fight, as she says, so gets a man to do it for her. In the end she is enclosed in the system, but it would be misleading if the play were to show her winning and somehow defeating violent patriarchy when she cannot. What the play does show, however, is something very unsettling – the second marriage of Claudio and Hero.

5   Look at a scene from Act V

After Don John's plot has been exposed, Claudio agrees that as part of his penance he will marry the daughter of Antonio, Leonato's brother. The marriage takes place in the final scene, with Hero playing the part of Antonio's daughter, though she does not reveal her face until after the service:

> CLAUDIO Which is the lady I must seize upon?
> ANTONIO This same is she, and I do give you her.
> CLAUDIO Why, then she's mine. Sweet, let me see your face.
> LEONATO No, that you shall not, till you take her hand
>   Before this friar, and swear to marry her.
> CLAUDIO Give me your hand; before this holy friar
>   I am your husband, if you like of me.
> HERO And when I liv'd I was your other wife; (*Unmasking*)
>   And when you lov'd you were my other husband.
> CLAUDIO Another Hero!
> HERO Nothing certainer.
>   One Hero died defil'd; but I do live
>   And, surely as I live, I am a maid.
>
> (v.iv.53–64)

Comedies end in marriage, the apparent marker of social order and harmony, but they do not end unproblematically. The second marriage of Hero and Claudio, far from establishing any new equality or new understanding, reiterates the terms of the first marriage: Claudio 'seizes', that is takes possession of Hero; she is still given away in an exchange between men, but what is extraordinary in her statement that she has died and is now another Hero, a duplicate but not the same person. In a sense the original Hero has died, taking upon her the sins attributed to her, whereas the new Hero speaks of herself as being a maid. What is curious about the scene, then, is that it is as if the first Hero has indeed been found guilty of having sex with a man outside marriage, and Claudio been put in the right. Far from establishing harmony and reconciliation, this second marriage may well leave the audience feeling nothing has been settled or solved. The action on stage may move towards its conclusion and the punishment of Don

John, but what the audience has seen is a more uncomfortable analysis of patriarchy and marriage than traditional criticism usually admits. For traditional criticism the play is more often than not regarded as a play about correct ways of seeing, about truth and deception; reading the play from a feminist perspective shifts its significance away from these surface features of the plot towards those problematic areas in the text which threaten to turn it into a different kind of play, one where the audience is asked to think about the wrongs of a society ruled by men, one where, as in *Romeo and Juliet*, death and desire seem entangled in one another.

Our analysis of *Much Ado* ends here, but we want to add a postscript. When we were writing this book, we had a long conversation with someone who had been teaching English for years and who told us she had no time for feminist approaches. The essence of her objection was that feminist readers had all their ideas worked out beforehand, and approached every Shakespeare play with the intention of imposing a standard feminist reading upon it. In her words: 'if you come looking for patriarchy, you're going to find patriarchy.' She felt that feminist criticism was blind to the poetry, the language of Shakespeare's plays. She isn't the only person who feels like this. Indeed, you might have exactly the same reservation.

Our answer was that she was confusing the informing principles of a critical approach with the critical reading itself. The whole point of the kind of feminist approach we have been outlining is that it gives you a 'hold' on the play, a set of ideas to start making sense of it, but that then, as one point leads to another, a lot more becomes involved. It is perhaps particularly obvious in the case of *Romeo and Juliet*, which might seem little more than a love story. A feminist approach, however, gives us a large key to start unlocking the text, and seeing what is inside. But that involves making connections – if you were going to stick to the one issue of how the play represents woman, the exercise would be a bit predictable, even pointless. What you should be doing, however, is relating it to all other aspects of love and death, politics and society, the law and human feeling, authority and freedom in the state. That is to say, you are looking at the issues people have always looked at, the things people have always seen as central in Shakespeare, but seeing them in a new light, with fresh perspectives, fresh dimensions. In other words, feminism isn't a dead hand that stifles a play, but a challenging way of opening up new facets of a play.

This is particularly true in relation to a play's language. Conservative Members of Parliament are particularly fond of talking about the beauty of Shakespeare's language, and how it would benefit everyone if they were to learn passages from Shakespeare by heart. Much of the time academic enthusiasm for Shakespeare's language is as empty as this – indiscriminate praise for how good it is, without much comment about what it all amounts to. In the first half of this book, we have already endeavoured to show that Shakespeare's language is complex and clever because it carries such a weight of meaning, incorporating so many themes, so many dimensions of an issue at any one time. The thing about feminist criticism is that it is also alert to the language of a text in this kind of way – by having a frame of explanation, by so often turning to the nature of the male discourse of the men in positions of authority, it has the kind of comprehensive theory that also has plenty of room for every nuance and subtlety within the text. In the end, the only answer to teachers of literature with no time for feminism is that they are wrong. Feminist criticism doesn't close options; on the contrary, it opens the plays up.

10

New Historicism and Cultural Materialism

THE preceding chapters have largely been concerned to show how the new ways of reading Shakespeare produce a very different kind of discussion and debate about the plays. One way of summarising this debate is to talk about the way recent criticism, and perhaps especially feminist criticism, makes it evident that Shakespeare's plays are not timeless or universal but are part of the struggles of the early modern period, the period usually referred to as the Renaissance. More narrowly, they belong to the final years of Elizabeth I's reign, the 1590s, and the early years of James I's rule (Elizabeth died in 1603; James as James VI was already king of Scotland, and became James I of England, so uniting the two kingdoms). The 1590s especially were a time of turbulence, with riots, food shortages and anxiety about who would succeed Elizabeth, an anxiety not lessened by the Earl of Essex's rebellion in 1601 and his attempted coup. James's succession was marked by a deepening rift between the crown and parliament as well as continued fears about Catholic conspiracies. The famous gunpowder plot of 1605 is symptomatic of this turmoil of the early modern period in which Protestant states like England and Holland were either at war or under threat from Catholic countries like Spain and France. If all of this seems remote, it may help to remember that many of the most violent events in Ireland's history belong to this period and that the consequences of those events have dominated much of twentieth-century life in Ireland.

There are obviously other historical details we could mention here, and, indeed, knowing about history has become one of the most useful tools for students interested in new ways of reading Shakespeare. There are several reasons for this. Whereas traditional criticism argued that the plays were not tied to any specific historical circumstances, nor even to any specific kind of theatre, but instead dealt with universal aspects of human nature, recent criticism has relocated the texts in their historical circumstances in order to emphasise the fact that change is possible and, secondly, to stress how history itself is a matter of crisis and conflict. Both of these points are worth expanding a little. First, the question of change. It has to be recognised that recent criticism is political, that it sees itself as a radical challenge to the status quo and that it is interested in change, in alternatives, in moving away from old values. This point might become clearer if we think back to the last section on feminism: there would be no point in a feminist analysis if you believe that human nature is universal and unchanging. What a feminist analysis shows is that human nature is an idea that is constructed according to certain values in certain periods: as the period changes, so do ideas about human nature. History becomes important because through it you can show difference, you can show how different meanings existed and therefore how change is possible.

But in addition to this is the second point above, that history itself is not a set of stable processes but more often a clash of voices and positions. Nor is history separate from literature: we know history largely through documents, through texts; we do not know it objectively but through interpretations. So we cannot close off the politics of the state from the literature of the period, nor the literature from the state. We know, for example, that Shakespeare's plays were put on at the court of Elizabeth; more revealingly perhaps, we also know that Shakespeare's company was paid by the Earl of Essex's supporters to put on a performance of *Richard II*, a play dealing with deposition, the night before Essex's attempt to dethrone Elizabeth on Sunday 8th February 1601: politics, court and theatre at this point are clearly inseparable.

There is, however, one further issue in all this which we have touched on in the reference to Ireland. If Shakespeare's plays are connected to the 1590s and 1600s, you might question whether they are still relevant to us in the late modern period. If they do not deal with human nature, what interest is it that they hold for us? One answer to these questions is that the political issues the plays raise and the questions they focus for us – questions about the power of the state, freedom, violence, class, gender, democracy – are still issues that concern us. We have, as it were, inherited them from the early modern period: we are part of that process of change and debate and crisis that begins with capitalism in the fifteenth century. But there is also a less clear-cut answer. It would be wrong to think of Shakespeare's plays as political tracts, as manifestoes about this or that issue. They are clearly spectacles of entertainment which involve us in their action on stage, but what we have to recognise is that theatre is always in this sense political: it addresses an audience about issues which are not always tied down to just one historical time. There are, for example, references to the striking of clocks in *Julius Caesar* which are obviously anachronistic – Rome had no clocks. The play floats free of its Roman world and we as audience recognise in its references to clocks and sixteenth-century dress how it bears upon the modern world of appointments and fashion: in other words we make connections with the play, interpreting its past in terms of our present. But at the same time because the language of the play resists our sense of something present, we are aware of historical difference, of gaps between ourselves and the play, gaps of meaning and ideas which point to the notion of change.

So far we have said nothing at all about the two critical approaches that provide the heading for this chapter, New Historicism and Cultural Materialism. What we have presented up to this point is an explanation of some of the issues that surround these two approaches, both of which are concerned to reposition Shakespeare's plays in the political struggles of the Renaissance and which involve a much more radical sense of history than the traditional notion of great events involving famous people. As we noted in chapter 7, both approaches are very much concerned with issues of power and control, with how the state seeks to order people, with what devices it uses, with how power presents itself to the public gaze. But going with this notion of power is the idea of resistance, of how power always produces a counter-force which resists its strictures. It is in this matter of resistance that the basic difference between the two approaches lies. New Historicism, usually associated with recent American criticism (especially the critic Stephen Greenblatt), is interested in the workings of power and how the state manages to contain resistance: in this view of things, rebellion is always contained, the state or the ruling classes, to put it crudely, always win. Cultural Materialism is associated with British critics (especially Alan Sinfield and Jonathan Dollimore) who emphasise instead how there is always resistance to the state which cannot be closed off, how power itself is always unstable, how the state is insecure, and how, indeed, the meanings of plays are always open to new interpretations which can be appropriated by criticism to further its own political agenda.

All of this may seem a little remote from Shakespeare's plays, but like much recent criticism both New Historicism and Cultural Materialism are not simply interested in the past for its own sake but in constructing a reading of the plays that does not insulate them either from other texts in the period or from the present political situation. They are much more flexible forms of criticism than the term 'critical theory' implies, and this is equally true of the sort of ideas they raise about power. Power is not seen as a single, monolithic idea but something that can assume various forms and configurations, as can resistance. In order to demonstrate this we want to look at two plays, starting with one of the Roman plays, *Julius Caesar*. Before we turn to the text it may be helpful to point out that Rome was much more important for Elizabethan than for modern audiences, because it acted as a sort of mirror for Elizabethan society. In an age when plays had to be licensed, writing about Rome gave dramatists a means of circumventing censorship while at the same time raising issues that went to the heart of contemporary politics, in particular the power of the monarchy. In order to understand why, it is necessary to remember that traditionally Rome was a republic in which the patrician classes enjoyed a freedom and liberty as well as rights that made kingship anathema to them. Many Elizabethan nobles saw themselves as the true inheritors of Roman nobility and liberty, a liberty under increasing threat from the attempts of the monarchy to establish itself as absolute, as having a divine right to rule. The Civil War that began in 1642, that is to say some thirty to forty years after the period when Shakespeare was writing, has its roots in this clash between an aristocracy pledged to its rights and freedom and a monarchy bent on absolutism, a clash seen in some of its aspects in the staging of *Julius Caesar* in 1599.

Julius Caesar

1   *Look at a scene from Act I*

As with previous discussions, we can begin our analysis by looking back at our earlier summary of the play. *Julius Caesar* is a history play. It begins with Caesar returning to Rome after his military triumphs. Various people in Rome are, however, beginning to turn against him, and a conspiracy develops in which even Brutus, an old friend of Caesar's, becomes involved. The conspirators murder Caesar. Mark Antony, who has not been involved, swears vengeance for Caesar's death. Antony is victorious in the subsequent battle at Philippi, and Brutus kills himself.

Underlying the play, we argued in chapter 2, is the standard pattern of the history plays in general, that is the gap between the ideal of an ordered society and the complicated reality of life. Such a reading of the play, though only a basic starting-point, is not without its difficulties for either a New Historicist or Cultural Materialist analysis precisely because it by-passes crucial questions about what sort of order is involved and what sort of society is assumed. There is, too, the further problem of the way in which such a reading offers little sense of crisis or conflicting positions and voices within the play itself or within Renaissance culture as it moved out of feudalism into capitalism. Rather than focusing on the gap between order and disorder, then, we need to revise our thinking about the play; we need to examine the sort of crises it dramatises and the contending forces involved, and how these relate to questions of power and resistance.

We can begin with the first scene, which shows the people's representatives in the senate, the Tribunes Flavius and Marullus, rebuking the citizens for their celebration of Caesar's recent victory:

> FLAVIUS Hence! home, you idle creatures, get you home.
>   Is this a holiday? What! know you not,
>   Being mechanical, you ought not walk
>   Upon a labouring day without the sign
>   Of your profession? Speak, what trade art thou?
> 1ST CITIZEN Why, sir, a carpenter.
> MARULLUS Where is thy leather apron and thy rule?
>   What dost thou with thy best apparel on?
>   You, sir, what trade are you?
> 2ND CITIZEN Truly, sir, in respect of a fine workman, I am but, as you
> would say, a cobbler.
> MARULLUS But what trade art thou? Answer me directly.
>
> (I.i.1–12)

We can see straight away that there is conflict here between the Tribunes, supporters of Pompey whose sons Caesar has just defeated, and the plebians, the artisan classes who have taken Caesar's victory as a cue for a holiday. As a result they have dressed up in their best clothes rather than their ordinary work clothes. The questions Marullus asks we might find odd: why does he want to know what these people are? why is he interested in their dress? One aspect of this has to do with Elizabethan sumptuary laws which specified what different classes should wear so that they could be recognised. It is one of the ways in which power operates, by prescribing dress – signs of professions – and by restricting what people could wear on labouring days. Put another way, Marullus and Flavius, even though they are in theory on the people's side, represent a type of authority which is bent on maintaining order and the status quo by preventing people from mingling work and holidays or going about without some clear sign of their class position. By contrast, the ordinary people in the scene are part of a festive order that refuses to be bound by petty rules and laws: they are the representatives of popular culture to whom questions of work and idleness are not central. Instead, what is stressed about the cobbler are his playful retorts and his witty evasion of direct answers to Marullus. His refusal to say directly what he is identifies him as a site of resistance: refusing to obey the rules of dress is accompanied by the refusal to conform to strict linguistic codes and answer directly.

The scene ends with Marullus and Flavius sending off the citizens and silencing their revelry. What matters in the first scene is this struggle to control the crowd, for they are to become the mainstay of power in the play. The citizens themselves do not belong to a party or hold power: they are a threat by their very crossing of boundaries between work and holiday and by their disregard for dress laws, but they are not in any sense like modern trade unions or workers. The danger they pose is their mobility, their lack of stability. Part of the play's concern with power will involve the struggle to control the crowd, though that will not be easy to do in a world where language, as in the case of the cobbler, can be used to undermine order.

2   Look at a scene from Act II

By Act II it is clear that Caesar intends to become king. Marullus and Flavius have been put to death for pulling scarves off Caesar's images, a gesture that shows their opposition to the way Caesar is venerated after his victory over Pompey's sons, a victory which leaves the way open for him to become absolute king. But by this stage a conspiracy against Caesar has been formed, with Brutus at its centre though not in total control of it. He is drawn in by Cassius and Casca who need the people's high opinion of him to validate their actions. What emerges from the conspiracy, then, is not just a sense of the nobles seeking to free themselves from the threat of absolutism posed by Caesar but how power is closely involved with questions of public presentation. What matters in a power struggle, and perhaps what power is on one level, is a certain style of presentation. This might become clearer if we look at Brutus's words to the conspirators in Act II scene i where he suggests to them how they should go about the killing of Caesar:

> Let's be sacrificers, but not butchers, Caius.
> We all stand up against the spirit of Caesar
> And in the spirit of men there is no blood.
> O that we then could come by Caesar's spirit,
> And not dismember Caesar! But, alas,
> Caesar must bleed for it! And, gentle friends,
> Let's kill him boldly, but not wrathfully;
> Let's carve him as a dish fit for the gods,
> Not hew him as a carcase fit for hounds;
> And let our hearts, as subtle masters do,
> Stir up their servants to an act of rage,
> And after seem to chide 'em. This shall make
> Our purpose necessary, and not envious;
> Which so appearing to the common eyes,
> We shall be call'd purgers, not murderers.
>   (II.i.166–80)

Brutus's advice to the conspirators is that they should perform the murder of Caesar as a ritual, as a sacrifice rather than as a piece of brutal butchery. He proposes this because he argues it is not Caesar's body but the spirit which he represents that they need to kill, the spirit of monarchy which will reduce them all through fear to mere servants, to subjects. They have, he argues, to present themselves in such a way as to make their act seem necessary.

There are several points in Brutus's speech here that bear on the larger questions of power and resistance. It is not enough, it seems, simply to take action: it is how the action appears that matters, and it can only appear right if it is staged in a certain way. New Historicist critics such as Leonard Tennenhouse have pointed out how power very often resembles a play in the Renaissance: for example, Elizabeth staged tournaments, and public executions can be seen as shows of power put on display for the public. One of the modes or styles that power employs in the Renaissance is theatricality, but not just this. Brutus in his speech draws a careful analogy between their actions and the idea of stirring up servants only to chide them. What Brutus is getting at here is the way the struggle for power involves both acting and manipulation of the audience.

There are, though, other aspects to Brutus's speech worth nothing. Brutus says they must be seen as sacrificers, not butchers, as if he is aware of the fact that actions can be interpreted in different ways. The republicans find themselves in a world where crisis in the state is reflected in a crisis of meaning. We have already seen how the citizens by their dress transgress and overturn the rules so that the Tribunes cannot make out which class or profession they belong to. Now there are similar problems haunting Brutus's speech. Despite his intention, our impression is that the killing will be as much a slaughter as a sacrifice. And there is another problem, too. Brutus speaks of making a sacrifice fit for the gods, yet he wishes to deny Caesar god-like power over the state. Curiously Brutus's speech seems to suggest the opposite of what he means, to imply a dignity and royalty about Caesar. This contradiction in the speech suggests something of how difficult it is to resist the discourse of monarchy: Brutus may wish to deny Caesar's kingship, but the idea has, so it seems, worked its way into the very language of the conspirators so that we are aware of just how difficult it is to resist. Brutus is trying to control a very complex situation and hold it together so that it has just one set of meanings, but like everyone else in the play he finds language slipping away from his grasp and control. At the same time, while the audience may be repelled by the imagery Brutus uses, they may also have some sympathy for his attempt to preserve the freedom of Rome against the encroachment of Caesar as god-like king, an encroachment that threatens to take over language itself.

Act II gives us, then, a complex sense of how resistance to state power involves wrestling not just with conscience and ideas of right and wrong but also with intricate questions of presentation so that the meaning of actions can be understood. It is, in a word, no use just stabbing Caesar: the significance of the action must be clear as must also be the threat posed by him. This, however, is something we can trace in the next act.

3   *Look at a scene from Act III*

In the first scene of Act III Caesar is murdered; Antony meets with the conspirators and is given permission to speak in the next scene to the people at Caesar's funeral, though Brutus is to speak to them first. The two scenes of the murder and the funeral are clearly of central importance to the play and it may be helpful if we look briefly at both.

We can start with the moment just before the murder. Metellus goes to Caesar and kneels before his seat to ask for the banishment of his brother Cimber to be repealed. Caesar refuses but then the other conspirators join in the request:

> BRUTUS I kiss thy hand, but not in flattery, Caesar,
> Desiring thee that Publius Cimber may
> Have an immediate freedom of repeal.
> CAESAR What, Brutus!
> CASSIUS Pardon, Caesar! Caesar, pardon!
> As low as to thy foot doth Cassius fall,
> To beg enfranchisement for Publius Cimber.
> CAESAR I could well be mov'd, if I were as you;
> If I could pray to move, prayers would move me;
> But I am constant as the northern star,
> Of whose true-fix'd and resting quality
> There is no fellow in the firmament.
> (III.i.52–62)

It is important to remember that, at this point, the audience is aware of what is about to happen: from their knowledge of history, they know that Caesar is about to be assassinated. The tension is, therefore, enormous. Ironically, by kneeling the conspirators seem to be treating Caesar as if he were king: he has not been crowned, but he is being regarded as the source of mercy and justice. By implication Caesar has taken over the role of the senate and its powers. The conspirators thus seem to be testing Caesar and making visible his actions as king: he allows them to abase themselves as low as his foot. Though they say they do not speak in flattery, the point is made that Caesar's court is one where the language of flattery and abasement will be evident.

The conspirators choose their words most carefully in asking for freedom for Cimber: it is freedom the republicans fight for, to be equal amongst other men. Caesar, in rejecting their plea, also rejects freedom for his subjects. But his reply goes beyond this point when he voices his claim to be different from other men, to be unmoved by prayers, to be constant and fixed. The image he offers of himself is of a superior force above the human, a being semi-divine like the stars. This discourse of absolutism, of kings alone being the rule of law, was in the process of being created in the Renaissance by rulers all across Europe in an attempt to secure their position and to lessen the power of the aristocracy. It was a move against the traditional position where aristocracy and kings were equally responsible for the security of the realm. The push towards absolutism is what threatens Rome, and is revealed in the way Caesar claims to be constant and unmovable. The identity that Caesar shapes for himself is that of the absolute ruler, but also therefore the role of tyrant who has total control and considers himself above justice. Once again it is worth pointing out how this connects to the crisis of the seventeenth century. The courts of Europe were notoriously corrupt and swayed by flattery, but also subjects more and more had to submit to the monarch. Elizabeth I encouraged the cult of herself as Astrea, the goddess of justice and as the virgin queen, a divine figure above mortal passions and weaknesses. We should not, however, try to trace the figure of Elizabeth in that of Caesar. The play is not an allegory. But it is important to see how the play is contiguous with political representations outside the theatre.

The representation of monarchy as divine continues in Antony's funeral address in the next scene. As we noted, Brutus speaks first, seeking to explain that the motives for the assassination were that he loved Rome more than he loved Caesar. Initially the crowd is convinced, but then Antony comes on and cynically sets about manoeuvring and reversing their judgements, manipulating their sympathies through his ploy of reading Caesar's will:

> ANTONY Here is the will, and under Caesar's seal:
>   To every Roman citizen he gives,
>   To every several man, seventy-five drachmas.
> 2ND PLEBIAN Most noble Caesar! We'll revenge his death.
> 3RD PLEBIAN O royal Caesar!
> ANTONY Hear me with patience.
> ALL Peace, ho!
> ANTONY Moreover, he hath left you all his walks,
>   His private arbours, and newly-planted orchards,
>   On this side Tiber; he hath left them to you,
>   And to your heirs for ever – common pleasures,
>   To walk abroad and recreate yourselves.
>   Here was a Caesar! When comes such another?
>   (III.ii.241–53)

Antony's reading of the will to the public focuses our attention on a number of aspects of power, not least his readiness to exploit the crowd in order to gain support for his own push to gain power. Ironically, the will itself sounds like a piece of democracy, that with Caesar's death has come a certain liberty for the people – they can walk abroad and amuse themselves as if free men. This, together with Antony's theatrical readiness to mingle with the crowd, are gestures calculated to suggest that it is Antony and Caesar, rather than Brutus, who are the true representatives of Roman freedom.

Underlying Antony's manoeuvring of the people are two further ideas. One is the notion of the state as a family: Tudor propagandists often made use of the idea of the state as a family in their political writings to create a sense of unity. Antony's reading of the will has a similar sort of effect in the way it turns the crowd into Caesar's heirs. While Caesar himself may have claimed to be different from ordinary men, the will associates him instead with 'common pleasures', as if to imply Caesar was like the people, a part of the same family. At the same time Antony is also flattering the crowd and playing upon their sense of self-importance and vanity: through Caesar's will they are to share the patrician life-style of walks and recreation. More obviously, we can see in Antony's words an appeal to greed and ownership of property which may link up with how the Renaissance witnessed a growing emphasis on money and class as the shift from feudalism to capitalism took place. Antony, then, fastens onto the material aspects of power. Where Brutus seeks to persuade and talks to the people of reason, truth and justice, Antony, with no time for republican values or respect for the common people, recognises that power lies not in reasoning with the people but in appealing to their baser instincts. If the play leaves us in little doubt which move is the most successful – by the end of the scene the crowd have become a mob ready to mutiny – it also makes clear which move ought to be right.

4   Look at a scene from Act IV

With the winning over of the crowd Antony has in his hands the means to take revenge against the conspirators, and by Act IV Rome has been plunged into civil war. The act begins with a meeting between Antony, Octavius and Lepidus to plan the next stage of their vengeance:

ANTONY These many, then, shall die; their names are prick'd.
OCTAVIUS Your brother too must die. Consent you, Lepidus?
LEPIDUS I do consent.
OCTAVIUS Prick him down, Antony.
LEPIDUS Upon condition Publius shall not live,
Who is your sister's son, Mark Antony.

ANTONY He shall not live; look, with a spot I damn him.
But, Lepidus, go you to Caesar's house;
Fetch the will hither, and we shall determine
How to cut off some charge in legacies.

(IV.i.1–9)

In this terrifying scene the three new rulers of Rome agree a death list of those who must be disposed of. They bargain across the table as brother is set against son, each ticked off. The ruthless exercise of power is seen here for the first time in the play, and for the first time we see exactly what tyranny is. Antony clearly has no right to the authority he exercises: having used the people he now exercises power in the most brutal way. What, however, is unclear is what relationship this tyranny bears to monarchy or absolutism. Is the play, we might wonder, suggesting that kingship, even a kingship giving the monarch absolute power, would be better than the chaos of civil war with its risk of tyranny? If so, the play wold seem to be saying that resistance, the sort of resistance Brutus has shown to kingship, is wrong because it leads to something far worse. As we noted above, this sort of reading which sees texts as serving to consolidate the established order is broadly referred to as New Historicist criticism. It is a criticism which sees subversion as being contained by the dominant ideology: in the case of *Julius Caesar*, this would amount to arguing that the play shows the conspiracy against Caesar as serving to reinforce the idea of monarchy since in the end the only alternative to monarchy appears to be anarchy, something unacceptable.

It is, however, far from clear that the play is underpinning monarchy in this way. The death of Caesar does indeed lead to civil war, but that does not mean that the play is advocating kingship or arguing that resistance is useless. A Cultural Materialist reading of *Julius Caesar* might argue that Antony's tyranny is in fact only an illegitimate form of Caesar's kingship, and that Caesar and Antony represent the same values and ideas. Certainly there can be little doubt that the play condemns Antony's ruthlessness in the extract above and his subsequent plan to exclude Lepidus from office. At the same time a Cultural Materialist reading might go on from this point to showing how the play also seems concerned with exploring how power involves not just violent physical force but also gaining control of the legal system and the paperwork that goes with it. In the extract above, Antony tells Lepidus to fetch Caesar's will so that they can set about changing it. Having used the will once, Antony now sees the need to rewrite it in order to maintain his grip on the wealth and freedoms Caesar would have given away. In this sense the world Antony inhabits is much more like our own modern world where power seems vested in documents rather than in the honour-culture Brutus represents, a culture where oaths bind men in actions for the communal good. To this extent we might conclude that *Julius Caesar* is not so much about a single idea of power as about a transition between an older order of power where resistance may have been possible, and a new order of things where what matters is the control of documents and how these are presented to the people.

5   *Look at a scene from Act V*

The final part of the play is taken up with the battle between Antony and Brutus. Antony's army wins, not least because it is efficient and in charge of its paperwork. And yet this is not quite the whole story. There seems no hope of defeating Antony's army or the Roman state. Beyond the power of the state, however, lies one last site of resistance: the suicide of Brutus in the last scene. The idea of suicide as an act of freedom by the individual against the tyranny of the state is brought out in the words of Strato, Brutus's servant:

> MESSENGER Strato, where is thy master?
> STRATO Free from the bondage you are in, Messala.
>   The conquerors can but make a fire of him;
>   For Brutus only overcame himself,
>   And no man else hath honour by his death.
> (v.v.53–7)

Brutus takes his own life; he resists capture and bondage by Rome by keeping control over his own body and its destiny. Elsewhere in Renaissance literature suicide is presented as an act of despair, but here it is presented as an act of defiance which enables Brutus to maintain his honour and freedom. The point of such action may seem utterly negative, yet the play praises Brutus as the noblest of all the Romans, so opening up at the very end of the play a debate about the nature of resistance and what might be the best way for the subject to act.

Much earlier in this chapter we made a distinction between New Historicism and Cultural Materialism as critical practices, that where the first of these sees the plays as showing how the state always wins, the second shows the way in which there is always resistance to state control. Is the reading above, you might be wondering, a New Historicist or a Cultural Materialist reading? As with many current readings it, in fact, falls somewhere between the two, opening up the issues in the same way that we believe the play itself does. *Julius Caesar*, that is, seems to us a p. / that investigates not just the nature of power or the nature or resistance but the interconnection between these two, dramatising the uncertain interplay between these concepts, and so foregrounding the question of whether power inevitably leads to and produces resistance, together with the question of whether that resistance is genuinely radical or merely serves to reinforce the status quo.

A purer theoretical approach might lean in one of two directions. If you took a New Historicist line your analysis would almost certainly want to make connections with the attempt by the Tudor monarchy to achieve absolute power and to demonstrate that power through both military force and propaganda. Your analysis, that is, would seek to position the play next to or as continuous with other shows of power in the age. This might involve a little bit of reading around, but it is easy to find, for example, references to the Tudor homily against rebellion that was read out in churches. If, however, you wanted to emphasise a Cultural Materialist angle, it would make sense to connect the play with some of the more obvious demonstrations of the power of ordinary people and the fear the authorities had, for example, of the crowd, especially at plays. One of the points New Historicism and Cultural Materialism have in common, then, is that they both seek to build outwards from the plays to the political events and documents of the period, but also to work from those documents back into the plays. This is another example of the way the new approaches to Shakespeare seek to be more fluid in their analysis of the texts, avoiding the old idea that somehow there is a background to the plays that we can set them in. There is no background, and no real foreground either; culture is a complex continuum involving everything that is done or said or written in a society. This, however, raises further questions, which can best be examined in a consideration of *A Midsummer Night's Dream* and the politics of comedy.

A Midsummer Night's Dream

One of the things we have stressed throughout the previous chapters is the way the new approaches to Shakespeare can open up new angles on the plays and make us much more aware of what we are doing as critics. We become, that is to say, much more conscious of the sort of reading we are pursuing as we follow a particular thread or slant. In the case of the comedies this can seem problematic: at first glance they seem unlikely material for any sort of analysis other than of the themes of love and marriage. There is, too, the question of whether comedy as a form of drama isn't too light to sustain the same sort of political weight that we attach to tragedy and to the history plays. And yet it is the case that, whether we realise it or not, we do read comedy as political, we do engage with comic plays not just at the level of whether or not they are funny but through a whole series of issues that bear upon the social and political order. It is this which makes discussion of Shakespeare's comedies such a tricky matter, especially a play like *A Midsummer Night's Dream* where there seems so little that is explicitly political to hold on to. What also complicates discussion of the play, however, are the different emphases of its multiple plots, something we take up in our initial analysis below.

1   *Look at a scene from Act I*

As usual, we need a summary of the play to begin our analysis. Theseus, the Duke of Athens, is to marry Hippolyta in four days' time. Later we see Nick Bottom, a weaver, and his fellow performers rehearsing their play of the tragical love-story of Pyramus and Thisbe in the wood near the city to celebrate their wedding. Meanwhile, Egeus appeals to the Duke to force his daughter Hermia to marry Demetrius rather than her choice, Lysander, but Hermia and Lysander decide to elope. Their plan is betrayed to Demetrius by Helena, Hermia's friend who loves Demetrius. In the wood a further quarrel is seen between Oberon, the fairy king, and his wife Titania over the possession of a changeling boy. Oberon decides to punish Titania by having Puck anoint her eyes with the juice of a magic flower that causes her to fall violently in love with Bottom, who, through the trickery of Puck, now has an ass's head. The lovers are also confused by the fairies' tricks, with both Lysander and Demetrius falling in love with Helena, until order is restored by Oberon. The next morning the lovers believe they have been dreaming. Hermia is now, however, to be allowed to marry Lysander, and Helena Demetrius, while Oberon frees Titania from her spell. Bottom awakes from what he also assumes has been a dream and rejoins his fellow-players to act their play before the court which is received with some humour. When all depart for the night, the fairies come to bless the bridal beds.

As with all Shakespeare's romantic comedies, the basic pattern we can see in this summary is the standard one of sane, rational behaviour being disrupted by people falling in love. What we witness is the absurd way people act when love takes them over, and this is evident in the confusion in the middle acts of the play where the lovers are made to change partners almost at random. The disorder love brings is, though, overcome at the end when the play ends with marriage. When we looked at *Julius Caesar*, however, it was fairly easy to see the political significance of this sort of basic pattern involving disorder in the state and to begin thinking about political questions of power and resistance. Here, with *A Midsummer Night's Dream*, there does not seem to be any-thing like that, there doesn't seem to be any kind of obvious concern with big political issues. Indeed, as we noted above, it might seem unnatural to look for such a pattern. And yet we can find plenty of evi-dence that this is more than just a light and fluffy comedy. In the summary, for example, we can see how much of the action takes place at night, and how it centres on sexual desire, including some odd sexual desires. All of this is most evident in the presentation of the fairies: when fairies are mentioned, most of us probably think of Tin-kerbell in *Peter Pan*, but the fairies in Shakespeare's play are not ethe-real and innocent in the usual manner. They are adults, playing with magic, playing at games of sexual conquest and deceit.

What is also evident is that the fairies echo the behaviour of the human world, the behaviour of those at court in Athens. The play's design allows us to see a number of parallels between the various groups on stage: Oberon and Titania as rulers of the fairies clearly par-allel Theseus and Hippolyta as rulers of Athens, but in their love quarrel Oberon and Titania also seem to mirror something of the quarrel of the young lovers. One way of reading *A Midsummer Night's Dream* would be to explore the play as a work dealing with sexual fantasy, in the sense that fantasies always explore the night-time world, the world of secret fears and repressions which are released in the wood. This, as we will see, is something that will be of importance in our analysis of the play, but it is not the only factor we have to take into account.

One reservation about approaching *A Midsummer Night's Dream* just in terms of ideas about sexual desire or, indeed, sexual politics is that it makes no allowance for the fact that *A Midsummer Night's Dream* is a play written at a certain time, for a specific audience, and, as such, inevitably commenting, if only in an indirect way, on the socio-political experience of that audience. An important aspect of this has to do with the fact that *A Midsummer Night's Dream* is an occasional play, a play designed to celebrate an aristocratic wedding at court. This has implications for the way we might begin to think about whether *A Midsummer Night's Dream*, as a piece of entertainment, in the end serves to endorse the existing social order. Here much will depend on what we make of Bottom's own play in the final act. The courtiers on stage are for the most part patronising and condescending. We do not have to share their attitude, but we might be unaware of how *A Midsummer Night's Dream* as a whole has positioned us out of reach of any class sympathy with Bottom, so that we see his play merely as an attempt to please the rather limited imaginations of the court lovers. Our response to the play becomes governed by ideas about how people should behave rather than shaped by any overt political ideas: we might forget that Theseus is, after all, using the folk theatre of Bottom and the people to celebrate his wedding and so affirm the value of the existing order.

The case we have outlined here has to do with the way plays can position their audience and take on different values according to where they are played and watched. It also has to do with what elements we choose to emphasise in our reading. So, for example, in looking at *A Midsummer Night's Dream* as an occasional play we could choose to make Bottom and his companions and the fairies seem fairly insignificant figures, aspects of the uncouth or irrational side of experience, but an uncouth or irrational side that can be contained – contained essentially within the social order. What becomes apparent in such a statement, of course, is that we have already arrived at a political reading of the play, a reading which sees the play arguing the need for social fusion to contain irrational impulses that threaten to overtake everyday behaviour. What is also apparent, we hope, is that there is nothing forced about arriving at a political reading of the play; indeed, once we start thinking about it, it becomes difficult to see how the play could be read any other way. We either, for example, see Bottom and the fairies as purely meaningless figures of fun and frivolity, or we see them – as we have done here – as characters created to serve a function and make a point.

So far we have looked, in general terms, at two aspects of the play, and suggested two sorts of reading. The first raised ideas about the fairies and sexual fantasy, the night-time world of the play. The second raised ideas about *A Midsummer Night's Dream* as an occasional play which seemingly endorses the social order. These are aspects of the text we will return to later. Theories of Shakespearean comedy, however, have developed along a number of different lines, and can offer a variety of emphases, even reversals of, the kind of analysis offered above. In order to explain this, we need to mention here three theories of comedy, those of Northrop Frye, C.L. Barber and Robert Weimann.

Frye argues that comedy has three stages. It begins with an anti-comic old society; then follows a period of confusion and loss of identity; finally, in the third stage, the confusion is resolved through marriage, resulting in a 'new society' in which all participate. This is to summarise Frye's ideas to a bare minimum, but underlying them is the notion of synthesis and harmony wrought through drama. It is an idea very close to the reading we have offered so far, a reading about how waywardness is contained. In Barber's view, by contrast, what is central is the idea of holiday and carnival which offers release from periods of constraint. According to Barber comedy stages an overturning of the social restraints of the everyday, a topsy-turvyness that celebrates those energies normally held in check by regulated life. At the end of such inversion, Barber argues, there returns social reconciliation and regeneration. In this last point, Barber seems to argue, like Frye, that comedy restores and amends the social hierarchy, but the big difference is that, within Barber's theory, there is potential for far greater significance to be found in, and room for the critic to make far more of, the period of disruption within the play. It is an idea that is taken further by Robert Weimann. Like Barber he puts an emphasis on the carnivalesque, on the overturning of the social order and on excess, but he sees this as something subversive, as perhaps expressive of class antagonisms or economic antagonisms. It is a much more overtly political approach which hints at the way plays might be seen in terms of rebellious gestures; but no more than that, for the gestures are restrained within the festive, the comic. The emphasis eventually falls upon reconciliation rather than violent overthrow.

Such theoretical thinking about Shakespeare might seem to take us away from the texts themselves, but this is not really the case. What is illuminating about such theories is how they allow us to grasp some of the nuances involved in concepts like power and resistance: power does not have to be a monolithic idea always involving force. It may, for example, include such ideas as social harmony as well as social control. Resistance may be something other than just fighting back: it may range from refusing to conform to refusing to speak. But the other point about such theories is that they connect, in their emphasis on carnival and festival, the play and the world beyond the play as reflected in such rituals as May Day, twelfth night revelry, folk games and customs, indeed the whole wider cultural world of the plays.

The normative world of *A Midsummer Night's Dream* – that is to say, the order that prevails on a daily basis in Athens – is one where the law, including the law of the father, holds sway. It is something we can see at the start of the play in Egeus's speech to the Duke about Hermia's refusal to obey him:

> And, my gracious Duke,
> Be it so she will not here, before your Grace,
> Consent to marry with Demetrius,
> I beg the ancient privilege of Athens:
> As she is mine, I may dispose of her;
> Which shall be either to this gentleman
> Or to her death, according to our law
> Immediately provided in that case.
>
> (I.i.38–45)

Egeus makes it plain that he expects the law to uphold his decision that Hermia shall marry Demetrius, that he has the right to determine the choice of her husband. It is clear, however, even at this stage that the play expects the audience to sympathise with the lovers against this representative of the 'old society'. This is in part underlined by the fact that this society not only makes use of the law, but will not hesitate to enforce the death penalty if members of that society dare to transgress. The difficulty in talking about a play like *A Midsummer Night's Dream*, however, is how to register such points without losing sight of the play's comic structure. We all see the reference to execution, but it might seem inappropriate to make too much of it, for this undermines our impression that the play is an entertainment rather than a social thesis. One answer, for the moment, is to recognise the important part tone plays in comedy and how it creates a sense of just how ridiculous, how pompously foolish these male figures are in their posturing attempts to rule. What we are getting at here is the way comedy doesn't just offer us a plot where we have to make up our minds whether or not the issues are serious; comedy as a form, as a specific genre of drama, already has an attitude towards the figures of power and authority on stage, that they are to be laughed at in their pompous foolishness, in their excessive self-importance and patriarchal pretensions. While they may not recognise it, the representatives of law and order are, in the eyes of comedy, every bit as stupid, silly, inadequate and bumbling as Bottom and his company.

Of course, for Hermia the threat posed by her father is real enough, but she refuses to be silenced or intimidated. The plot to escape is quickly hatched, and the action moves rapidly away from the city and its restrictive law. The very fact that flight is so easily possible reinforces our sense of a comic structure at work which will end in marriage and harmony. At the same time, we have already become aware of how the play adds up to something more than just a comic structure.

That, necessarily, is just one reading of the opening of the play, a reading that you may disagree with, preferring to stress the way patriarchy is represented as violent and cruel, an issue we will come back to. What we are initially interested in exploring, however, is some of the ways in which comedy registers its concern with wider issues while remaining comic. It is precisely this combination of an ordered structure that celebrates social disorder which gives comedy its ambiguous nature and potential for subversion.

2   Look at a scene from Act II

By the end of Act II the four lovers have fled to the wood and Puck has spread confusion by squeezing the flower love-in-idleness not just on Titania's eyelids but also on Lysander's eyes, causing him to fall in love with Helena. The action on stage moves swiftly to create a sense of the comic chaos Frye notes as belonging to the second stage of comedy, a stage marked by the loss of identity and topsy-turvy changes. Central to this process is Puck, the spirit of mischief and fun. At the same time, what we may notice is the way in which social realities keep intruding into this world of comic inversions. For example, at the start of Act II we discover that the breach between Oberon and Titania has not only disrupted the seasons but destroyed the crops. Such details may be no more than part of the comic disorder described by Frye's theory, but in this account of bad harvests the play may also be glancing at the bad weather of 1595–96 which led to a rising in Oxfordshire of some poor

working-class figures not unlike Shakespeare's artisan actors. Such
social distress is kept at the margins of the play, but placing the play in
its immediate historical context helps to suggest why *A Midsummer Night's
Dream* is more than a fantasy. It also suggests why comedy is a more
ambiguous form than it initially appears, dealing with issues that take it
beyond its apparent confines.

But it is not just social realities that enter into the play's fabric.
Within its world of fairies and lovers there are traces of other elements,
moments when the language of the play disrupts any simple idea of
comic celebration. For example, this dialogue between Oberon and
Titania:

> OBERON Why should Titania cross her Oberon?
>   I do but beg a little changeling boy
>   To be my henchman.
> TITANIA   Set your heart at rest;
>   The fairy land buys not the child of me.
>   His mother was a vot'ress of my order;
>   And, in the spiced Indian air, by night,
>   Full often hath she gossip'd by my side . . .
>   And for her sake do I rear up her boy;
>   And for her sake I will not part with him.
>   (II.i.119–37)

The exotic language here moves the play outside the realm of the law
of the city into a richer, more symbolic landscape where we may well
be puzzled by Oberon's insistence on having the changeling boy from
Titania. There are, though, a number of points we can make about
this. One has to do with the wood or forest, commonly a symbolic
place in the Renaissance of the emotional world, a sort of psychological
landscape where fantasy and desire may take over. In this sense we can
talk about the way in which psychological, sexual realities constantly
force their way into the play's pattern, complicating its politics of marriage and love. But going with this point is the way the boy here seems
to symbolise the bonding between Titania and the child's mother, a
bonding that excludes men and heterosexual love. It is clear from the
play that Oberon is jealous of the boy and wishes to break the link
between Titania and his mother, her devoted follower. The way he
does this is to substitute Bottom as the object of Titania's love, consequently humiliating her but also limiting her power. Like Egeus,
Oberon seems bent on physical control over woman, afraid of her
desires which exclude him.

Where this analysis leads us is to a recognition of the extent to which the play's action works to create a number of complex parallels between plots. Through the struggle of Oberon and Titania, we begin to see some of the unstated gender issues that underlie the actions of the human world. It is as if the Oberon plot works to trace some of the erotic or psychological implications of the Theseus–Egeus plot in their desire to control women while at the same time generating further sympathy for women who resist such patriarchal control. What is interesting about the play is the extent to which the resistance of Titania mirrors that of Hermia, both refusing to be subjugated by threats. Again, both Egeus and Oberon seem to regard human life in simple physical terms of property and ownership, whereas Titania invests the changeling with a symbolic resonance that has no place in it for the destructiveness which Oberon wishes to train him in. What we start to see here, then, is the way the sexual and psychological aspects of the play are linked through the question of gender to the social aspects, and how these various aspects undermine any simple sense of the play as endorsing the social order.

3   *Look at a scene from Act III*

The dialogue between Titania and Oberon takes us towards a much clearer grasp of the play's interest in sexual control and resistance and how this is enacted in the magical world of the forest. Titania, we know, is to be punished and humiliated for her love and devotion to the memory of her female follower while at the same time the parallel bonding between Hermia and Helena is to be dissolved into bickering and quarrelling. It is as if the play enacts a series of resistances by women to the dominant male power structure at both the social and sexual level. The punishment for this resistance in the case of Titania is to be made to fall in love with an ass; in the case of Hermia it is to be robbed of all love; for Helena, the torment of an excess of lovers. Here she protests at her treatment at the hands of Lysander and Demetrius who now both claim to love her:

> O spite! O hell! I see you are all bent
> To set against me for your merriment.
> If you were civil, and knew courtesy,
> You would not do me thus much injury.

Can you not hate me, as I know you do,
But you must join in souls to mock me too?
If you were men, as men you are in show,
You would not use a gentle lady so.

(III.ii.145–52)

Helena's words are curious insofar as all her references are to social codes and to social values. Here, in the forest, her fear and sorrow at being, as she sees it, the object of scorn lead her to reassert the need for social values, for 'normal' codes of behaviour between men and women. It is an interesting speech because of the way in which it works to remind us that even in the forest the figures on stage are still governed by the social codes they carry with them. To that extent escape and resistance are difficult, if not impossible: we carry with us social values and social disciplines. But the second point we can make here is how, even as Titania is being punished for her resistance by having to love the grotesque Bottom, Helena seems to ask for the ordinary rules of society to be restored, that is for a return to heterosexual love between members of the same class. It is in such speeches that we can once again detect the idea of how the comedies are conservative in reinforcing ideology: it is better, the argument seems to suggest, to endure Athenian law than this mock world of cruel merriment. If, however, we remember the start of the play we may realise that it is only a fantasy that society is less menacing than the wood.

4 Look at a scene from Act IV

Let's take stock. We began by suggesting that *A Midsummer Night's Dream* is an occasional play celebrating marriage. To this extent it follows the standard pattern of romantic comedies, as described by Northrop Frye, in which an old society is replaced by a new one. The opening of the play, we might argue, shows us a society in need of change; its law is archaic, out of touch with human feeling and manifestly unfair to women. In looking at the play we have also seen how it generates sympathy for both Titania and Hermia and Helena in their rebellion against patriarchal power. At the same time there seems little sense of the play wanting to abandon the hierarchical structure of society; indeed, Helena's speech above seems to suggest just the opposite, that the play for all its sense of wrongs against women and for all its sense of the foolishness of male power, is in the end deeply conservative, interested only in preserving the status quo. To this extent we might argue that the play supports a New Historicist reading, that its fantasy serves to reinforce the social hierarchy and contain resistance.

This, though, is not quite the whole story of the play. So far we have said very little about Bottom and his fellow actors. We have, however, noted the way Theseus appropriates their folk drama to celebrate his wedding. Such appropriation was widely practised by the Tudor and the Stuart hierarchy, in the way they presided over holidays, such as the May games, and turned, in Elizabeth's case, her Accession day celebrations into a tournament. Elizabeth also made sure there was a firm eye kept on the theatres by way of her patronage. We can see, then, how Bottom's company points us towards the idea of state control of both holiday and theatre, something witnessed in the way the artisans take excessive care about the interpretation of their play so that it should not be seen as frightening or threatening to the ladies (III.i.9–21). At the same time, Oberon's plot against Titania clearly takes it for granted that underclasses such as Bottom can be used to humiliate Titania because of their position in the social body.

In this analysis of Bottom's part in the play there seems little room for resistance to the sort of control exhibited by either Elizabeth or Oberon. And yet watching the play our experience of what Bottom does and says does not quite match this view. He is not at all nonplussed by being taken up by Titania into her bower and readily commands the court. Bottom is not only translated into an ass, he is translated socially. And after he awakes he is no less in charge of circumstances:

> I have had a most rare vision. I have had a dream, past the wit of man to say what dream it was. Man is but an ass if he go about to expound this dream. Methought I was – there is no man can tell what. Methought I was, and methought I had, but man is but a patch'd fool, if he will offer to say what methought I had. The eye of man hath not heard, the ear of man hath not seen, man's hand is not able to taste, his tongue to conceive, nor his heart to report, what my dream was.
>
> (IV.i.200–9)

Bottom's words problematise his role and function in the play by drawing attention to their potential meaning as being more than that which is stated. On one level, of course, Bottom is no more than a comic butt used to mock Titania; on another level he seems the very spirit of inversion as the lower orders of the social body take over the court world and command it. But Bottom's words seem to suggest that beyond this, on another level, there is another significance if we can but see it, a significance lying outside the usual social discourse and political structures. What Bottom's dream hints at is a subversion of all the usual forms of society, of all the usual ways of understanding and interpreting meaning. In this sense we might think of Bottom as a sort of deconstructionist critic challenging the conventional ways of understanding language and society, and mocking its attempts to reduce everything to simple meanings. In this we might see the play as offering us the possibility of a more radical position from which to view and judge its action, a position questioning the very structure of the state, something that is also evident in the last act.

5   Look at a scene from Act V

In the final Act of the play Bottom and his company perform their 'tedious brief scene of young Pyramus/And his love Thisby'. Their play-within-the-play mirrors the events of the play itself, so creating an ironic perspective on the court party who, apart from Theseus, mock the laboured performances and lack of skill of the artisan actors. By contrast Theseus advocates a more subtle judgement:

> HIPPOLYTA This is the silliest stuff that I ever heard.
> THESEUS The best in this kind are but shadows; and the worst are no worse, if imagination amend them.
> HIPPOLYTA It must be your imagination then, and not theirs.
> THESEUS If we imagine no worse of them than they of themselves, they may pass for excellent men.
>
> (v.i.209–14)

Theseus's words are for a more generous attitude to the players than the shallow mockeries that come from the court party on stage. Because they are unexpected, they are words that may cause us to reflect on their social implications. The antagonism that prevailed at the start of the play, like the confusion that ruled in the wood, has been resolved; reason once more governs the state, with love finding a place in the social framework of marriage. In a word, the new society that Frye speaks of has been established, the festival carnival and inversion is over. Yet out of this new society comes not new values but cheap jibes against men who work for their living. There is something grating and offensive about the court, something complacent and smug about their attitude which was not there before. For the first time in the play the court is presented in a critical light which finds it wanting not just in its behaviour but in itself as a social group. It is, we might argue, a dangerous moment in the play, a point at which an audience may start to wonder why there is such a social group.

Paradoxically, it is Theseus, the head of this court, who argues for a more imaginative understanding of the social matrix than that of merely judging the actors by their holiday parts. Instead he suggests that the court party try to see that these are excellent men, that they should not be patronised or viewed as lowly creatures, that they are men who already know their faults, their shortcomings, their lack of acting talent. But there is also something more to Theseus's words. His defence of Bottom and his company is not just a recognition of the value of ordinary working men's efforts, they are also a recognition that these are the men on whom the state depends, loyal subjects who are ready to please their ruler. Ironically this would seem to make Theseus a critic of the very power structure he represents, a power structure that humiliates the artisans encouraged to celebrate his marriage.

To some *A Midsummer Night's Dream* seems the perfect comedy, the perfect celebration of the harmony brought about through the imagination. Its plot, however, is a curious combination of erotic jealousy, artisan drama and social analysis focusing on the issue of sexual control and in particular the control of women's desires. It is this contradiction that makes comedy the double-edged form that it is, inescapably political while still being funny. It is also this contradiction that makes it difficult to decide whether comedy serves, as New Historicist criticism might suggest, to endorse the status quo, or, as Cultural Materialists might argue, whether comedies offer us a critique of the dominant power structure. There is perhaps in the end something profoundly ambiguous about the nature of comedy which leaves it open to both kinds of reading.

11

Conclusion

IF you look back over the last four chapters as a whole, it should be apparent that what we have been describing is a massive change in Shakespeare studies. It is a change that involves new terms, new ideas and new topics. Where before there was imagery, character and themes, critics now focus on language, gender and politics; where before there was the idea that plays were unified, critics now look for contradictions in the text; where before everything centred on the author's intentions, now we have plural readings of texts; where before there was a seeming absence of theory and history, now there is both. And we could go on listing these changes: where before there was a stress on the desirability of order, now the very question of order, like the question of what is natural, is under intense investigation.

One way of summing up these changes is to draw attention to the title of a book edited by John Drakakis called *Alternative Shakespeares*. What is implied in this title is the idea that there is not just one view of Shakespeare, and indeed not just one Shakespeare. Rather, Shakespeare is seen as something produced by criticism and produced in a number of different ways. *Alternative Shakespeares* itself contains a series of essays all employing different critical positions: there are psychoanalytic readings, feminist readings, Cultural Materialist readings. What all these alternatives have in common, however, is that they are an attempt to change our understanding of the way Shakespearean drama works, to open up the texts to the new ways of thinking about society and language that have developed since the 1960s. We might think of them as bringing Shakespeare into the late twentieth century, of bringing together the plays and the ideas that now influence a whole range of academic disciplines.

It is perhaps this last point that we should stress most. What is different about the new approaches is that very often they cross into one another, drawing upon ideas from different disciplines, including, for example, linguistics, psychoanalysis, philosophy, history, politics. If you look back at our analysis of *A Midsummer Night's Dream*, for example, you will see that it switches from talking about the play in terms of formal theories of comedy, such as those of Northrop Frye, to relating the play to contemporary events as well as discussing its concern with sexual drives and urges. Behind this sort of combining of approaches lies the desire to do fuller justice to the play, to see it not in terms of a single theme but as a complex piece of writing that engages with a whole set of issues.

One result of this exchange between different approaches, as well as between different subjects like history and English Literature, has been the growing sense that the study of Shakespeare is now perhaps best seen in a larger framework which can be called cultural history. We cannot, that is, simply cut Shakespeare off either from the other dramatists of the age or from the social, historical or political events of the age. Nor can we readily draw a line between issues in Shakespeare's plays and issues dealt with in, say, pamphlets or poems. Shakespeare did not write in isolation from his age; texts do not exist in a vacuum.

For the student, however, all of this can seem overwhelming, as if suddenly you are expected to know much more about the Renaissance, about criticism, indeed about everything. This, though, is not really the case. What we hope you have gained from the previous chapters is a sense of how stimulating and challenging the new approaches can be and how they open the texts up to suggestions, ideas, possibilities. In addition, we hope the chapters suggest how you can make a change to your critical practice by using just a few of the basics of the new approaches. Nobody becomes a critic overnight: it is a matter of writing, thinking and reading, of extending your range and making connections between your ideas. What may help in this is if we outline two further sets of pointers to the new approaches and how these relate to traditional criticism.

For many years it was suggested that *The Tempest* was a sort of farewell to the stage by Shakespeare, that in the figure of Prospero Shakespeare created an image of himself as artist. This approach to the play tied in with a wider interest in the development of Shakespeare's art and with attempts to relate the plays directly to his life. It is not an unattractive approach since it seems to offer a coherent view of the play. Its shortcoming is that constructs a rather romantic view of the text, with Shakespeare about to retire to Stratford. What it omits is a sense that the play adds up to much more than a personal statement, that its language carries more weight and meaning than this. It was not, however, until Frank Kermode's Arden edition of the play in 1954 that this weight of meaning became clearer. In his introduction to the play Kermode opened up the themes of the play, including its concern with art, represented by Prospero, and nature, represented by Caliban, and the significance of these ideas. The shift was from seeing the play autobiographically to an analytic discussion of its ideas.

In his introduction Kermode also examined the connection between *The Tempest* and some pamphlets describing a shipwreck on the Bermudas in 1609, as well as Shakespeare's probable knowledge of some of the members of the Virginia Company concerned with setting up the American colonies. What he was interested in was showing how Shakespeare's thinking about ideas such as providence and life as a voyage may have been reinforced by his reading, and how the play draws upon common Renaissance attitudes and values. The introduction, however, also makes it plain that not a little that was written in the Renaissance about the new world was half-propaganda, half self-justification for exploiting the indigenous population. In other words Kermode's introduction started to sound out some of the political issues and concerns that have come to occupy recent criticism of the plays more generally, and of *The Tempest* in particular. The difference is that, where the Arden edition of the play still continues to praise Shakespeare's art and ideas, more recent critics have come to see how that art may be less straightforward than it appears.

To put that more simply, it was not until recently that critics have begun to see the racial and colonial implications of *The Tempest*. Up until the 1980s the play was assumed to be politically neutral, as if its depiction of Caliban as a savage slave was an entirely objective matter. What has happened to *The Tempest* is that critics have stopped reading it as if it were a moral treatise about, for example, the need for forgiveness and examined how it constructs non-white Europeans as savage outsiders who threaten because they are black; they have looked at how the play justifies colonialism by presenting other peoples and other countries as uncivilised and lacking culture and education. As a result, *The Tempest* has become a much more problematic play, a play that, instead of expressing something individual to Shakespeare or rather bland moral ideas, is now seen to be part of the political thinking of the modern period in which contact with countries beyond Europe threw into question traditional assumptions and ways of reading the world.

We can perhaps see something of this in Act IV scene i where Prospero stages an elaborate masque to bless the love of his daughter Miranda and Ferdinand, son of the King of Naples. For a moment it seems as if nature and the gods, through Prospero's art, can join in celebration of human love, but the masque is brought to a sudden close by Prospero when he is reminded of Caliban's plot against his life. The end of the masque is sudden and uncomfortable: it is as if we are suddenly made aware of all the elaborate fictions we invest around marriage, and how those fictions collapse when they confront a culture that is different. Far from being a confident exploration of the themes of art and nature, *The Tempest* comes to seem to be a play only too aware of the fragility as well as shallowness of social forms.

Other readings of *The Tempest* have gone on beyond this to explore the relationship between the play and plays such as *Othello* and *Titus Andronicus* and their construction of outsiders. In other words, there has remained an interest in Shakespeare's texts, but an interest that looks beyond the traditional groupings of the plays as tragedies and comedies, early and late. Indeed, more and more critics have come to question the traditional divisions of the plays into comedies, histories, tragedies, often preferring to examine issues across genres. This is not to say, however, that recent criticism has stopped looking at individual plays. What it does mean, as in the case of *Hamlet*, for example, is that the sort of criticism written has begun to change our whole thinking about the play.

Traditionally *Hamlet* is seen as a revenge play in which the Prince for one reason or another cannot bring himself to kill Claudius, his father's murderer. For many critics the play is a brilliant study of Hamlet's powerful mind as he examines the conflict between duty and morality: Hamlet, it is argued, sees he ought to avenge his father but is held back by his conscience. At the same time traditional criticism was interested in exploring Hamlet's psychological state, and especially his highly charged feelings towards his mother. It is a reading of the play, then, that focuses on the hero, his character and thoughts, but which takes in the question of revenge and moral action.

How has this reading changed over recent years? To begin with, *Hamlet* is no longer seen just in terms of the prince. Many traditional studies all but exclude the other characters from the play or see them as merely contrasts to the hero. More recent criticism, however, has, for example, examined the representation of women in the play, how Ophelia and Gertrude are seen in stereotyped terms signifying either purity or corruption, yet how their presentation disrupts these categories. This involves, too, seeing how the play is the tragedy of more than one figure: the deaths of both Gertrude and Ophelia are matters that should give an audience pause for thought about the play's violent sexual politics and their cost.

But as well as coming to see how the play is about more than Hamlet's indecision, recent criticism has become much more interested in ideas about madness. In the play Hamlet adopts an antic disposition, a temporary state of madness, in order to protect himself against Claudius's attempts to find out what he knows. After he kills Polonius, however, Hamlet is sent away to England by Claudius on the pretence that he is dangerously mad. This use of the idea of madness in the play lends it the same sort of political significance that recent criticism has suggested it has in wider culture. We often label as mad those who do not fit in with our ideas; madness is often the only position from which people can speak if they wish to challenge the state. The threat of madness is something the state often uses to silence people, as, for example, in the former Soviet Union. Once again we see a broadening out of the issues in the play and how they come to take on a new interest and significance: Hamlet's madness is no longer regarded just as a symptom of his indecision but as a much more powerful idea in the play. We can perhaps grasp something of its rich dramatic plurality in Hamlet's words to Rosencrantz and Guildenstern when he tells them that his 'uncle-father and aunt-mother are deceived':

GUILDENSTERN In what, my dear lord?
HAMLET I am but mad north-north-west; when the wind is southerly I know a hawk from a handsaw.

(II.ii.373–5)

Madness is, it would seem, by its very nature unstable, but its nature may itself be something that throws into doubt where the border between reason and madness lies.

A third, and possibly the most important, area of *Hamlet* that has been explored by recent critics is connected with how the Renaissance sees the beginning of a new individuality, of figures who look inward and examine the self. This new individual is termed, in recent criticism, the subject, meaning both the political subject and also the subject who speaks the word 'I', the first person. The most obvious example of such a subject is Hamlet. It has been suggested that Hamlet is a sort of representative figure who stands on the edge of modern subjectivity. His identity is still largely fixed in terms of the court and the social body, but time after time he turns inwards in his soliloquies to try and find answers to why he cannot act. He finds, it is suggested, only a hollowness: the new individual subject has yet to be shaped in the modern period, but Hamlet is, as it were, a precursor, a figure divided between the modern period and an older world where identity is outside rather than inside. Again, we can perhaps see this in the way Hamlet both turns inwards in self-examination but also outwards as he tries to work out his relationship to other revenge figures in the play, to Lucianus who poisons the king in the play-within-the-play, and to Fortinbras, another revenging son.

This summary of how criticism has changed and is changing both *Hamlet* and Shakespeare studies as a whole is deliberately intended to lead into the further reading section of the book where we have tried to pick out a range of books that will help you explore the new approaches for yourself. What we have tried to demonstrate in the last four chapters is that if you continue to work from the text, taking small extracts and building your argument stage by stage, you will find it much easier to use the new critical approaches. The mistake many students make is to learn the new terms without realising that what is actually central is the critical activity of reading and thinking about the text. Working from the text will allow you to ask yourself what sort of difference it makes if you look at a scene in terms of its politics or gender or in terms of the values it seems to endorse. It is, as we said above, a matter of practice as well as extending your reading. The rewards, we think, are the challenge of a new set of ideas to consider and a much more open attitude to the study of Shakespeare.

Further reading

Which edition of Shakespeare should I buy?

This is not usually a problem as most often you will be told which particular edition of an individual play you should use. If you are free to choose your edition, you will obviously want to ensure that it is both reliable and as helpful as possible. The following series all have good notes, sound critical introductions, and are fully annotated: the *Arden Shakespeare* (a new, revised series will start appearing in 1995), the *New Cambridge Shakespeare*, the *New Oxford Shakespeare* (being published in paperback by World's Classics), and the *New Penguin Shakespeare*. In addition, you will find it useful to have a copy of Shakespeare's complete works both for further reading and for reference. The standard *Complete Works* is that edited by Peter Alexander for Collins (we have taken our quotations from this); the Oxford edition of the *Complete Works* edited by Gary Taylor and Stanley Wells has many non-standard features; the *Riverside Shakespeare* (edited by G.B. Evans) has useful introductions to the plays.

What critical books should I read?

If you have read the play you have been set to study, but cannot see what it is about, what you need is a book that gives you an idea of the significance of the play. An introductory volume in this respect is Marguerite Alexander's *An Introduction to Shakespeare and his Contemporaries* (1979). Similarly Philip Edwards's *Shakespeare: A Writer's Progress* (1986) will provide some starting-points, as will Richard Dutton's *William Shakespeare: A Literary Life* (1989). More advanced but still very approachable is Leah Scragg's *Discovering Shakespeare's Meaning* (1988), which provides a sound general introduction to many aspects of Shakespeare. A lively book that offers both clear analyses and a way into more recent criticism is Kiernan Ryan's *Shakespeare* (1989).

The most directly useful books are obviously those which offer a close reading of the particular play you are interested in. The volumes published by Penguin in their *Penguin Critical Studies* series provide sensible and clear analyses of individual plays. A single view of a play, however, can appear to be the only view, and this is why it is helpful to look at a collection of essays on different aspects of a play by critics with different approaches. Two series of this kind are *Twentieth Century Interpretations* published by Prentice Hall and Macmillan *Casebooks* (General Editor: A.E. Dyson), which include collections of essays on most of Shakespeare's plays. The *Casebooks* offer a broad selection of critical views from the first appearance of a text through to the early 1970s. By contrast, the *New Casebook* series, also published by Macmillan (General Editors: John Peck and Martin Coyle), focus on current criticism and new approaches to Shakespeare. Each volume contains about ten essays together with an Introduction that explains the kind of critical thinking that lies behind the essays. The *New Casebooks* complement rather than replace the original *Casebooks*, and together they provide a very good source of critical material. A similar series but focusing on topics rather than individual plays is *Longman Critical Readers* (General Editors: Raman Selden and Stan Smith). Three volumes are particularly helpful: *Shakespearean Tragedy* edited by John Drakakis; *Shakespeare's Comedies*, edited by Gary Waller; and *New Historicism and Renaissance Drama*, edited by Richard Wilson and Richard Dutton. The emphasis of the volumes is on new approaches to Shakespeare; some of the material, though, is very difficult.

Use critical books in a sensible way. Many students waste a great deal of time making huge piles of notes from critical books, even copying out whole sections. If you have read and thought about the play you are studying you should be able to *make use* of criticism rather than relying on it: you should be able to read a chapter, or an essay, or even a few pages, see what the critic is saying, and then go back to the text to test the ideas against your own reading of a speech or scene. At school there is no need to read vast amounts of criticism: read just enough to discover what literary criticism is and to stimulate your own thinking. At college or university you will be encouraged to read more, but always as a complement to your own thinking. Don't fall into the trap of relying on other people's ideas and discussions. Criticism is there to help you extend your ideas and explore your responses, not as a substitute for reading and thinking about the text.

What general books about Shakespeare should I read?

At the end of this section we provide the sort of list of books on Shakespeare that you are likely to be given at college or university. It mixes some classic works on Shakespeare with more recent volumes. Confronted by such a list, the best tactic is to start with the most recent book. This is likely to offer a sense of the current ways of looking at Shakespeare and also provide a view of earlier criticism. All criticism works by discussing previous discussions of the text, but this is an especially important aspect of recent Shakespeare studies which in various ways are a reaction against earlier criticism. Very often recent critics will refer to traditional criticism in order to clarify by contrast their own critical position, and, indeed, there is very often an expectation that the reader already knows their way round the critical map. What follows here, therefore, is a very brief survey of the century's most influential traditional critics and books, and then some equally brief notes about recent critics and books.

Any account of twentieth-century Shakespeare criticism has to start with A.C. Bradley's *Shakespearean Tragedy*, still probably the most famous book on the tragedies. Bradley is often criticised for his 'character approach' to Shakespeare, in which he treats the characters as if they were real people (speculating, for example, on how many children Lady Macbeth had). His analysis of the action of the plays, however, and his comments on the structure of tragedy, are altogether more complex than is sometimes suggested.

The next phase in Shakespeare criticism begins with G. Wilson Knight's *The Wheel of Fire* (1930). Bradley focused on character and action in the tragedies, but Wilson Knight is interested in the imaginative, symbolic impact of the tragedies. He concentrates on the vision of life they offer and the moral values they embrace. His way of getting at this is through the language, in particular through the broader, universal implications of the imagery. This shift from an interest in character to an interest in language is also evident in the work of L.C. Knights. Knights argues (in, for instance, *Explorations*, 1946) that Shakespeare's plays should be regarded as 'dramatic poems', as essentially poetic explorations of themes and ideas. A similar interest in Shakespeare's language is also found in Caroline Spurgeon's *Shakespeare's Imagery* (1935).

Another strand in Shakespeare criticism is exemplified in the work of E.M.W. Tillyard. His best-known books are *The Elizabethan World Picture* (1943) and *Shakespeare's History Plays* (1944). Tillyard focuses on the religious, social and political ideas in the plays; in particular he is interested in the kind of moral investigations the plays offer of political issues.

The approaches listed so far could be said to centre on character, language and themes, the central concerns of traditional criticism. The next significant development came with critics such as Maynard Mack and Northrop Frye, who focus more on the form and structure of the plays. In *'King Lear' In Our Time* (1965), Mack examines how the play achieves its larger significance, how the play draws on parable and myth. Frye is also interested in the structure of the plays, but his approach, as in his discussion of the comedies in *A Natural Perspective* (1965), focuses more on the underlying structure, the pattern behind the individual plays.

With Frye we can say that criticism has moved beyond the concerns of the traditional criticism into new ways of reading and thinking about the texts. Frye's approach is basically that of the structuralist: he is interested in the plays as cultural artefacts, and his theory of comedy is based on ideas drawn from anthropology. Similarly, C.L. Barber's theory of comedy put forward in his *Shakespeare's Festive Comedy* (1959), and which draws on ideas to do with popular festivals, pushed Shakespearean criticism towards the new directions and approaches that became established in the 1980s. There are the approaches discussed in chapters 7–11, that is structuralism, poststructuralism, deconstruction, feminist criticism, New Historicism and Cultural Materialism, as well as those approaches such as Marxist criticism and psychoanalytic criticism which many recent critics also draw upon.

At first the new approaches were worked out in books on critical theory but using Shakespeare for illustration, books such as Catherine Belsey's *Critical Practice* (1980), probably still the best introduction to modern critical theory. Or they were worked out in books dealing with the Renaissance more broadly, as in Stephen Greenblatt's *Renaissance Self-Fashioning: From More to Shakespeare* (1982), which paved the way for the growing interest in cultural history as well as New Historicism. But for students the changes in critical approach started to become accessible and influential with a stream of books in the mid-1980s. There is the collection edited by John Drakakis, *Alternative Shakespeares* (1985) which contains essays using a variety of new approaches, including feminism, psychoanalytic criticism and Marxism. In the same year appeared Jonathan Dollimore's influential *Radical Tragedy* (1985) and the collection he edited with Alan Sinfield, *Political Shakespeare: New Essays in Cultural Materialism* (1985), both of which helped establish Cultural Materialist criticism. Also in 1985 appeared Catherine Belsey's *The Subject of Tragedy*, a book combining cultural history with feminist criticism.

Important to establishing feminist criticism of Shakespeare were Juliet Dusinberre's *Shakespeare and the Nature of Women* (1975) and Marilyn French's *Shakespeare's Division of Experience* (1981). An influential reading of the plays combining feminist criticism and psychoanalytic theory is Coppélia Kahn's *Man's Estate: Masculine Identity in Shakespeare* (1981), while three more recent feminist volumes are Lisa Jardine's *Still Harping on Daughters: Women and Drama in the Age of Shakespeare* (1988), Kathleen McCluskie's *Renaissance Dramatists* (1989) and *The Matter of Difference* (1992) edited by Valerie Wayne. Each of these offers different feminist approaches to Shakespeare and to the debate about how we read the plays today.

It would, of course, be possible to extend this survey for many pages, but that would not significantly alter the outlines of the sketch we have drawn. The sketch shows a radical break in Shakespeare criticism during the 1970s as modern critical theory came to be established and influence contemporary thinking about the study of English Literature, and especially of Shakespeare.

Bibliography

C.L. Barber, *Shakespeare's Festive Comedy* (1959)

Catherine Belsey, *The Subject of Tragedy: Identity and Difference in Renaissance Drama* (1985)

A.C. Bradley, *Shakespearian Tragedy* (1904)

Dympna Callaghan, *Women and Gender in Renaissance Tragedy* (1989)

Jonathan Dollimore, *Radical Tragedy: Religion, Ideology and Power in the Drama of Shakespeare and his Contemporaries* (1985)

Jonathan Dollimore and Alan Sinfield (eds), *Political Shakespeare: New Essays in Cultural Materialism* (1985)

John Drakakis (ed.), *Alternative Shakespeares* (1985)

John Drakakis (ed.), *Shakespearean Tragedy* (1992)

Juliet Dusinberre, *Shakespeare and the Nature of Women* (1975)

Terry Eagleton, *William Shakespeare* (1986)

Marilyn French, *Shakespeare's Division of Experience* (1981)

Northrop Frye, *A Natural Perspective* (1965)

Stephen Greenblatt, *Renaissance Self-Fashioning: From More to Shakespeare* (1982)

Andrew Gurr, *The Shakespearean Stage 1574–1642* (1970)

Terence Hawkes, *That Shakespeherian Rag: Essays on a Critical Process* (1986)

Terence Hawkes, *Meaning by Shakespeare* (1992)

Graham Holderness, *The Shakespeare Myth* (1988)

Jean Howard and Marion O'Connor (eds), *Shakespeare Reproduced: The Text in History and Ideology* (1987)

Lisa Jardine, *Still Harping on Daughters: Women and Drama in the Age of Shakespeare* (1988)

Coppélia Kahn, *Man's Estate: Masculine Identity in Shakespeare* (1981)

L.C. Knights, *Explorations* (1946)

G. Wilson Knight, *The Wheel of Fire* (1930)

Jan Kott, *Shakespeare Our Contemporary* (1964)

Kathleen McCluskie, *Renaissance Dramatists* (1989)

Stephen Mullaney, *The Place of the Stage: Licence, Play and Power in Renaissance England* (1988)

Annabel Patterson, *Shakespeare and the Popular Voice* (1989)

Kiernan Ryan, *Shakespeare* (1989)

Leonard Tennenhouse, *Power on Display: The Politics of Shakespeare's Genres* (1986)

E.M.W. Tillyard, *The Elizabethan World Picture* (1943)

E.M.W. Tillyard, *Shakespeare's History Plays* (1944)

Gary Waller (ed.), *Shakespeare's Comedies* (1991)

Valerie Wayne (ed.), *The Matter of Difference: Materialist Feminist Criticism of Shakespeare* (1991)

H. Aram Veser (ed.), *The New Historicism* (1989)

Robert Weimann, *Shakespeare and the Popular Tradition in the Theatre: Studies in the Social Dimension of Dramatic Form and Functions* (1978)

Richard Wilson, *Will Power* (1994)

Richard Wilson and Richard Dutton (eds), *New Historicism and Renaissance Drama* (1992)

A list of Shakespeare's plays

All dates are approximate.

1589–90	*Henry VI Part One*
1590–1	*Henry VI Part Two*
1590–1	*Henry VI Part Three*
1592–3	*Richard III*
1592–4	*The Comedy of Errors*
1593–4	*Titus Andronicus*
1593–4	*The Taming of the Shrew*
1594	*The Two Gentlemen of Verona*
1594–5	*Love's Labour's Lost*
1594–6	*King John*
1595	*Richard II*
1595–6	*Romeo and Juliet*
1595–6	*A Midsummer Night's Dream*
1596–7	*The Merchant of Venice*
1596–7	*Henry IV Part One*
1597	*The Merry Wives of Windsor*
1598	*Henry IV Part Two*
1598–9	*Much Ado About Nothing*
1599	*Henry V*
1599	*Julius Caesar*
1599	*As You Like It*
1600–1	*Hamlet*
1601–2	*Twelfth Night*
1601–2	*Troilus and Cressida*
1602–3	*All's Well That Ends Well*
1604	*Measure for Measure*
1604	*Othello*

1605	*King Lear*
1606	*Macbeth*
1606–7	*Antony and Cleopatra*
1607–8	*Coriolanus*
1607–8	*Timon of Athens*
1607–8	*Pericles*
1609–10	*Cymbeline*
1610–11	*The Winter's Tale*
1611	*The Tempest*
1612–13	*Henry VIII*
1613	*The Two Noble Kinsmen*